MW00466114

quick to listen

UNDERSTANDING VIEWPOINTS THAT CHALLENGE YOUR FAITH

"Everyone should be quick to listen."
(James 1:19)

Samuel Degner | Christopher Doerr
Nick Schmoller | Luke Thompson

NORTHWESTERN PUBLISHING HOUSE
Milwaukee, Wisconsin

Cover Photos: Openculture.com, Pixabay, Shutterstock, Twenty20
Art Director: Karen Knutson
Designer: Pamela Dunn

All rights reserved. This publication may not be copied, photocopied, reproduced, translated, or converted to any electronic or machine-readable form in whole or in part, except for brief quotations, without prior written approval from the publisher.

All Scripture quotations, unless otherwise indicated, are taken from the Holy Bible, New International Version®, NIV®. Copyright © 1973, 1978, 1984, 2011 by Biblica, Inc.™ Used by permission of Zondervan. All rights reserved worldwide. www.zondervan.com.

The "NIV" and "New International Version" are trademarks registered in the United States Patent and Trademark Office by Biblica, Inc.™

Northwestern Publishing House
1250 N. 113th St., Milwaukee, WI 53226-3284
www.nph.net
© 2018 Northwestern Publishing House
Published 2018
Printed in the United States of America
ISBN 978-0-8100-2913-2
ISBN 978-0-8100-2914-9 (e-book)

18 19 20 21 22 23 24 25 26 27   10 9 8 7 6 5 4 3 2 1

CONTENTS

FOREWORD

This is not an easy book. You should know, dear reader, what you've gotten yourself into.

In these pages, our writers have asked real, flesh-and-blood people just exactly what it is that they find so implausible about Christianity, in part or in total. These interviews open up a space for atheists and evolutionists, Bible skeptics and practicing homosexuals (among others) to freely voice their viewpoints from various positions outside of biblical truth. After the interviews are quotations from a variety of popular thinkers and gifted writers who represent the broader intellectual climate as they chime in their hollow "amen."

And you are being asked to hear them—truly hear them—to take in their stories, to acknowledge the humanity of people who disagree with you, to let them get under your skin. It's even possible that some stereotypes might explode along the way, for example, if it should come as a surprise to you that they can be quite nice and interesting people. These conversations are not without good humor and genuine tolerance. Yes, there's some sarcasm here too, and no small amount of pain. Each person, in his or her own way, will step out from the undifferentiated crowd of "postmoderns" or "agnostics" or whatever other label might apply. They make themselves unforgettable.

Listening to them will be, in a word, uncomfortable.

It is uncomfortable even briefly to imagine your way into a Christless framework, to look around and take in that smaller world, and to think of (or in some cases, to remember) what it is like to not believe. After all, we are not dealing here with the denial of some abstraction, but with the denial of your Brother and your Lord, your Savior and theirs. How long would I casually discuss the matter of, let's say, whether my bride is faithful to me? To be dispassionate about *that*, to listen politely, or even to take up such a conversation at all, well, in the very act I would allow our relationship to slip into something other than what it is meant to be. I do not want to speak idly and lightly of the destruction of a deep, precious, and abiding trust in someone who has brought me *immeasurable joys. Yes, that conversation would be uncomfortable—and intensely personal. How much more when it comes to the matter of Jesus—does he live for us or does he not?—when what is at stake is precisely everything!*

*With that in mind, it may be that what gets to you, like it gets to me, is what our generous participants are **not** saying, indeed, what they seem not to know. Not a single one of those who left Christianity outright (not all the participants are in this category) describes a time when the full beauty of Jesus broke through, like nothing this world contains, made more real to them by Word and Spirit than any competing vision of the good. You will catch in their comments much talk about some dimly recalled church and all the reasons they don't look back. If they have ever known the astonishment of forgiveness—as the only sun in their sky, of being dressed in Jesus' own righteousness, having found none of their own—they aren't saying. Have they ever once tasted, in Christ, the very reason beyond reason to wait in hope, to doubt their doubts, to take every thought captive to him as to the one thing they could not do without? It doesn't seem so. What, then, to make of the accounts they offer to us?*

It is probably not safe to assume that the conversations you are about to read necessarily arrived at the whole story or got down to "what it's really all about" for these people. That would be asking a lot of a single encounter, no matter how much trust was achieved, how penetrating the questions, or how open the disclosures.

Besides the limits of these single encounters, there are the limits of self-understanding, especially of those who have not yet at all seen themselves how God sees them. It is just as Jesus said. People simply do not want to come into the light because of the way their life would be exposed, naked and quivering, in that unrelenting brightness. Certainly, other reasons coexist and should not surprise us, even as we have each learned to be suspicious of ourselves. But the truth is that they, like the rest of us, are in the wrong—fully, awfully, and completely. It is we, not God, who are on trial. To think otherwise is the great miscalculation. And when the verdict comes down—Not Guilty for Jesus' sake—and the soul first learns who God is and what the singing is all about, well, nothing can ever be the same. My point is that it may only be in hindsight that the mind, newly alive and fully awake, can come face-to-face with itself or that a person can come to properly read their own history.

So while it is only fair to take these people's stories at face value, such as they are, to receive them as a tentative exchange of friendship and to honor their honest questions, we should not imagine that we have fully penetrated their diverse experiences. They are not two-dimensional cardboard cutouts, after all. There is so very much more to them than that. And they compel us to admit how much more difficult it is to answer, not questions—"Isn't the church full of hypocrites?"—but actual living and breathing people, living their particular lives, who do more than blandly nod their heads.

No, this is not a comfortable book.

You may even sense some risk in this project, risk in publishing and spreading the influence of anti-biblical viewpoints.

If so, please consider some recent research into the experience of Christian college students at the secular university. One study reveals that it goes too far to say that the barrage of intellectual challenges, the very air you breathe at such places, is somehow able to destroy the faith of any young person who dares to enter. It is more accurate to say that the university environment merely **exposes what is superficial** about the faith of Christian students, the questions that never once occurred to them, the hard work they have not done in making sound theology their own, and what are the untested skin-deep places of their Christian understanding. The university merely exposes the vulnerability of young believers who were already, long before they left home, at least partially disconnecting from the life of faith and from the community of worshipers gathered around the means of grace. Above all, the jarring experience in the philosophy classroom or the coed dorm will expose those tentative disciples who have no mature Christian mentor in their own back pocket, no one to receive their text message, "I'm so confused," no one who will run and pull them to their chest.

I'm thinking of my own daughter. She received a top-shelf education at a highly respected university. I saw the look on the face of one of her mentors as she presented a senior seminar in the psychology department; he beamed at her with at least as much pride as I did. Her world opened up in college, and some wonderful people stepped inside. All in all, it was a very impressive and stimulating place. Only that's not the whole story. Bear with me, because I need to take you there, if I can.

The "Christian bubble" burst for her, so to speak, and it happened on the first day. What one Christian philosopher terms "naive faith" is no longer possible for her and never will be again. That is to say, she can no longer believe in God in the taken-for-grantedness of "Well, what **else** would I believe?" She is no longer unable to imagine the alternative to trusting in Jesus or what it could possibly look like to navigate the world in any other way. Because there she sits in the midst of that colorful, smiling diversity, finding out that she represents only one among dozens of **apparently** viable options. This was her first five minutes.

My daughter is not told but intuits at once what mumbling, "The Bible says . . ." would sound like there. The Christian life—the life lived in and with, by, and for Jesus and, along with it, the gray-haired church down the street—can be dismissed out of hand. Ask the person on the street what the word **evangelical** means to them or what the Bible is all about. First, you might want to brace yourself.

Intolerance. Bigotry. **Hatred.**

And in an intellectual climate in which Jesus has come to strike many ears like some sort of fairy tale or the weird legend of a remote culture, why in the world would they give him a second thought? What we have here is a quite appalling failure to communicate. More than that, it is the grotesque agenda of Satan at work, the terrible obscuring of the very glory of God that has come to us in the form which we could bear, that is, the face of Christ.

My daughter tries to tell me what it felt like to go to college, how it dawned on her in the first class she attended, in her words, "None of my Christian teachers have ever sat where I sit right now. Not even my dad." The characterization of evolutionists she had picked up somewhere along the way turned out to be a fiction. These are **not** stupid people. Certain rational arguments for a biblical view of the world, the ones that were supposed to send scientists running, plainly did not. They were batted away like flies. As to the actual vulnerabilities in the reasoned arguments that say this world we can see is all there is, she would have to discover them on her own (for just one example, the mystery of consciousness). And while the "sage on the stage" in the college classroom reached for her mind, what is even more formative about the college life—think dormitories and Friday nights and cliques of people anyone would want to break into—would reach for her love, her desire, her imagining of who else she could be, and what else there might be to want out of life.

Of course there are other Christians there, but they will have to find one another. That is precisely what she did. Simply put, that is how she survived. She went to church. It seems like such a small thing to say it that way. But there it is.

She went to church.

*She started a fledgling campus ministry of four or five peers. They met in a quintessential 1970s-style church basement. The worship style there was liturgical, the kind performed in a transcendent style— in mystery, beauty, symbol; in confession and absolution; in the high and holy pleasure that God finds in saying to his children, again, "I forgive you. I am for you. **I Am.**" We drag our poor halfheartedness to the sanctuary (or the sanctuary basement), to kneel and pray, to sing and genuflect our worldview, to lay our old arguments and questions at the foot of the dear cross. A heart-pounding glory stretches out before us, our future having been conquered as well as our past. It is pure joy, **his** joy, and it does not end.*

Yes, my daughter survived with a faith made much more her own, burning brightly. And yet, for my part, did I even begin to comprehend what I was letting her in for as I drove away from her dorm that first late-summer day? Not in a million years. If her experience is unfamiliar to you and you've never sat in that desk either, this could be the whole value of Quick to Listen, *precisely when it creates the most discomfort. Surely, we need to know something about such things or at least have some inkling about what it feels like to be there.*

Surely, we cannot be content with tired and dated straw man arguments, continuing to pitch our favorite battles while the real war rages elsewhere. Surely, we do not want to display a sort of religion that is secure only because we have managed to close our eyes and stop our ears, preferring the Christian "echo chamber." The journey is worth it. It is so that we who hope to be able to call ourselves mature followers of Jesus can say to the vulnerable among us, "This world will eat you alive! Dear ones, it will eat you alive if you do not stay connected to the Word of God and the family of faith!" To do so with convincing and helpful urgency, we need to know what we're talking about.

If this is you—vulnerable, already all too familiar with the slippery case against Christ, perhaps losing your grip on him, sensing a creeping skepticism in yourself as you pick up your Bible or leave it alone; if your Jesus doesn't seem quite as real anymore compared to the shimmering, flattering world; if you are out there somewhere working things out all on your own—this may not be the book for you. Read your New Testament instead and immerse in its narratives and letters, like coming home. Throw open again a window on your life. Read a psalm out loud on your walk. Set your Sunday morning alarm. Invest in a uniquely Christian friendship and find a good coffee shop or take over a corner booth. See to your own soul.

Then again, this may yet be a book to bless you profoundly.

*Because, don't get me wrong, although the purpose of this book is unique in keeping with its title and our guest skeptics are given something like equal time, our writers do have answers, quite good ones in fact. The answers they offer may, in fact, be precisely what the tentative believer most requires. They are grace-saturated and Christ-obsessed, wrapped in the warmth of human skin and informed by long experience, and they come from educated people who do their best to be winsome and thoughtful. Let the defense we provide at the "sites of struggle," those meeting places where Christian truth is contested, be free of the "gotcha" or any hint of weaponized rhetoric. To speak about the grace of God with a hostile or superior tone is to contradict ourselves. We want **what** we say—in our myopic focus on Jesus, in this spotlight fixed on a cross—to be in harmony with **how** we say it and, in fact, an expression and extension of who we are becoming by grace so that, come what may, **they know that we love them.***

You should know, however, that this book does not take pains to answer the skeptic point-for-point. In fact, the interviewers you are about to meet are kind enough to let their interviewees get away with a few things. They don't pounce when one of their questions is met with something quite flimsy. They do not interrupt to say "you're wrong" every chance they can, just because they can.

*The Christian players in this book model a rare and gracious style of interaction designed to "change the moment." This seems necessary given how predictable in this time and place are the patterns of resistance to anyone transparently Christian. They mean to keep down the psychological guard of the other person, if they can. They go to identify and to share in human stuff, the hunger for relationship and the striving for significance. They are not immune to all possible influence— who wants to talk to people like that?—but come expecting to gain a more complex view of all that still divides, prepared to be thankful for the education. They bring with them their openness, not to error—God forbid—but an openness to people, being profoundly interested in how they have come to think and live as they do. They ache for a communication moment in which, as someone has put it, "a person becomes a person before their very eyes." That is to say, not a label. Not a stereotype. A human being. A soul. A **somebody** whom Jesus loves.*

Ah, to just stand side by side at the Lord's table and be two sinners with our hands held out.

*The listening that is modeled here includes taking care not to dismiss the unrelenting pain or contradict the deep disappointment that animates at least some of the resistance they meet. Our writers do not casually excuse the dismal ways in which the church has failed these people when they hungered for a word of grace and belonging and none came. Instead, their better impulse is to question their own self-righteousness and the way they have not represented Jesus in their lives. Further, their impulse is to reach for the heart of the other, to forge a human connection, even by means of connecting with what is most painful in themselves, if that's what it takes—"I too have lost a child, though I too prayed and prayed." They meet those stray moments within these interviews, instances of bitterness or dogmatism, with something **else**, namely, gentleness and respect. They would have stereotypes explode on **both** sides.*

These conversations are instructive. Please notice how this posture of grace—of self-questioning and of genuinely wanting to understand—allows slim plots of common ground to appear. Listen for those uncommon admissions by the participants in this project about what they envy or admire in people of faith, what they miss, what they honestly don't know, and how they too have been wrong. We can grow those hopeful spaces. "Tell me about the God you don't believe in. Maybe I don't believe in him either," or, "Tell me about the religion you've left behind. I might just breathe a sigh and say, 'Well, thank God you did.'" We might just surprise them.

There is a reason, if only temporarily, to take on a posture with people whose lives we have not lived—one that says, "You are the teacher. I am the student. Teach me."

I, for one, do very much want to know the psychological barriers that exist between us: the unnecessary offense we cause (as opposed to the necessary scandal of the cross) and the outward reasons—intellectual, social, and personal—that these people are hanging onto. I want to know the stories they tell themselves, such as they are. I want to know them simply because the way they feel about Christianity makes its own kind of sense within the way they have come to tell their story. If it had been incomprehensible before—their disillusionment, their sense of betrayal, or whatever the case may be—it will not be any more.

I want and need to know what the "defeaters" are for these people—that's the term a prominent Christian has coined. He has in mind a set of ideas that have come to feel self-evidently true to non-Christians and which, if they are true, then Christianity cannot be. An example would be, "It is wrong to claim that your beliefs are superior to those of other people." Like all such ideas, this one could stand to be examined and gently deconstructed.

I want to know the things these people aspire to—identity, meaning, freedom, connection—which I can passionately affirm even as I disagree about where they think such things are found. I want to know what it is that they cannot live without—whatever would tell them at last that they are someone in this world—so that, as a kindness, I can gently probe whether they understand how each falsehood ultimately will break their hearts. I want to know these things in order to strike at the root of their idolatries, and mine at the same time, using the living and active Word of God.

I want to clear the stage for the brilliant sentence of the apostle, "For to me, to live is Christ and to die is gain" (Philippians 1:21). If you live for anything else in this world, then you will die a thousand deaths as the years strip that thing away. It will happen in bits and pieces, if not in one terrible, inevitable swath. "For to me, to live **is Christ**"—this and only this will mean that "to die is **gain**," with the blessed day already on its way to bring you completely and at last into that which you called your real life all along. It is brilliant.

All this is to answer the call to be "imitators of Christ" as people who are dearly loved. How like Jesus it was that day he turned, in a jostling crowd, to a woman who had touched his clothes and was healed. It is at that moment that we are treated to the exquisite detail that she "told him **the whole truth**" (Mark 5:33). We can only try to mentally construct the scene: the sort of attention he paid her, the manner, the look on God's face saying, "Go on." The all-knowing One found a reason to hear her, to—I don't know—just let her talk. Certainly there must remain some very good reasons for us, the not-so-omniscient, to want to hear people. I want to be able to explain their point of view to them, their "whole truth," if I can, better than they can explain it themselves. I want to give words to how it all looks and how it all feels to hear someone exclaim now and then, "Yes, that's it exactly!" and maybe even, "Thank you!"

Why? So that by understanding, I can be understood. So that I can speak words that are not superficial, words that stick, into another mind and heart. So that I can tell that better, grander, and more dramatic God-so-loved-the-world story, the one that is absolutely true, told faithfully in the Bible, guaranteed by the Spirit himself. The One Grand Miracle of Christ's incarnation. The Big Fact of Easter. By grace, these resonate. To become caught up in that story is not anti-reason but reasoning of a higher kind, as the mind soars to Christ, for whom I am willing to be a fool. What makes sense within **that** story, as we tell it to one another, is all peace, all hope, all joy.

We are talking about spiritual friendship, an esthetic achievement... and humility is the price of admission. I do not wish to win arguments, but only to arrive at the moment when I get the chance to leave a new friend alone with a Word of Christ, leaving it to the two of them to work it all out. (Meanwhile, I will speak to Christ about the other person at least as much as I have spoken to the person about Christ.)

Just imagine the redeemed version of all these fascinating interview subjects, when the Spirit does with them what only he can do by the Word of God to which he has married himself. Imagine what fresh air they will bring with them into our circle, what sanctified insight and what heartening encouragements they will uniquely have to offer in our Upper Room, when they've learned to tell their story in a new way. We do not want to miss out on them. If it will get us **there**, then yes, I'm willing to learn.

This book goes out in search of its ideal reader. It will find that in all of you who are like-minded in Christ and, likewise, are not content with a shallow understanding of all those many people who live without him. Jesus did not sit in some basement to write a blog about what's wrong with the world. God came in the flesh, drawn by our misery all the way down and all the way into our human existence to wade out into that sea of ignorance and suffering, to give himself outright to a world all lined up together in its hostility toward him. God in hell. God himself in the sort of pain no one else can possibly know, and it was all for you. Imagine. It is by this unfathomable grace that he has made you, his natural-born enemy, into his friend. There is no basis for self-righteousness and no need to isolate ourselves. Secure in the knowledge of him, you are now hungry to be drawn fully into the real world, to learn there what it means to be thrown onto Christ and to rely on his Word, as all you really have, in the places where faith and unbelief collide.

Knowing what you know, you are able to tolerate some ambiguity, that gap in time between the hard question and the hard-won, costly answer. You've been at this a while, so you've been in that place before, and no matter the dilemma, time and time again you have come out the other side to the warm reality of Jesus: the release of forgiveness, *the gift of an identity that does not crush you because you did nothing to earn or deserve it, the resilience of hope and joy, and the Spirit that does not give you up without a fight. You are kept by the power of God. It is **he** who is holding **you**.*

And so you are hungry to model in all your talk of faith a serene, Spirit-worked confidence in Jesus, in whom God, your "God who hides himself," has revealed his very heart. No, you don't have him all figured out. His very thought transcends our own like the heavens spin impossibly high above the earth. But you trust him, asking that his will, not yours, be done. You trust him because he has won that much from you. You trust him, so much so that it renders all defensiveness plainly unnecessary. There is no need for panic if, for a time, you have no clue what you can say. It's going to be alright.

Grace has awakened this feeling in your bones that we who know Christ need to know who these people are as well, to let our hearts be broken, and to love them as well as we can. But how? The apostle James lights up for us a very good place to begin: "Everyone should be quick to listen, slow to speak" (James 1:19).

—Mark Paustian,
Professor at Martin Luther College,
New Ulm, Minnesota—July 2017

quick to listen

EVOLUTIONISTS
TALKING TO CHRISTIANS

by Samuel Degner

LISTENING TO GREG

This isn't a topic I've had to really wrestle with too much. I'll just start with my faith background. I'm Eastern Orthodox. The Eastern Orthodox Church doesn't really have concrete views on this issue; there aren't any dogmas associated with it. So in thinking about creation and Genesis and evolution, or any question you could ever pose, the starting point is always the cross and the crucifixion and the resurrection. Everything in the Old Testament is interpreted through that lens of the cross, and everything in the New Testament as well. But also everything in human history, creation history—everything is through that lens. And so I guess I might come back to that with my answers. But I would say the overall general view of the Orthodox Church is the idea of not feeling obliged to partake in the wrestling match of trying to reconcile everything—always leaving as much room for mystery as possible and, at the same time, acknowledging that science is in our toolbox to arrive at truths about the world that we live in. And that those truths don't have to detract from who God is and what he's done through his Son for the salvation of the world. So that's a starting point, I guess. I haven't done extensive research into patristic literature on the subject, but from some of the secondary sources I've read, it seems like historically, in the early church, there were various opinions from a lot of the Eastern fathers and some of the Western fathers too. Augustine, Gregory of Nyssa, Gregory the Theologian, Basil the Great, and a lot of these early fathers didn't adhere to a literal interpretation of Genesis and the creation narrative as depicted in Genesis. So there was a lot of room for interpretation with that.

Why do you think they didn't?

I don't think they had to. Perhaps just due to where the scientific community was at that time, there wasn't a pressure to have to. I don't think trying to justify a creation story in scientifically accurate terms is necessary to understand the heart of the gospel message. And I think that's what the main concern was and still is.

Do you think our understanding of the cross and resurrection is affected by how we view the origins of the earth?

That's a good question. I don't think it needs to be. One of the lines [of the Bible] that pops out for me is from Revelation, where it talks about the Lamb that was slain before the foundation of the world. That's kind of a mysterious line to think about. But I think the important thing is understanding the role of God in creation. And the second person of the Trinity being Jesus Christ (who from the gospels it's clear that he is pre-eternal, together with God the Father and the Holy Spirit, in one essence) orchestrated creation in some way, and I don't think scientists have a great explanation of how all this happened. So for me, however all this came to be, there is a real mystery to it and there is a real beauty to both the complexity and simplicity of our world. Going back to the cross, I think Christ died to redeem humanity but also all of creation. And exactly what that "new earth" is going to look like, I don't really know. For me, though, those origins don't really detract from the cross.

It sounds like the origins don't really matter and you're okay with having some mystery and some unknowns. Would you say you have a leaning, or predisposition, to believe one thing or another?

I'd say I lean more toward the evolution side. I'm definitely not an expert in that. For example, I still need to read *The Origin of Species,* and there's a lot of stuff I want to further explore to better understand that. In terms of the world I see and the evidence, I think the alternative would be that God made the world to look old. There's some deception there, some things that, for me, are less plausible.

So you're saying that the "God created the world to appear old" theory doesn't really resonate with you?

Yeah. And I'm not an expert on carbon dating, but yeah, from what I know.

Do you want to say what you do?

I'm a PhD student in biomedical engineering, starting my fifth year studying muscular dystrophy.

So if you imagine an evolutionary origin to the world and to life, how does the origin of man, the soul, and sin fit into that picture? Because I think if we're viewing everything through the cross, those questions are relevant.

Big questions. I don't know how it happened, but I think there was a point at which human beings became human beings—woke up one day and had that self-awareness. And not just a self-awareness but an awareness of the Creator in a way that consisted of a dialogue, a relationship—the birth of the soul and of human consciousness. I think one of the points of the story of the fall (and even its position within Scripture) is the fact that it was just [snaps his fingers] right away. The time in paradise of perfect union with God walking in the cool of the evening was so brief that, for me, there was this creation of a creature that has the potential of perfection, who was made in the image and likeness of God, but from the very beginning that creature turned away. Sin was introduced so early on that to isolate that incident isn't something I feel the need to do. But just knowing that from the very beginning there was this attempt to be our own gods, to be god without God, and that from the very beginning there was free choice, there was free will—one of the greatest gifts God gave to man. I don't think God was surprised when Adam and Eve sinned and rejected his commandment at the time. I don't think he was so thrown off like that, like, "Crap! Plan B, Plan B!" But then I think perhaps all of that was part of the plan from the beginning. And even death [was part of the plan]. You know, the issue of death is something I've thought about a little bit, and it can pose a problem, I think, this idea of the wages of sin being death and death being introduced into the world as a result of sin.

You mean it's a problem because, with the way you're describing it now, death would have already been in existence.

Exactly. And I don't know if death is now something different when it involves a creature with a soul and a conscience, and that's one of the things I've thought about: death being something different in that sense. But also I think the revelation of death as an enemy is also part of the gospel, and in the Jewish tradition, death wasn't really confronted as much; it was just kind of accepted as a mystery, as separation or repose—I don't know too much about it. But I think in the gospel we see death for what it truly is. We see that in the Saturday before the crucifixion, with Jesus weeping, standing at the foot of his friend Lazarus who had been dead four days. And then we see that with the cross too, with death being the last enemy to be destroyed through that. Now death is no longer separation from God or the end of the story, but it's that passage from this world to the kingdom. And I don't know exactly what that's going to be like. I don't know how the rest of creation gets redeemed in that.

Can you describe evolution in your own words to a lay person?

As far as I understand it, the terms that pop into my head are *natural selection* and *survival of the fittest,* that over time living organisms adapt in order to best survive. And there's a process where those traits that are favorable will kind of stick around and others will not. So these adaptations are influenced by the environment, geographic location, a lot of different ecosystems, predators—very complex in that sense. It's essentially a theory that explains biological diversity that happens over time, and it can also explain why certain organisms may become extinct whereas others will thrive.

Do you think that believing in one theory of the origins of the universe over another could detract from God's character or omnipotence, or does it change it in some way? Does it change how we relate to him?

My gut tells me it's perfectly possible, but I don't think having a perfect understanding of that is necessary for salvation, and it might be different for different people. This type of question has a different context and expression for a peasant worker, compared to an elite researcher or someone whose career is highly involved [in evolution] and may be in jeopardy. Going back to your question, I think having the truth is important and beneficial, but in terms of the necessity of having that particular truth for salvation, there are other things that are much more necessary in terms of just having proper understanding. It really manifests in daily life. I don't know, do you have any examples of how one view or the other would affect someone's actual practice as a Christian?

If you believe in a big bang origin to the universe, you're taking away the miracle of creation just coming into existence and you're relying on random chance and death and accidents to shape both the tree of life[1] and the human species.

But don't you still have, with the big bang, a creation coming into existence out of nothing?

How do you describe the authority and veracity of Scripture?

I think the Bible is foundational to the Christian faith, that it is God-breathed and inspired. An important aspect is not just the reading of the text, but the interpretation, in that no one is interpreting Scripture in a vacuum, and so I think we just have to be cognizant of the lens through which we are interpreting. I would also say that there needs to be a congruence throughout Scripture, and there is that, but in terms of interpretation, there should be a harmony that's preserved.

You mean a harmony as far as interpreting different parts of Scripture?

Yes.

Would you say that Scripture is infallible?

With the proper interpretation, yes. I mean, depending on how nitpicky you want to be, we have different manuscripts that are all slightly different, and even in terms of canonization, in different traditions you have apocryphal texts that are recognized [in some but

---

[1] That is, all living organisms. Just as we record genealogies with a family tree, biologists often use a similar tree (called a phylogenetic tree) to plot calculated evolutionary relationships between organisms. When referring to all organisms, this tree is often called the tree of life.

not others]. But I believe in Scripture as it has been collected and preserved through the canonization process, and I think the truth of Scripture is infallible.

On the spectrum of interpretive to literal, where do you stand when it comes to interpreting Scripture?

It's very context-dependent. Because Scripture has so many different texts—it's not just one book in one genre, but it spans numerous genres—I think you have to pick up on the author's style in a certain book. The gospels are written very differently than Genesis or some of the wisdom literature; they're just different. For the gospels I would lean much more toward a literal interpretation because a lot of it is documenting the life of Christ and what he did and what he said, but I think particularly some of the Old Testament texts are written in a very different style.

Do you think that science and Scripture contradict each other? If so, how do you reconcile those contradictions?

I think they can appear to, but I don't think they do. And I think they seek to answer different questions in different ways. Science is unequipped to answer some of the questions that the Holy Scriptures can answer, such as, What is the meaning of life? What is the purpose of existence? No matter how hard science tries to answer some of those questions, it's going to fall short, just because it's not equipped to do it.

Do faith and science intersect?

I don't think we can compartmentalize so easily. In some ways for me, they can even be one and the same thing. Francis Collins, the director of the National Institutes of Health, has some books on this very topic. He talks about his own medical research being a form of worship in many ways. To look at a human cell under a microscope and to think about the complexity of just that one cell, there's something astonishing about that. Having been a scientist for a few years, I think there's even a lot of faith that goes into being a scientist. With every assay that you run, especially if you're working with things you can't see. For example, you have this tube, and there's nothing in it, but apparently there's some DNA in the bottom of it. That's kind of a cute example, but I think we're too quick to compartmentalize and put things in conflict that shouldn't be in conflict. I understand coming from a perspective where you want to preserve the integrity of Scripture and its authority. You might be more defensive against science as something that is threatening that. But I think, just like the early fathers, we have some freedom of interpretation, freedom to allow mystery to really permeate, and just go back to the cross for the essentials as the foundation of our faith. Maybe I just haven't wrestled enough with this, but part of me doesn't think I have to.

Do you think that believing in a six-day creation is detrimental to either (1) somebody's faith or (2) society?

Assuming that person is already living the faith, I don't think it's detrimental. I can just speak for the Orthodox Church: There are people on various sides, there are six-day creationist people, and there are big bang evolutionist people, so there is that flexibility. One thing we do have to be mindful of is that for many people in our society, modern science, and even the rhetoric associated with it, is one of the biggest detriments to people accepting Christ and believing in God and going to the church. I'm thinking of Richard Dawkins and some of these New Age atheists, who are very much leveraging science in juxtaposition with a very rigid, six-day creation viewpoint that outright rejects some of these findings that the scientific community feels very strongly about. So in that sense, it could potentially threaten some people's faith. And that's where the freedom to say, "I don't know" could be a comfort to some people and could help usher very scientifically rooted people into the faith. For someone who trusts that Jesus Christ is their Lord and Savior who died on the cross for the sins of the world, I think you could believe either way and it's not going to be a detriment to knowing that fact and believing it and having that transform your life.

Is there anything you'd like to say to six-day-creationist Christians reading this?

I challenge myself to do this as well, but I think there's a lot of benefit to studying the early church and some of the patristic literature and then seeing how some of these holy people in the first couple centuries grappled with this and how they interpreted Genesis. It's interesting to see the breadth of different opinions and to think about the implications of those differences and whether or not they even have huge implications in terms of being rooted in the core of the Christian faith. I would challenge others, as well as myself, to look into that, because I think there is some freedom there.

LISTENING TO NATE

I was essentially raised a highly educated, liberal version of Southern Baptist. My dad was a nuclear physicist, but he also received at least a couple years of religious training from Dallas Theological Seminary and was religious his whole life. He always taught us directly from the Bible and wasn't ashamed to disagree with anyone else in the church. So we were always taught that whatever someone wants to call themselves, their ideas could be flawed and not at all representative of the textual authority they claim to be following. I think the strongest training that I received from my father was, "Don't necessarily accept what people claim is the only way to interpret the Bible, because oftentimes it is misused and misinterpreted." But conventionally speaking, it was pretty clear-cut Southern Baptist—you know, you have to ask for forgiveness of your sins, there is a heaven, and there is a hell. I don't really recall my Dad's beliefs about creation. Other than that, on some level, he obviously felt God was responsible for it. But I would say that I've just taken the critical analysis a lot farther than he would have. And, yeah, I just don't really buy the whole thing. I would say I was partly religious until I was 13, and then in those years, as I developed my own identity and thoughts, I just kind of left it behind.

Was the way you see the world shaped by the way your dad taught you about religion and how to approach religion?

A lot of the religious teachings stayed with me, but I just believe them for a different reason. There's a lot of moral things I believe that I don't attribute to the existence of a god but because they make me happy or even that it's the path of least resistance. So, yeah, a lot of those teachings stick with me for completely nonreligious reasons. But I was still taught them through religion.

Do you remember when you became religious, or is that just something you were raised with?

It's something I was always raised with.

Was there a clear-cut moment when you decided to leave religion behind? Or was it sort of a gradual transition?

It was mostly just a gradual, continual realization. I guess it started as a general acceptance that even most of the religious people I knew, knew less about what they professed to believe than me, who was skeptical about a lot of these things. So I would say it kind of started that way. But it was also as I learned about other religions, the history of many of these religions, and the ways in which some of these stories were related or drew from each other. And then, conversely, as I learned more about science and learned many of the things that can explain the, well, literally miraculous powers that [science] has, it just seemed like a pretty easy choice to follow one of those lines of teaching over the other.

Some people use the miraculous powers of science (as you just said) as an explanation for there being a God or as an argument that there's no way that it all could have happened by chance. I'm thinking right now of how a protein works and how proteins would have come into existence. What do you think about that?

The problem is that these arguments are kind of aloof. I would counter with, "Well, look. If we are a product of random chance, if we believe in the process of evolution on any level, even just on a behavioral level, then an appreciation of beauty where there is none could have very good fitness advantages, right?" In general, you'll just be happier because obviously a shoreline or beach—we don't necessarily believe anyone created that, but appreciating it as beautiful can have good benefits. You might even say that humanity's proneness to believing in some higher power watching over them—that itself we could understand would be a product of the selective process.

That people who have a belief in a higher being were somehow selected for?

Yup. So purely because we experience these emotions doesn't make them real.

If I can fill in the gaps of what you're saying, you're saying that people who are more likely to have a blind trust in something may also be more likely to have a blind trust in their fellow human beings, may be more likely to form cooperative societies, and thus may be more likely to survive but also to follow a supreme being as a by-product.

Exactly.

So is faith or religion any part of your life at this point?

Not really. I mean, philosophy and morality are, and also these social ideas about how we treat others. So certainly moral discourse is, but I wouldn't classify that under religion. I'm always happy to engage with people on any of these topics, so in that regard it includes religion, but that's just part of this wider thing that I have now. So outside of that I would say, "Not really."

Would you define yourself as agnostic or atheist (or somewhere in between)?

I would say technically I'm agnostic, but socially I kind of prefer to be atheist, just because I've met too many people who clearly don't know what they're talking about. So that's how I would describe myself. But if someone's willing to have a reasoned debate, I'll clearly take agnosticism.

In a sense, it takes just as much faith to be atheist as it does to have religion. Because it's kind of an unprovable thing, that there is or isn't a God, right?

Certainly, but I would also say that, as any mathematician can tell you, [it is harder to prove] that something doesn't exist than [it is to prove that] something does exist. In that regard, technically what you're saying is true, but at the same time, I think it's a little unfair. But yes, I agree.

What do you think about the creation story in Genesis, how it came to be, and whether there's any truth to it?

I haven't thought about it in a while, and honestly I'm probably a bit hazy, but I think how it came to be is . . . we know storytelling has played a large process in human development and evolution and, certainly, culture. Storytelling is a very powerful force in not only forming but maintaining these cooperative groups that it created. So from that perspective, I think it's an early story, like many others, that was also used to try to help maintain social order. I think that's how it came about, and I think it's just a story.

Do you think that faith and science intersect? If so, how?

I would say they can. I mean, everything we do always has some faith in it. Maybe one of the first people to really drive this point was David Hume and the problem of induction. Basically, the scientific method assumes that if I perform this experiment today and get this result, then if I repeat the same experiment tomorrow, I should get the same result. But how did we come about having that belief? Only by the practice itself. We knew that experiments performed three days ago could be performed today and it would be the same thing, but that means we're proving induction by the logic of induction, so there's a circularity there. So, ultimately, we believe in the scientific method entirely on faith—that this law of induction will not change tomorrow or any other day. And all of our best theories rely on that. So at the end of the day, there are logical holes in any belief system that you choose to live by, but I would still say that there's a lot more evidence for induction, however flawed and circular the underlying logic is. I don't know. It's just a belief system I'm more comfortable with. But beyond that general idea of faith, I don't really see . . . again, unless you choose to try to bring the two together, they don't have to be necessarily so related. Because while what I just stated about faith is true, as a scientist you don't think about that every day to do your work. Just as a religious person, you don't have to think about science every day to go about your religious life.

So there isn't too much intersection between the two. Do you think there can be?

Yeah, I mean, as I just said, good scientists should be aware of the logical faults with what they're doing and the aspects in which our practice is based on faith. You should always be aware of these things, just as I think it would be good practice for any religious person to be aware of the science of the day. I definitely think they can be closely connected.

I agree with that. Would you say that both the religious right (i.e., the six-day creationists), and the liberal left could both benefit from learning more about each other?

Yes? But not necessarily, for example, about each other's philosophy. Oftentimes for people from such disparate groups, it isn't so much the schools of thought that they need to be closer with, but the other stuff—the culture and the lifestyle that surrounds it—that really empowers those very different schools of thought. Because when you hear someone with a philosophy different from your own, it's easy to think, "Wow, that person must be stupid," and not realize that their experience is so different from your own, that unless you understand their experience first, you'll never understand why they live by that philosophy. So they definitely need to know each other better, but not necessarily philosophically. Just on a human level, there needs to be more connection.

Would you say that there's harm to believing in a six-day creation (either personally or societally)?

I think there can be a lot of harm, but at the same time, the same is true of the liberal left. Any belief system, or any story, whether it's the scientific birth of the universe or the religious creation of the universe, any such worldview can be co-opted and used for harm— great harm. There's evidence of that on both sides. Of course you build in harmless stories, because then you hide the power structure. You say, "Oh, I generally believe in this religion," or in this set of moral values, but then you claim moral authority to deliver justice any which way you want.

I'm not sure I follow.

For example, the Crusades. Clearly there was a religious power with a vested interest that abused that power. And so perpetuating these stories maintains that power. And again, it's whether that story is scientific or religious. Because you have the opposite thing with Stalin: a declared atheist state. So there's always harm in perpetuating any kind of system of moral absolutes. Because whoever created and commands that system has the power to dole out justice however they please, on some level.

On an individual level, do you see harm in a six-day creation belief?

Probably not. These philosophies are so complex. For example, believing in the creation story is probably harmless. But people who believe in that story, at least in our day and age, tend to share other values that can be very harmful. And again, I think these narratives are built to build a following, that you can believe other, more harmful things.

For example?

Well, at various times Christianity has been prone to anti-Semitism or other forms of xenophobia and antagonism of any other religion, and I think that can be extremely harmful. Maybe you're not arguing about the creation story, but whatever you are arguing about can breed violence. So even by having someone believe in a harmless story, you can then turn them against someone else who chooses not to believe in that harmless story. It sounds ridiculous now, but we know it's happened. You could have the most innocent philosophy in the world that says, "Do no harm to others." But as soon as someone doesn't believe that, you're like, "Well, guess we have to kill him." It's like, Wait, what? When—how—did that happen?

Aside from present company, what sorts of interactions have you had with six-day creationists? Have any been particularly positive or negative?

Recently? Since I left high school, I haven't had many such interactions. Even mostly by high school, I just started avoiding those people. Because, I don't know, I just had nothing to learn from them, didn't have a lot in common with them.

What turns you off from wanting to speak to people like that?

Oftentimes they're not willing to—they're not really open-minded. You can't even take a different interpretation of the Bible with them—like it isn't up for debate or discussion. Just, "No, it's this way. You're wrong." So there's no point. Why even disagree at that point? I learned nothing; you learned nothing; thanks. And I did move to circles where I could discuss these things. For a long time I was on a religious side, but as I learned more, the religious answers didn't satisfy me.

Do you think that learning more, in general, leads to agnosticism? Is it the more you know, the more you realize you don't know?

Not necessarily. But people who are prone to questioning probably end up questioning more. Skeptics, who are less willing to take an answer that they don't have good reasons for, are more prone to becoming agnostic. I started with my experience with my dad. What I learned the most from my dad was to question. That led me to here. It's not that I'm saying, "I know more." In fact, I'm claiming to know less. It's just that a lot of people don't take the time or don't care to ask those questions. And that's fine. It's just not necessarily about knowledge.

Barring something supernatural, what would it take for you to believe in God, or is there anything that could change your mind?

I don't think there is anything beyond the natural world. The way I would put it is this: If you're implying that God is outside the world . . .

What I meant more is like, if you saw an angel come and pick that motorcyclist up and set him gently on the sidewalk while a car crashed into it, you would probably believe in a God, right?

Right, yeah. I'd have a lot of questions.

So beyond something obviously, blatantly miraculous, is there . . .

Again, this goes back to being a skeptic. The natural world is one that we can question and maybe gain some understanding about, but obviously there's still a lot of faith involved. But the fact that we have this world, that we're able to scrutinize on this level, I just don't see—it's kind of hard for me to believe in other worlds. You could call that shortsighted, but I don't know.

So, basically, without evidence for something it's difficult to . . .

I would say this: The biggest reason I'm skeptical of religion is because humans lie, cheat, and steal, and there are many reasons why humans would create such a big lie. So that made me a skeptic and makes me less prone to believe when someone's like, "Hey, there's a pot of gold." Does that mean I'm maybe throwing God out with the bathwater? Like, "Well, my bad. He'll forgive me, right?"

LISTENING TO ELIZABETH

Could you briefly describe your religious background?

Ahh . . . religious background . . . raised Catholic, went to Catholic schools all my life. The type that if we were away on vacation, we'd stop and go to church on the weekends.

And is faith or religion a part of your life now?

I'm not one of those people who would say, "I'm spiritual and not religious." I like the establishment of the Catholic church, and I like even the history and tradition and all that. I don't really go to church anymore, but I usually enjoy it when I do; it's just that I don't really feel that way anymore.

When you say you don't feel that way anymore, can you elaborate on that?

I'm a bit more agnostic now.

Why is that?

Lots of reasons. I guess faith is believing in something that you can't see, but it's hard when people . . . I don't know if I can point to a specific instance or case or anything like that. It's more that it's just harder and harder to believe there's a God out there. For instance, when would this manifest itself in our lives, you know? I would like there to be one, but then there's also so many questions. Like why are we just left on our own? And I don't know, maybe the science part too—you just kind of start growing away from religion and believing.

Can you elaborate on the science part? What do you mean by that?

You're always questioning: what can you prove, what can you see, what can you actually think about with experiments? Although I say that, and I'm working in phylogenetics, and it's reconstructing things [that you can't see] that happened a hundred million years ago. [Laughs.] It's kind of like this different type of analytical, critical thinking where you always need to have something to hold on to. If the Bible can't be taken literally, then what can you get out of it? I believe that there was a person, "Jesus," but if some things can't be taken literally, then what?

Would you say that being a scientist contributed to your shift to agnosticism?

I'm not entirely sure. It might have just been as I got older and began to think about things differently.

I know you said it happened over time, but if you could estimate a time in your life when you would have said you were more agnostic than believing in God, what time was that?

It probably started in college, slowly, and then during my master's [program], so I was 22 or 23.

What's your view on the Bible now? Is there truth to it as far as historical truth? Is there a lot of fable in it? Does it have value for people other than Christians?

I do think there's truth in it, and actual events and happenings and all that. But, yeah, I feel like a lot of the parts of it are open to interpretation or should be interpreted. And if we think it was written in a whole different society—one that is so far removed from us—maybe the way their society worked influenced things that were written.

Can you elaborate?

I don't think I know the Bible well enough to elaborate, but I think their value system is going to make its way into all of the writings. . . . [trying to remember] . . . For example, that there's two different stories of creation: the one where Eve is made out of Adam's rib, and then the other one where they're both formed at the same time.

In bringing that up, are you thinking that there are contradictions in the Bible?

Yes, I guess a few. I don't know. Even the gospels have slightly different stories, in the way that things were revealed. But I don't know a lot of specific instances. Just, if there's one contradiction, then how can you read the whole thing literally? It's much more like, "This happened. Here's the story." But if passed down verbally, things are going to change.

So what do you believe about the creation story? Do you believe there's any value to it or any truth in it?

Hmm. Any truth? As in, if the world had been formed in six days type of truth? I would say no. I think historians are coming at it from a more scientific sense. For example, all different societies have some sort of creation story. You can kind of see how things are the same and different that way around the world.

When did you first learn about earth's (or the universe's) origins?

I was really big into being an astronaut when I was in kindergarten and first grade. So I suppose at that point I was reading about it, but I honestly couldn't tell you.

Was there ever any hint in your upbringing saying that the earth was created in six days? Or was it pretty much always, "There's this story in the Bible, but it's not entirely true"?

I'm guessing in elementary school we probably did learn that the earth was created in six days. But I don't remember the details of what we learned.

Do you think it's important, from a Christian's perspective? Or do people make a bigger deal of it than is necessary?

The issue of the creation story? I suppose if we're going to have a discussion of what the Bible says, then, yeah, it would be important that people know what it says. So in that respect, yes. And I think the Bible has been extremely important through all of history, since so many laws are based on it—and art. It's engrained in some of the things we do and we don't even realize it.

Can you explain evolution in your own words to someone who has little formal education on it?

In a nutshell, evolution is gradual change in species over time, but then there's microevolution and macroevolution. Although even for evolutionists, there are arguments of whether it's gradual or if there are big jumps. The traditional idea, especially if you go back to Darwin, would be the gradual change over time and that some sort of interbreeding populations have genes and DNA (DNA is what replicates in our cells and basically can pass on genetic information for the next generation), but there can be little changes, little mutations in the DNA through different processes. Especially if the population is small, a few little changes can easily kind of take over and change the whole genetic makeup of that population, and so it would be small, gradual changes over time—microevolution. And then above the species level, that's macroevolution, that you have actual species that are splitting apart from one another and no longer interbreed.

How does that happen, speciation?[2]

I think that's a really huge question itself. If you think in a geographic sense, you could have sympatric[3] speciation (i.e., species are slowly growing away from each other or something happens or

---

[2] Speciation is the process by which one species splits into two. Depending on your working definition of species, this isn't always a black-and-white scenario. For example, sometimes similar species can still interbreed but their offspring may be sterile (think horses and donkeys) or poorly adapted to their environment so the offspring themselves don't reproduce. For speciation to occur, some sort of reproductive barrier must be in place so that the genetics of two groups of the same species are separated. An obvious case of this is geographic isolation. For example, if two birds migrate away from the majority of their species and begin a subpopulation on an island, there would be no genetic mixing between the two groups. After many generations, their offspring may have adapted to the new island or evolved new or different traits. If those changes make the island birds incompatible with the original population, then speciation has occurred.

[3] Sympatric speciation is when two species split even though they are geographically in the same place. They live in the same location, and may even encounter each other, but something causes a reproductive barrier. For example, one group may mate during the day and the other at night, and so the two groups are reproductively isolated by their behavior.

maybe there's an important mutation and all of a sudden there's some group that can't interbreed). Or maybe there's a change where some part of the population is mating during the day instead of the night. But then there's also the idea that some sort of boundary comes up in between two populations, maybe a river goes through and separates these populations, and so they're split into two different pieces that can't really cross and get to each other.

Can you talk about timescale?

With speciation? I guess it can happen quickly. Darwin, in *The Origin of Species*, was also talking about varieties of things; you have farmers who are breeding sheep together to get certain characteristics, so you can start seeing changes within a matter of generations. Or especially in fruit flies in a lab. A lot of species do persist for a few million years—like insects and stuff—up to several, even 20 million years. But speciation itself can be protracted, so scientists who try to model how speciation works take that into account: that it could be a very slow and gradual process, over several million years, but it could be faster.

Why could some species persist for 20 million years but not others?

Changing environmental conditions, how well-adapted these species are to the environment. I mean, if a meteor comes in and wipes out a whole bunch of things, like the dinosaurs, there you go, that's the end of that. But it might just have to do with their life history traits: are they producing a whole bunch of offspring, or is everything invested into one or two offspring? And if something detrimental happens, that could make a difference.

If a creationist came up to you and said that they didn't believe in evolution, would you change your answer to them? How would you try to describe it?

I'd probably try to pull up more examples on a smaller timescale. For example, the peppered moth in industrial Europe: that's a good example of microevolution; the population is slowly shifting. Before pollution, the moths were white on the trees, so they blended in with the white bark. But after pollution, the population changes. There was already genetic variation in the population, but the moths with the dark-colored traits persist better in the polluted environment because they're now camouflaged against the dirty trees. So you can see those small-scale shifts. Another example is viruses. You can see how things can change on a scale of just years, basically. Pulling out smaller-scale things, you could argue different things with micro-evolution vs. macroevolution actually making new species—you can see how things could change.

Would you say that the earth or the tree of life (and the genetic code in the tree of life) has evidence against a young earth?

Well, I guess fossil evidence, and with carbon dating. Or Baltic amber, being 44.1 million years old.

Talk more specifically about what you do. You're a phylogeneticist.[4] Would you say that there's evidence within the genetic code of organisms against a young earth, or is DNA compatible with a young earth?

I don't know if I could answer that the most accurately. But basically, we're pulling out little pieces of DNA that we can match up across all sorts of different organisms. We look for pieces that are similar between organisms, but then there are differences in those pieces. In order to get the dates, we have to calibrate that with an outside source. So we would find evolutionary relationships, basically, and a family-tree-like structure of how things are related. But in order to put an age anywhere on that or to date a branching point in that tree, then you need some sort of outside information. Like a fossil, for example, or a point at which two continents had moved apart. So, usually, to get an absolute age, you need some sort of outside information. Although this is not the case with viruses, because you can collect genetic information from samples from a decade ago or more and you can actually date branching points in the tree that way. But, otherwise, just in the DNA, I don't know if there's necessarily a signature of that.

---

[4] A phylogeneticist is a biologist who studies the evolutionary history and relationships between organisms or individuals.

In your opinion, is there harm to believing in a six-day creation? Is there a detriment to either personal well-being or society?

I guess you could have a different worldview if you believe that and not that the world is really old and all the changes that happened over millions of years. I don't think it's tied to a specific story; it's probably tied to a whole different way of looking at the world.

What do you mean?

If you believe that story, I don't know, what about the dinosaurs? How does that work? Then how do you accept any other evidence we're trying to collect from the earth? Like soil cores and what's happened to Antarctica or how humans came across the Bering land bridge. How old would the earth be, then, for a literal interpretation [of the Bible]?

It depends on how literally you take it.

I feel like, honestly, I wouldn't even understand how you would view the world differently. But you must, otherwise how do you believe that humans came across the Bering land bridge 12,000 years ago? How would you interpret history in that case? I just feel like it would be a whole different ball game.

Do you think there's harm to believing in a young, biblical time frame for the origin of the universe?

I don't know. I don't think necessarily, but it probably means you're not open to any more historical science, like fossils and things like that. Then it's kind of a rejection of what scientists would believe. And to extrapolate, if you're taking that literally and other parts of the Bible literally, then it is maybe affecting some of your opinions and you're just going to reject other things.

What opinions do you mean, specifically?

For instance, man having dominion over the world so you can do with it what you want. But then maybe it's a different thing, like the world has actually been around for a really long time and we weren't just put here to take care of it, although now we should. So, things like that—kind of tangential. I don't know that you'd be hurting anyone if you believe in a creation story.

Have you had any particularly positive or negative interactions with creationists?

I don't think I've really had many, or at least it hasn't come up.

There were never, say, protesters outside your building at [major public university].

No, I can't think of anything that sticks out in my mind.

Creationists will sometimes claim that both believing in a six-day creation and believing in evolution require faith. How would you respond to someone who said that?

I don't feel like faith is needed for evolution. You can see small examples, just in your lifetime.

Can you extrapolate those small examples to longer timescales?

What if you go into geology and the history of the universe? People are seeing how fast light travels or seeing stars that are many billions of light years away; everything's so old. You don't have to just look at life itself; you can look at the universe. I would say that there are other examples there. I guess it depends if you believe calculations or carbon dating.

What misunderstandings do you think creationists have about evolution?

That humans descended from apes. That sort of thing. We didn't really descend from anything that is alive right now. Any species that exists now may have descended from a common ancestor, but it's not like we came from an ape. So at some point in the past—a million, two million years ago—there was some sort of different-looking organism that was the ancestor to humans, orangutans, gorillas. I would say that's a big misunderstanding.

Is there anything you want to say to Christians who might be reading this book?

I feel like anything I'd say would be asking them to go against their religion. If you have to interpret the Bible literally, obviously, I've shown I believe in evolution.

Would saying something to someone that goes against their religion give you pause? I get the impression that would make you uncomfortable.

Well, as I said, I was raised Catholic, and I think religion is important. And religious people are good people. I've just never been in a position to have to interpret the Bible literally, so I guess that's hard for me to even understand—that viewpoint. I'd just say, "Keep an open mind to science." But if that directly conflicts with what you believe . . . I don't know if I have anything.

What would it take for you to become religious again or to believe in God again?

I don't know, I've thought that I'd like my kids to go to Catholic schools and things like that, but even then, I think it would have to be more of an internal thing. Something would have to change in me, like it changed before, but it would have to change again. I don't know what it would take. Quite honestly, if there was something like a miracle, if I have no faith, I guess that's what I need, you know? Even experiences like ghosts and stuff like that, like if something supernatural . . .

Do you believe in ghosts?

Kind of. But if I believe in them, then I could believe in supernatural things, right? But . . . yeah. So some ghosts, that might start me off in the right direction.

It's interesting to me how many people believe in ghosts but don't believe in God.

If I believed, obviously a ghost would be something—if a person's soul was still here, then how would I not believe in religion?

What would it take for you to believe in a six-day creation, or could that ever happen?

That part would never happen.

Why not?

I just don't think you need to interpret the Bible literally. And I feel like there's too much evidence to the contrary. So I would have to say that part I would probably never believe in.

A young woman sits on a bench and stares into the vast canyon below. Her wide eyes take in hues of pink and red, purple and blue, arrayed in bands stacked all the way down to the river, barely visible at the bottom. The breeze wafting up from the warmth of the canyon's lower reaches plays with her hair and serves to reinforce the enormity of it all.

After a few minutes of taking everything in, she breaks the silence. "I can't believe anyone could look at this and think it all came about by accident," she says to her husband, without taking her eyes off the sight. He smiles and nods. He too has been marveling at the grandeur of the scene and recognizes the fingerprints of the Creator.

Meanwhile, a short walk along the rim, there is another woman sitting on a bench, basking in the same soft colors, breathing in the same pine-scented air, mulling the meaning of what she sees. "I can't believe someone can look at this and imagine it just appeared in six days," she says. Her husband smiles and nods as he looks at those exposed layers of sedimentary rock and sees clear evidence for a land- scape laid down and carved out over eons.

How could the second couple come to such a drastically different conclusion? You may sympathize with their point of view. If so, read on to hear how others explain that perspective in their own words—and to hear what God says in his.

On the other hand, seeing the second couple's perspective may seem as difficult to you as spotting the rapids in the river from the can- yon's edge. Yet people with this perspective are just down the rim. They live down the street. They study or work with you. They may even sit in the pew with you on Sunday. They may be blinded to the work of their Creator or, even worse, to their need of a Savior. But their views—and the reasons for them—may not be what you expect.

1.

The young-earth creationist's worldview is built on the supposition that the book of Genesis is meant to be read as perfectly preserved, literal history. . . . Unfortunately for YECs, they do not have to go very far into scripture to run into problems with this approach. That's because the first couple chapters of Genesis contains *[sic]* not one, but two creation accounts, and—if read entirely literally—they are completely contradictory and irreconcilable.

—Tyler Francke,
founder of godofevolution.org

It's not uncommon for evolutionists who know a bit about the Bible to talk about the first two chapters of Genesis as two different, contradictory creation accounts. Naturally, it's easy for those who read them that way (or hear someone talk about them that way) to doubt their truth and dismiss it all as a myth.

This is frustrating for young-earth creationists. It seems so clear that the first two chapters of the Bible give the same history. Chapter 1 of Genesis gives us the play-by-play of God's creating activity. Chapter 2 gives a quick recap of the first five days and a close-up, slow-motion replay of that all-important day 6, zooming in on the crown of his creation. It's no different than a flashback scene in a movie or news coverage of an event from multiple angles. In fact, it may seem so obvious that it never even occurred to you that someone might see these two chapters as different, contradictory accounts.

Why would a creator put plants that are fundamentally different, but look so similar, in diverse areas of the world that seem ecologically identical? Wouldn't it make more sense to put the same species of plants in areas with the same type of soil and climate? . . . Again one must ask: If animals were specially created, why would the creator produce on different continents fundamentally different animals that nevertheless look and act so much alike?

—Jerry Coyne,
Professor Emeritus of Biology,
University of Chicago; author,
Why Evolution Is True

A six-day creationist might respond like this: Well, why not? Surely an almighty God can design his creation the way he wants. You might question why your friend decorates her house the way she does, but that wouldn't lead you to assume that it decorated itself by accident. The Lord's words to Job come to mind:

Who is this that obscures my plans with words without knowledge?
Brace yourself like a man; I will question you, and you shall answer
me. Where were you when I laid the earth's foundation? Tell me, if
you understand. Who marked off its dimensions? Surely you know!
(Job 38:2-5).
A little humility is in order, isn't it?

Why does anyone need to wear glasses with corrective lenses?
Wouldn't you, as the designer, have just specified perfect vision for
everyone? Why do so many of us get sunburn? Why isn't our skin
more sensitive and tougher all at the same time? Same with hips,
knees, and anterior cruciate ligaments: Why not make them a lot
more durable? We wouldn't be having all these replacement and
repair surgeries.

—Bill Nye,
PBS' *Bill Nye the Science Guy;*
author, *Undeniable*

It's called sin! There is a designer, and his design was perfect. Then
his creatures rebelled against him. Since then sin's curse has worked
its way through the whole system. "We know that the whole creation
has been groaning as in the pains of childbirth right up to the present
time" (Romans 8:22). This is why eyesight fades, skin burns, and knees
blow out. This is why decay, destruction, and death are everywhere in
the universe. The chapter that immediately follows the account of cre-
ation tells us all about it.

We creationists find it frustrating when evolutionists misunderstand
and misinterpret our point of view. And these are just a few tame quotes,
to say nothing of the mean-spirited things people write in blog posts
and the comments sections of online forums. Or say on late-night TV:

This week Georgia's Board of Education approved a plan that allows
teachers to use the word 'evolution' when teaching biology. Though
as a compromise, dinosaurs are now called 'Jesus Horses.'

—Jimmy Fallon,
Weekend Update news anchor on
Saturday Night Live

How does it make you feel? Annoyed? Indignant? Exasperated?

*Okay . . . now has it ever occurred to you that **this is exactly how evolutionists feel** when they hear creationists misquote, misconstrue, and
even mock what they believe?*

*This is a complaint of many who subscribe to the prevailing scientific
theory of the origin of life:*

"Creationists just don't understand evolution."

*So many of the books written about evolution have as their stated
purpose to educate a public that remains, in the view of their authors,
largely ignorant of what evolution is. Here's a quote from the introduction to one:*

Darwin's ideas were simple, powerful, and they explained so much
that today evolution is the foundation of the life sciences. But after
nearly 150 years, evolution is still commonly misunderstood by the
general public, particularly in the United States, where a number
of myths about evolution have arisen. . . . Many of these myths are
based on ignorance, for which the best remedy is knowledge. Some
are perpetuated because evolution is inadequately taught in high
schools, although many teachers do an excellent job. The media also
contribute a fair share of confusion, from the misleading depictions
of evolution sometimes found in science fiction movies to the poverty of science programming on commercial television. There are
even more troubling forces at work in America that make it hard to
debunk these myths, such as the people who believe that their religious texts and traditions can provide us with scientific answers even
though those answers come from prescientific times.

—Cameron M. Smith and Charles Sullivan,
The Top Ten Myths About Evolution

*Note that the authors are worried not only about creationists but the
general public. If it's true that people on the whole have misunderstandings about evolution, it's surely truer yet about those of us who
believe in creation!*

*Many of us grew up in Christian homes. We went to Christian Sunday
schools, perhaps Christian elementary schools, maybe Christian high*

schools, and even Christian colleges. What a blessing! But that also means that many of us may know very little about how actual evolutionists talk about the theory of evolution, other than what we may have picked up reading National Geographic *or watching episodes of the previously quoted* Bill Nye the Science Guy. *On the one hand, it's good to have been spared in this way; on the other hand, we may have to learn a bit more in order to engage evolutionists.*

If you're in this boat, here's a one-sentence summary of evolution from the man who made it popular:

One general law, leading to the advancement of all organic beings, namely, multiply, vary, let the strongest live and the weakest die.

—Charles Darwin,
19th-century naturalist;
author, *The Origin of Species*

Here's a slightly longer summary:

Darwin described evolution as "descent with modification." This simply means changes in the properties of organisms over generations. These changes are explained by at least three independent processes that when taken together form what we mean by evolution. These are replication, variation, and selection, and they are all observable facts. Replication is simply reproduction. Variation is genetic differences between parents and their offspring. And selection refers to natural selection, the process whereby those best adapted to their environment tend to survive and pass on their genes to the next generation.

—Cameron M. Smith and Charles Sullivan

That's the essence of it. But for those who don't know much more than that about evolution, there's always the risk of mischaracterizing it, even if unintentionally.

For example, have you ever heard evolution described as the theory that people come from monkeys? Evolutionists would jump all over that statement.

People don't come from monkeys. Around thirty million years ago, the African primates diverged into two distinct groups, taking up different diets, habits, and habitats, as their environments changed and opportunities arose. One group developed into apes, which included—much later—chimpanzees, gorillas, and humans. The other group developed into monkeys, and DNA and other studies prove that we belong in the ape group instead of the monkey group. Do people come from monkeys? Not at all. We do share a common ancestor with chimpanzees, and before them, with the group that became monkeys. But to say that we came from monkeys is simply wrong, and evolution has never claimed it.

—Cameron M. Smith and Charles Sullivan

Any species that exists now may have descended from a common ancestor, but it's not like we came from an ape. So at some point in the past—a million, two million years ago—there was some sort of different-looking organism that was the ancestor to humans, orang-utans, gorillas. I would say that's a big misunderstanding.

—Elizabeth,
see above, "Listening to Elizabeth"

To say we "share a common ancestor" with chimpanzees may not sound all that different to you than saying that we come from monkeys. But that's missing the point. To someone well-versed in evolution, it's the kind of fundamental misunderstanding that provokes annoyance, just like so many statements about creation do for us.

Here's another one: A favorite argument against evolution is the one demanding proof in the form of a missing link. Evolutionists hear this all the time and, as you can see, get quite tired of it:

Creationists are deeply enamored of the fossil record, because they have been taught (by each other) to repeat, over and over, the mantra that it is full of "gaps": "Show me your 'intermediates'!" They fondly (very fondly) imagine that these "gaps" are an embarrassment to evolutionists. Actually, we are lucky to have any fossils at all, let alone the massive numbers that we now do have to document evolutionary history—large numbers of which, by any standards, constitute beautiful "intermediates."

—Richard Dawkins,
evolutionary biologist,
author, *The Greatest Show on Earth*

Again, we could jump on an answer like this and say, "You're admitting there are gaps!" But we are trying to listen first. Harping on the missing links will often come across as ignorance of the vast numbers of fossils that have been found.

Here's one more caricature that evolutionists find troubling:

Many creationists and science deniers, especially in the United States, cite randomness as part of the process of evolution and go on to insist that since evolution is random it cannot explain the rich complexity of life. . . . Creationists often use the example of a hypothetical tornado swirling its way through a hypothetical junkyard whose contents include all the pieces to build one of my beloved old 747s. (This is sometimes called the junkyard tornado argument.) What are the chances, they ask, that you'd end up with a perfectly assembled, operable airplane? Obviously, zero, because it would be random.

The problem with this argument is that the premise is wrong. Evolution, and the selection of reproduction-worthy genes that drives it, is the opposite of random. It is a sieve that living things have to pass through successfully, or we never see them again.

—Bill Nye,
Undeniable

These are just a few examples. The purpose of this chapter is not to give you a crash course in evolution. Rather, it's to point out that harboring such misconceptions or using such clichés can short-circuit the kinds of conversations we're hoping to have.

In other words, a little humility is in order.

Would you like to engage an evolutionist? Recognize that you may not know as much about what they believe as you might think. Be willing to let them tell you more about the theory they adhere to, and they just might be willing to let you tell them more about the truth you know.

You might even start in a surprising place: by confessing your faults. The stereotype of Christians as backwards and ignorant may be offensive to us, but the one that likely hinders our witness even more is that of Christians as judgmental and condescending. What if, in your conversations with evolutionists, you conceded that you've been ignorant of their perspective? What if you admitted that you've sometimes harbored uncharitable thoughts or judged others without getting to know them? Such an honest confession could be very disarming. It also gives you the perfect opportunity to talk about your Savior. Once your guilt is on the table, you can describe what God did with it for the sake of Jesus—how he washed it away and erased it from his record book (Psalm 51:1,2). How he sent it away, as far away as east is from west (Psalm 103:12). How he stomped on it and sank it to the bottom of the ocean (Micah 7:19). And how he does the same for all who believe in Jesus.

*This is the truth you want a chance to speak. Some patient listening may get you there. "Always be prepared to give an answer to everyone who asks you to give the reason for the hope that you have. **But do this with gentleness and respect**" (1 Peter 3:15).*

2.

Thus, from the war of nature, from famine and death, the most exalted object which we are capable of conceiving, namely, the production of the higher animals, directly follows. There is grandeur in this view of life, with its several powers, having been originally breathed into a few forms or into one; and that, whilst this planet has gone cycling on according to the fixed laws of gravity, from so simple a beginning endless forms most beautiful and most wonderful have been, and are being, evolved.

—Charles Darwin,
The Origin of the Species

With these words, Darwin concluded the book that started it all, his The Origin of Species. *A century-and-a-half later, another author concluded his book in similar fashion:*

We are surrounded by endless forms, most beautiful and most wonderful, and it is no accident, but the direct consequence of evolution by non-random natural selection—the only game in town, the greatest show on Earth.

—Richard Dawkins,
The Greatest Show on Earth

The way they describe the natural world with such wonder almost sounds like it could come from a psalm:

> *The grasslands of the wilderness overflow;*
> *the hills are clothed with gladness.*
> *The meadows are covered with flocks*
> *and the valleys are mantled with grain;*
> *they shout for joy and sing.*
> *(Psalm 65:12,13)*

Of course, in that same psalm, David recognized that all of nature's grandeur points to the greatness of its Creator: "The whole earth is filled with awe at your wonders" (Psalm 65:8). Those of us who agree with David may find it tempting to assume that those who do not see the Creator in nature must be lacking in awe and wonder over the creation, that those who see nature as the result of a gradual process see it only as an object to be categorized and measured instead of a work of art to be admired.

Evolutionists are aware of that characterization and find it unfair.

The tactical genius of the ID [intelligent design] movement is that its very name has maneuvered the defenders of Darwin into a losing position, one in which they are made to seem as if they are arguing against meaning and purpose, to be claiming there is neither rhyme nor reason to the universe in which we live.

The great irony of this situation is that defenders of science are well aware that that caricature is wrong. Scientists are, in fact, the very ones who search for order in our existence, who are best equipped to marvel at nature, and who find the deepest fulfillment in their exploration. Like others who have been lucky enough to make a career in science, I find the natural world filled with wonder and delight, and shake my head at those who would depict the scientific enterprise as something that would rob our existence out of its meaning. Quite the contrary: The more we understand of nature, and the more thoroughly we investigate our past, the more deeply we can appreciate just how remarkable our lives truly are.

—Kenneth R. Miller,
molecular biologist, Brown University;
author, *Only a Theory*

In other words, they would say:

"I can see nature as marvelous without seeing it as miraculous."

Often evolutionists are the ones with their faces up to the microscopes and telescopes, studying the intricacies of the world in here or the one out there. They do see beauty and complexity. They see something bigger than themselves.

Science assures us that we are indeed the products of evolution, but it certainly does not tell us that we are its "casual and meaningless" products. The scientific insight that our very existence, through evolution, requires a universe of the very size, scale, and age that we see around us implies that the universe, in a certain sense, had us in mind from the very beginning. It is very much, in the memorable words of physicist Freeman Dyson, a "universe that knew we were coming."

—Kenneth R. Miller

They marvel at the way that everything fits together to form life as we know it.

Though I have no doubt that the origin of life was not in fact a miracle, I do believe that we live in a bio-friendly universe of a stunningly ingenious character.

—Paul Davies,
physicist, professor at Arizona State University

They even find purpose in evolution.

A clearer understanding of our relationship to nature leads, without question, to an appreciation of the unique role our species plays at this moment in the history of our planet. It is certainly correct to remind ourselves that we are just one species among millions that share the earth, but it is even more important to have a realistic view of our own value to that living world. We may be one among many, but we are the only one that can actually catalog and value that diversity, and the only one that can act in a way that will directly and consciously affect the future of this planet. That is an awesome responsibility, and it infuses every human life with meaning and value.

—Kenneth R. Miller

Now, we recognize that the meaning they see is but a shadow of life's real purpose. We are to care for the world because God put it in our care.[5] And God has entrusted to us not only his creation but also his Word, which tells us that this world is beautiful for a reason (God made it) and for a purpose (to point to him).

Ultimately, evolution can become idolatry. When Darwin talks about the "most exalted object which we are capable of conceiving," we wish he were talking about God instead of "the production of higher animals." Such praise of creation, without giving credit to the Creator, denies God his glory as the source of life and truth. Indeed, Satan has succeeded in convincing many to take God off his pedestal in favor of the false gods of Nature or Life or Evolutionary Process.

We see it for the idol that it is. Like the wooden statues of old that the Lord derided (Isaiah 44:6-23), humans have fashioned this theory and look to it for answers it cannot give. Yet instead of trying to topple the idol from its stand, we could strive to raise up something higher to marvel at: the cross, on which the most exalted Son of God was willing to die in humility for us.

Here's one way you might do that: Let your evolutionist friends tell you about the things they've learned from science that cause them to marvel at our world. Join them in their wonder. Discuss with them how such awesome things could have come into existence. As you're marveling together at creation, you'll have a chance to express your faith in the Creator. "You know, the more I learn about amazing things like that,

---

[5] Here we may find a point of connection with those who espouse evolution. People sometimes assume that Christians do not care about the environment, since we (rightfully) say that God gave us dominion over the world and we know that he, not we, will bring it to an end. But we know that we have the greatest reason to care for this world: God has entrusted it to us. When you express concern for the earth, evolutionists may be surprised to hear it—and interested in hearing more.

the more impressive it is to me that a God who's smart enough and powerful enough to make all these things would want me as his child." Then talk about how God made that happen. Invite them to stand with you on Calvary and see the sun stop shining as its Creator dies for our sins. Have them listen with you as Jesus speaks extraordinary words of forgiveness. Put your arm around their shoulders and point up at the love streaming down from the bloody face of the Son of God.

Remember, it is only through this gospel message that Jesus takes up or firms up his rightful rule in human hearts . . . and idols crumble before him.

In other words, when we hear evolutionists speaking in such glowing, almost religious terms about nature and its processes, there's a better path than to rage about the foolishness of talking about purpose and meaning without a God there to give those things. Instead, we can be thankful that God's creation is catching people's attention, just as it was meant to do.

> The heavens declare the glory of God;
> the skies proclaim the work of his hands.
> Day after day they pour forth speech;
> night after night they reveal knowledge.
> They have no speech, they use no words;
> no sound is heard from them.
> Yet their voice goes out into all the earth,
> their words to the end of the world.
> (Psalm 19:1-4)

Of course, the "voice" of the heavens—the divine beauty and power that the skies proclaim—is only the introduction. Another Voice must be heard. Just before quoting those Psalm verses in his letter to the Romans, the apostle Paul reminds us of the only way anyone can truly believe: "Faith comes from hearing the message, and the message is heard through the word about Christ" (Romans 10:17).

In our time, Satan, the "god of this age" (2 Corinthians 4:4) has blinded many hearts, so that they see the signs but not the One to whom the signs point. But as long as people are marveling at the wonders of nature, we have a little patch of common ground as a place to start. Like Paul in Athens (Acts 17), we can offer them something they may not realize they're searching for. We can tell about the God who not only brought life into the world but also brought life from the grave.

3.

The cellular biologist hunches over his microscope. The tiny lens transports him into an even tinier world, a world with magnificent organization. His frame of view is wall-to-wall membranes and mitochondria, chromosomes and ribosomes, and all kinds of other organelles—the building blocks of life as we know it. He marvels at its complexity. It all works together so remarkably. It does things that no human machine can do, and all of that in a space many times smaller than the period at the end of this sentence. It's almost as if it were designed that way . . .

*He sits up abruptly. **No, that can't be,** he thinks. He grunts and shakes his head. **I know there's no God. There must be some other explanation.** So he puts his face back to the scope and comes up with a way to explain away the inexplicable complexity. **Something about gradations and mutations . . . yes, that's it.** He's found his answer. He publishes a paper. Another scientist builds on his work. And so evolution marches on, all because scientists are intent on finding an explanation for what they see—any explanation, no matter how far-fetched—that leaves God out of the picture.*

Or so we might imagine it.

If that kind of ignoble laboratory scene ever really plays out, it is the exception. Yes, there are evolutionists who are atheists. There may even be a few whose denial of God leads them to willfully deny any evidence of God's existence in the natural world and look for some—any—other way and then stubbornly charge down that path while ignoring all other possibilities.

But that's not what we hear from most of those who subscribe to evolution. To start with, most of them would say that they are not atheists[6] (more on that later). And whether they believe in God or not, many would say something like this:

"I believe in evolution because it works."

---

[6] According to a recent survey, 57% of Americans believe in evolution, and over two-thirds of that group believe that God guided the process. (Swift, Art. "In U.S., Belief in Creationist View of Humans at New Low." Gallup News, May 22, 2017, http://news.gallup.com/poll/210956/belief-creationist-view-humans-new-low.aspx.)

Why insist on explaining the world through blind law when you might well believe that something else might stand behind everything? The answer given by the scientist, including the evolutionist, appeals to the pragmatic. Methodological naturalism[7] works!

—Michael Ruse,
philosopher of science, Florida State University;
author, *Darwinism and Its Discontents*

Since Darwin popularized the theory of evolution in the late 19th century, scientists in many different fields have been testing and using his hypothesis. While there has been (and continues to be) much disagreement along the way, most of the scientific community feels that the basic principles of that theory continue to explain what they can observe, measure, and study.

The creationists repeatedly assert that evolution is a theory, and, indeed not a scientific theory at all because it is unable to predict future developments. Both statements are untrue. Evolution is a fact, not a theory. It once was a theory but today, as a consequence of observation and testing, it is probably the best authenticated actuality known to science. There are theories concerning the mechanisms of evolution, but no competent student doubts the reality of evolution.

—Ashley Montagu,
anthropologist and author, *Science and Creationism*

This touches on another great annoyance among evolutionists today— people attacking evolution by calling it "just a theory." We would disagree with calling evolution a fact, of course.[8] But that's because we

---

[7] Methodological naturalism is the philosophy that scientific inquiry should only consider natural processes and that supernatural explanations are not valid.

[8] Be careful with terminology. *Evolution* in a general sense happens all the time. It's why some antibiotics no longer work against certain bacteria, for example. We have no reason to deny it; it is observable in real time and does not contradict Scripture. In fact, understanding it is extremely useful for research that has positively affected our lives in countless ways. Our problem is with large-timescale, "molecules-to-man" evolution, so-called *macroevolution*. This is how the term *evolution* is being used here and is commonly understood. Of course, those who adhere to evolution would say there's no difference between "microevolution" and "macroevolution;" it's all the same process to them.

have a higher standard for truth. We know that what God says is truth. Period. Nothing else can be fact in the same way. Even what we see with our eyes can deceive us.

But for those who prefer the scientific method as a tool to find the truth, a theory is about as solid as it gets:

A theory is a well-substantiated explanation of some aspect of the natural world that can incorporate facts, laws, inferences, and tested hypotheses. The contention that evolution should be taught as a "theory, not a fact" confuses the common use of these words with the scientific use. Theories do not turn into facts through the accumulation of evidence. Rather, theories are the end points of science. They are understandings that develop from extensive observation, experimentation, and creative reflection. They incorporate a large body of scientific facts, laws, tested hypotheses, and logical inferences.

—*Science and Creationism:*
A View from the National Academy of Sciences,
2nd Ed.

*You may have noticed that even this defense of evolution reveals some of its flaws. "Creative reflection" and "logical inferences" invite the subjective. They hint at the unproven assumptions that underpin this theory.[9] One of our interviewees even admitted that there's "a lot of faith" involved in science. It's good for us to be aware of these weak spots, and if we listen patiently, we may have a chance to say where we put **our** faith.*

*It's **not**, however, something to throw in an evolutionist's face as some kind of "gotcha" response. Likewise, we may want to avoid speaking dismissively about evolution as "just a theory." That would only prove that we're not listening because, in science, a theory is something that consistently works. It answers a question or solves a problem and*

---

[9] An example of such an assumption is *uniformitarianism:* the idea that the natural laws and processes we observe now are uniform across space and time (i.e. they have been in operation everywhere, uninterrupted, from the beginning). This type of presumption underlies the various dating methods (e.g. radiocarbon or molecular clock) that produce ages of millions or billions of years. Such presuppositions are not only unprovable but also incompatible with the existence of miraculous events.

remains in force until it is proved wrong. For now, evolution carries that kind of weight in most of the scientific community.

We've seen that calling evolution "just a theory" involves a misunderstanding of what a scientific theory is. Evolution is a fact, and the three main processes that make up evolution—replication, variation, and selection—are observable and undeniable. While scientists do sometimes disagree about specific hypotheses within evolutionary theory, they don't reject the theory of evolution itself. Indeed, the theory of evolution does such a good job of explaining so many observations that the biologist T. Dobzhanksy wrote, "Nothing in biology makes sense except in the light of evolution."

—Cameron M. Smith and Charles Sullivan,
The Top Ten Myths About Evolution

Surely we would disagree vehemently with that last point. But this is the confidence that many people have in the theory of evolution.

Hard problems often yield before science, and though we still don't understand how every complex biochemical system evolved, we are learning more every day. After all, biochemical evolution[10] is a field still in its infancy. If the history of science teaches us anything, it is that what conquers our ignorance is research, not giving up and attributing our ignorance to the miraculous work of a creator.

—Jerry Coyne,
Why Evolution Is True

Science has indeed accomplished great things in our time. Much of that science was based on principles that include evolution as a background and achieved by people who were guided by evolutionary tenets. There's no need to pretend that's not true. We can thank God for those advances and breakthroughs, no matter how faulty the motives or undergirding ideas may have been. All our human endeavors are

---

[10] Essentially, this field tries to answer the question of where the first biological molecules came from and how they could have replicated themselves to ultimately make the first organisms.

flawed; that God provides for us through them at all is pure grace! Let's not be afraid to acknowledge scientific progress with thanks, even while being wary of putting too much confidence in it.

Because scientists have persisted in taking a methodologically naturalistic approach, problems that hitherto seemed insoluble have eventually given way to solutions. . . . The methodological naturalist says that this is a moral for us all: although there are indeed many unsolved problems, notably the origin of life, past experience suggests that these problems will be solved eventually by a methodologically naturalistic approach.

—Michael Ruse

The idea that naturalistic methods will eventually resolve all questions about nature can only yield disappointment. Evolution may seem to fit a lot of the evidence at this time. But, given enough time, it's possible that some new evidence could unseat the reigning theory of the origins of the universe. Such paradigm shifts have certainly occurred in the past.

Still, for the time being, there are two competing worldviews, as the opening quote in this section admits. There's this one:

If I were to give an award for the single best idea anyone has ever had, I'd give it to Darwin, ahead of Newton and Einstein and everyone else. In a single stroke, the idea of evolution by natural selection unifies the realm of life, meaning, and purpose with the realm of space and time, cause and effect, mechanism and physical law.

—Daniel C. Dennett,
philosopher, cognitive researcher,
and author, *Darwin's Dangerous Idea*

Then there's this one:
   Your word, Lord, is eternal;
   it stands firm in the heavens.
   Your faithfulness continues through all generations;
   you established the earth, and it endures.
   (Psalm 119:89,90)

Only one worldview is true. Only one can tell us with certainty what (really, **who**) came before and what will come after what can be observed now. (Books on evolution tend to be conspicuously silent about the former and wildly speculative about the latter.) Only one will stand the test of time. In that we can take comfort.

In the meantime, we have work to do. Even if no other scientific theory manages to dethrone evolution, one day the regime change will be even more dramatic.

> Above all, you must understand that in the last days scoffers will come, scoffing and following their own evil desires. They will say, "Where is this 'coming' he promised? Ever since our ancestors died, everything goes on as it has since the beginning of creation." But they deliberately forget that long ago by God's word the heavens came into being and the earth was formed out of water and by water. By these waters also the world of that time was deluged and destroyed. By the same word the present heavens and earth are reserved for fire, being kept for the day of judgment and destruction of the ungodly. (2 Peter 3:3-7)

How can we rescue those who do not know God and warn those believers whose subscription to evolution poses a real danger to their soul? Let's start by recognizing that, while they are indeed denying some or all of God's creative work, **they may not realize it**. They may not see it that way. They probably see evolution as the most plausible way to put the puzzle together. It simply makes logical sense.

Our job is to place before them something that makes no sense at all: a God who was willing to die in the place of the creatures who disobeyed him so that they could live with him forever. Who would have conceived of such a thing? It defies logic. Better said, it defies **human** logic, but it is perfectly in line with what God has revealed to us about his love for all people.

Remember that the default mindset of fallen humans is that we have to earn whatever good we want to receive from God—or from other people or from the universe, for that matter. Some even think this is what Christianity teaches. So surprise your friends, as Jesus did, by telling them about a Father who welcomes home his wayward children with open arms—no lectures, no conditions (Luke 15:11-24). Go against all logic, as Paul did, by reminding your friends how the Son of God died for us, even while we were still ungodly sinners (Romans 5:6-10).

This radical message may not sweep through the entire scientific community, but it will put—or keep—Jesus on the throne of many hearts. *"For the message of the cross is foolishness to those who are perishing, but to us who are being saved it is the power of God"* (1 Corinthians 1:18).

*Remember, we believe the Word because **it works.** That is, it has worked on our hearts—and it has the power to work on many others.*

4.

Have you been to the Creation Museum? Have you checked out the website Answers in Genesis? How about the creation videos hosted by Kirk Cameron? There are very intelligent and devout Christians out there who love their Lord, know his Word, and have been blessed to learn much about his creation. Many of them are working hard to show how science corroborates the Bible's account of creation or to poke holes in the teaching of evolution.

*We may like what they say. We may learn much from them. We may cheer them on in their quest. But what matters here isn't what **we** think. It's what an evolutionist thinks, which is generally this:*

"Creation 'science' doesn't impress me."

You may be offended by those extra quotation marks, but they're often used when evolutionists write about the subject.

The "Scientific Creationists" may call themselves so and refer to their manipulations as "creation science," but they are no more scientific than Christian Scientists or Scientologists. A scientist is characterized neither by a willingness to believe or a willingness to disbelieve, nor yet a desire to prove or disprove anything, but by the desire to discover what is, and to do so by observation, experiment, verification, and falsification.

As a scientist, no scientist can be a fundamentalist in his attitude toward the truth. Scientists do not believe in fundamental and absolute certainties. For the scientist, certainty is never an end, but a search. . . . As Leonardo put it, "Wisdom is the daughter of Experience, Truth is only the daughter of Time."

There are people who have taken degrees in one or another science or technology, but that doesn't necessarily make them scientists. They may be scientists in the practice of their particular science, whatever it may be, but the moment they step out of their special field of competence their opinions on any other field or subject are not necessarily of any more value than those of the proverbial man-in-the-street. Their opinion can be of value only when it is based on the application of scientific method to whatever it is they are evaluating.

—Ashley Montagu,
Science and Creationism

There's a lot to disagree with here. Surely many excellent scientists, published and trusted and lauded in their fields, have believed in "fundamental and absolute certainties" regarding God and creation.[11] And Leonardo was wrong about wisdom and truth. "The fear of the LORD is the beginning of knowledge," said a man much wiser and almost 2,500 years his elder, inspired by the Spirit of God (Proverbs 1:7). "Your word is truth," said the eternal Son of God in the flesh to God the Father (John 17:17).

But our purpose here isn't to debate. Our purpose is to know what evolutionists think. And many seem to think of creationists as either biased, incompetent, or both. It doesn't help that well-meaning creationists have, at times, championed their findings as the ultimate proof for the Bible only to have those findings later thoroughly discredited or debunked. The bottom line is that many evolutionists have deep disdain for creation science.

---

[11] Making lists of such scientists is tricky. Their views on God and Scripture—and their personal lives—were often complicated. However, in their own writing, such pre-Darwin giants as Johann Kepler, Carl Linnaeus, Isaac Newton, and Blaise Pascal acknowledged God as Creator. James Joule fought against the rising tide of Darwinism in his day. Wernher von Braun, father of rocket technology in our country, wrote and spoke about his faith in a Creator-God. Dr. Raymond Damadian, pioneer of MRI scanning technology, is an outspoken advocate of the Bible's creation account. While dropping these names in a conversation with an evolutionist may not be helpful (and may even be counterproductive), they are given here simply to show that there have indeed been great scientists who believed in a Creator, some of whom would even be considered "fundamentalist" in their attitudes toward the truth because of their belief in Scripture.

Compared to the evidence of geology, the claims of Young Earth Creationists are so ridiculous that no legitimate scientists believe them.

—Cameron M. Smith and Charles Sullivan,
The Top Ten Myths About Evolution

This is not at all to say that creationists should abandon all scientific pursuits. Thank God for Christians who are scientists! In a sense, they understand creation better than their peers because they know its true origins and purpose. Nor is it to malign those who publish creation science. They are trying to testify to the truth. They are using their God-given gifts to explore God's creation and explain it to others. They often point out flaws and inconsistencies in evolutionary science. They show Christians that science is not somehow the exclusive domain of evolutionists and that evolution is not the only paradigm that exists.

Their work can even help Christians combat the arguments of their sinful reason by showing that evolution isn't the only way to read the empirical data. When it sounds like every scientific voice out there is speaking the language of evolution, it can be refreshing to listen to a creationist, who knows his science equally well yet uses the vocabulary of Scripture.

Still, perhaps a few cautions are in order.

We can begin by reminding ourselves that creationists and evolutionists are coming from opposite worldviews. Evolution is a naturalistic[12] explanation, based on observation.

All that's required of scientists is that they recognize that science is limited to using natural methods and natural explanations for what it studies.

—Cameron M. Smith and Charles Sullivan

Creation is a supernatural explanation, based on God's Word: "This is the account of the heavens and the earth when they were created, when the LORD God made the earth and the heavens" (Genesis 2:4).

---

[12] In other words, it excludes the possibility of divine involvement from the start. It may be helpful to ask—humbly and respectfully—about these kinds of assumptions when talking with an evolutionist.

One problem with some creation science is that it wants to try to prove something supernatural using naturalistic methods. In a sense, this is like conceding home-field advantage to the evolutionists. Whether it's fair or not, once we enter the world of observational science, we step onto what evolutionists feel is their home turf, where their theory prevails, their people are more numerous, and their findings carry more weight.[13]

It would be good to ask ourselves: What is our purpose in using creation science? Is it to "prove" that what the Bible says is true? Build a scientific case for scriptural truths? God's Word needs no such help! It stands on its own. "'Is not my word like fire,' declares the Lord, 'and like a hammer that breaks a rock in pieces?'" (Jeremiah 23:29).

Is the purpose to confirm the faith of our people? Help them feel confident in the Bible's truth? Again, God's Word needs no help in that regard. Besides, what happens when the latest scientific find that we used to support creation is discredited? What happens if someone shows that our arguments were incorrect? If we have taught ourselves to rely on outside support of Scripture and that support is knocked out from under us, we have put our faith in jeopardy of falling.

Or is the purpose of creation science to convince evolutionists to believe in a Creator-God? First, they don't seem all that impressed by it. Second, not the finest arguments or most fully vetted, journal-approved science can do that. Only God's Word has that power. Consider Jesus' story about the rich man and poor Lazarus. When the rich man in hell wanted Lazarus in heaven to go back and warn his living brothers, Abraham told him, "If they do not listen to Moses and the Prophets, they will not be convinced even if someone rises from the dead" (Luke 16:31). To put it into our context, if they do not listen to the words of the prophets and the apostles in the Bible, they will not be convinced, even if the fossilized skeleton of a man with a missing rib is discovered east of the Tigris and Euphrates Rivers, dated to around 4,000 b.c. and found to contain half the genetic information of the world's inhabitants.

---

[13] To be accepted by the scientific community, any new finding must be substantiated and picked through with a fine-tooth comb by experts in the field—the revered peer review process. The expertise of reviewers is based on their own experience, but also all of the findings and conclusions that precede the new, supposedly conflicting evidence. So to file a charge against the status quo in this system means that a creation scientist must fight an uphill battle against an enormous body of literature and a large community of experts, whose careers and egos are dependent upon the findings they have reported. In sum, it is a battle that is unlikely to be won.

Sixteen centuries ago, the church father Augustine offered some good advice along these lines:

> Even a non-Christian knows something about the earth, the heavens, and the other elements of this world, about the motion and orbit of the stars and even their size and relative positions, about the predictable eclipses of the sun and moon, the cycles of the years and seasons, about the kinds of animals, shrubs, stones, and so forth, and this knowledge he holds to as being certain from reason and experience. Now it is a disgraceful and dangerous thing for an infidel to hear a Christian talking nonsense on these topics; and we should take all means to prevent such an embarrassing situation, in which people show up vast ignorance in a Christian and laugh it to scorn. . . . If those who are called philosophers, especially the Platonists, have said things which are indeed true and are well accommodated to our faith, they should not be feared; rather, what they have said should be taken from them as from unjust possessors and converted to our use.

Some evolutionists like to quote Augustine here, making him sound like he's saying that Christians should leave the science talk to the scientists. But that's not his point. His point is that we be careful not to give evolutionists good reason to ridicule us. They'll mock us surely enough, but let it be for standing on the truth of Scripture, not for making shaky scientific arguments to try to support what we know by faith. What can easily happen when we enter that kind of debate is that evolutionists listening in are hardened in their opinions and our own people may find it troubling to see the other side "win" the argument.

Jesus didn't tell us to go and make creationists. He said to make disciples (Matthew 28:19) and to do so with the gospel. We won't be ashamed to teach everything he has commanded us, including a six-day, miraculous creation. But we don't have to start there. "By faith we understand that the universe was formed at God's command, so that what is seen was not made out of what was visible" (Hebrews 11:3). "Faith comes from hearing the message, and the message is heard through the word about Christ" (Romans 10:17).

So we speak that message, the good news about the Messiah, and trust it has the strength to firm up the feeble soul and the power to shatter the hardest heart.

5.

My practise as a scientist is atheistic. That is to say, when I set up an experiment I assume that no god, angel, or devil is going to interfere with its course; and this assumption has been justified by such success as I have achieved in my professional career. I should therefore be intellectually dishonest if I were not also atheistic in the affairs of the world.

—J. B. S. Haldane,
scientist and science popularizer, 1892–1964,
introduced the "primordial soup" theory

There are plenty of atheistic evolutionists like this out there. Many evolutionists would even claim that the concept of God is itself a product of evolution.

Religions are largely (although by no means entirely) group-level adaptations.[14] In their explicit behavioral prescriptions, theological beliefs, and social practices, most religions are impressively designed to provide a set of instructions for how to behave, to promote cooperation among group members, and to prevent passive freeloading and active exploitation within the group. The features of religion that appear most irrational and which have always made religion such a puzzle to explain from a scientific perspective can be largely understood as part of the "social physiology" (to use a term employed by social insect biologists) that enables the religious group to function adaptively.

—David Sloan Wilson,
evolutionary biologist, describing the
central thesis of his book, *Darwin's Cathedral*

---

[14] This is one of several hypotheses for how religion may have evolved. Consider how this could impact a conversation with an evolutionist. We may point to creation (as does Scripture) and say, "Look what God made." But some evolutionists would point to the concept of God and say, "Look what evolution made!"

So would you be surprised to learn that nearly half of the evolutionists quoted so far also profess to believe in God? In fact, most evolutionists would say this:

"I can believe in God and evolution too."

I believe in evolution. But I also believe, when I hike the Grand Canyon and see it at sunset, that the hand of God is there also.

—US Senator John McCain

Imagine that you have an artist friend who tells you she just finished a watercolor painting. You know her abilities in watercolors and wouldn't have any reason to think she actually used oil paints or even bought the painting already made from a store. But when she shows you her painting, it sure looks, smells, and feels like an oil painting. So you're left with a conflict. Do you call your friend a liar? Do you question everything your senses are telling you? Or perhaps you try to find some middle ground, some way to make it make sense—maybe she used a different technique than you would expect with watercolors, or maybe she misspoke. Then again, maybe you just shrug it off and say, "Who cares? It's a beautiful painting."

You see where this is going. This is creation to Christian evolutionists. To them, the scriptural record and the scientific evidence in front of them don't line up. How do they handle it? Naturally, different Christians deal with this issue in different ways. Some don't deal with it at all. Some don't even think it's an issue. Beliefs on this issue are diverse—undoubtedly as diverse as the views on so many other biblical teachings throughout Christendom. Here are a few examples, which are not exhaustive nor mutually exclusive:

For someone who trusts that Jesus Christ is their Lord and Savior, who died on the cross for the sins of the world, I think you could believe either way and it's not going to be a detriment to knowing that fact and believing it and having that transform your life. . . .

Because Scripture has so many different texts—it's not just one book in one genre, but it spans numerous genres—I think you have to pick up on the author's style in a certain book. The gospels are written very differently than Genesis or some of the wisdom literature. It's just different. For the gospels, I would lean much more toward a literal interpretation because a lot of it is documenting the life of Christ and what he did and what he said, but I think particularly some of the Old Testament texts are written in a very different style. . . .

I lean more toward the evolution side. . . . I think that in terms of the world I see and the evidence, the alternative would be that God made the world to look old. There's some deception there, some things that, for me, are less plausible.

—Greg,

see above, "Listening to Greg"

With regards to the presence of dinosaur fossils, I think for us to question God's intentions is a dangerous proposition. Earlier today, I was reading Isaiah 55, and he says, "My ways are not your ways . . . " I don't think there's much to gain by questioning his intentions. I think we can guess all we want, but we're not going to know.

—Joe,
behavioral biologist, personal interview

God has graciously provided us with two sources of information: in the Bible and in nature. . . . Of course, for the most important things in life—for learning about God and how He wants us to live and love—the Bible is more important. But we don't have to make an either-or choice, and by using both sources of information our understanding of total reality (spiritual plus physical) can be more complete and accurate.

—Craig Rusbult, PhD
former chemistry teacher at UW-Madison

When I am asked how I manage to "reconcile" evolution with my religious faith, I often shake my head and try to explain that I don't "reconcile" them at all. If two ideas are not in conflict, they have no need of reconciliation. But isn't there a basic conflict with faith in the notion that God needed natural processes to accomplish his ends? . . . As Thomas Aquinas was later to point out, if God exists, he is the author of nature itself, and the cause of causes. Therefore, finding a natural cause for any phenomenon does not take it out of the realm of divine providence. If all of nature is part of God's providential plan, as the Western monotheistic religions teach, then the science of natural cause exists within that providence and does not contradict it.

—Kenneth R. Miller,
Only a Theory

I don't think evolution takes away from the miraculousness of creation. I think evolution is incredibly miraculous. If it's true that we did start as a single-celled organism, and to think of where we're at today, and to think that God guided that process through all of time—it's so cool for me to think that he was there at every step, every single DNA mutation, every selection event, and somehow it all came out to create us, full functioning beings that think and speak and worship him.

—Joe

The Bible itself speaks to us of the origin of the universe and its make-up, not in order to provide us with a scientific treatise, but in order to state the correct relationships of man with God and with the universe. Sacred Scripture wishes simply to declare that the world was created by God, and in order to teach this truth it expresses itself in the terms of the cosmology in use at the time of the writer. The Sacred Book likewise wishes to tell men that the world was not created as the seat of the gods, as was taught by other cosmogonies and cosmologies, but was rather created for the service of man and the glory of God. Any other teaching about the origin and makeup of the universe is alien to the intentions of the Bible, which does not wish to teach how heaven was made but how one goes to heaven.

—Pope John Paul II

Keep in mind that you are likely to see people who held these views in heaven someday. The truth is, as gravely dangerous as it is to explain *away the first two chapters of the Bible, you **can** believe in God and evolution. That is, it is definitely possible, and many do.*

Though creationists seem to accept the literal truth of the Biblical story of creation, this does not mean that all religious people are creationists. There are millions of Catholics, Protestants, and Jews who think of the Bible as a source of spiritual truth and accept much of it as symbolically rather than literally true.

—Isaac Asimov,
science fiction author and professor of biochemistry

Clearly the question of interpretation is a big part of the equation. As the quotes have shown, a common way Christians attempt to reconcile their faith with evolution is by reading the Bible's creation account as symbolic instead of literal—as a genre other than history, meant to answer spiritual rather than historical questions. However, nothing in Scripture gives us reason to interpret it that way. Moreover, the rest of the Bible clearly teaches the truth of creation. There are dozens of passages from many different books in both testaments that mention God's work of creation either directly or indirectly. We could know with certainty that God made the heavens and the earth and everything in them out of nothing, by his word, in six days, even if Genesis 1 and 2 did not exist![15]

What is more, many other biblical teachings are explicitly connected to the creation account. The Lord bases the Sabbath on his resting on the seventh day (Exodus 20:11), after creating everything in six days. Paul says that sin and death came as a result of Adam's fall (Romans 5:12-14). Jesus' family tree is traced back to Adam (Luke 3:23-38). Jesus himself quotes from the creation account and says that God instituted marriage "at the beginning," not after billions of years of evolution (Matthew 19:4-6).[16]

---

[15] For example, see Exodus 31:16,17; Psalm 33:6; Colossians 1:16; Hebrews 4:3,4; 11:3; and Revelation 4:11.

[16] Passages like this one, in which Jesus places his stamp of approval on Genesis chapters 1 and 2, may be especially helpful with someone who questions other parts of Scripture but still holds Jesus in high regard.

*Clearly, those who use the question of interpretation to seek middle
ground between the Bible and evolution are standing in a slippery
place. Even evolutionists recognize that:*

If the Bible can't be taken literally, then what can you get out of it? I
believe that there was a person, "Jesus," but if some things can't be
taken literally, then what?

—Elizabeth,
see above, "Listening to Elizabeth"

*Here's one answer to Elizabeth's question, an example of the kind of
thinking that can result from interpreting a portion of Scripture figu-
ratively—for any reason—when there is no cue in the text itself that it
should be read that way:*

The Christian believes that humans can be saved by the death of
Christ on the Cross and his subsequent Resurrection. The Christian
believes that this salvation will come after death—or at the Second
Coming. On these matters, Darwinism is silent. But what about the
Resurrection? . . . The real miracle was not some reversal of life-death
processes, but that, on the third day, the disciples who were down-
cast and lonely suddenly felt a great lift and that life was meaningful for them—that Jesus had left a message and example that they
wanted to promulgate. If some psychologist explains this in terms
of mass hysteria or whatever, so be it. There will always be a natural
explanation. This leaves the meaning of the event untouched.

—Michael Ruse,
Darwinism and Its Discontents

*We would argue that with this kind of interpretation, the meaning of
the event is utterly destroyed. The meaning of the resurrection is that
Christ rose from the dead! Without the resurrection, all is lost, as Paul
wrote: "If Christ has not been raised, your faith is futile; you are still in
your sins. Then those also who have fallen asleep in Christ are lost" (1
Corinthians 15:17,18).*

*If that's the danger for many evolutionists, here's the danger for us
who would engage them: Assuming they are all at that point or on their
way there. Putting people into that box—or a box constructed from any
of these examples—can put up walls as fast as we'd like them to come*

down. *Everyone we come across who professes to be a Christian evolutionist will have a slightly different interpretive lens, a slightly different past that has shaped what they believe, and slightly different values based on their experiences that craft how they wrestle with (or don't wrestle with) the apparent contradictions between Genesis and science. Regardless of where they stand in that, it's our job to listen.*

When we do that, we may have an opportunity to explain how God's Word itself has convinced us to read it the way we do. A good start would be to express genuine joy over the fact that the other person shares our faith in Jesus. At the same time, we recognize how potentially lethal it is to think that one can "believe either way" with regard to something God says. But rather than getting stuck on the first chapters of the Bible, we can zoom in to its beating heart. We can remind our friends about the "second Adam," Jesus Christ, whose obedience is our righteousness (Romans 5:19) and whose resurrection is our life (1 Corinthians 15:22). Then, in time, we can zoom out and show how God's creation was the beginning of that wonderful plan of salvation.

It takes patience. We don't want to snuff out a smoldering wick by demanding a hasty choice: "It's Jesus or Darwin!" Believers may continue to struggle with this particular question of faith—as we all do with our own doubts. In fact, we can join with them in praying, "I do believe; help me overcome my unbelief!" (Mark 9:24). In the end, we will ask the Holy Spirit to keep that person's faith in Christ—along with ours— alive and strong until we can enjoy God's new creation together.

6.

It's February 4, 2014. Creationist Ken Ham stands on a stage at his Creation Museum in Petersburg, Kentucky. Scientist Bill Nye stands to his right. Their televised and much-hyped debate is nearing its conclusion.

Moderator: What, if anything, would ever change your mind?

Ham: The Bible is the Word of God. I admit that that's where I start from. I can challenge people that you can go and test that, and you can make predictions based on that; you can check the prophecies in the Bible, you can check the statements in Genesis, you can check that—and I did a little bit of that tonight—but I can't ultimately prove that to you. All I can do is to say to someone, look, if the Bible really is what it claims to be, if it really is the Word of God and that's what it claims, then check it out. . . . [As] Christians, we can say we know. And so, as far as the Word of God is concerned, no one's ever going to convince me that the Word of God is not true.

We would agree with him on that last point. And we pray that we might speak as plainly as Mr. Ham did about our own reliance on God's Word. But it is good for us to realize how that kind of immovable position drives some people crazy. Here was Nye's response to the same question:

We would need just one piece of evidence. We would need the fossil that swam from one layer to another. We would need evidence that the universe is not expanding. We need evidence that the stars appear to be far away, but they're not. We would need evidence that rock layers can somehow form in just four thousand years instead of the extraordinary number. We need evidence that somehow that you can reset the atomic clock and keep the neutrons from becoming protons. Bring out any of those things, and you would change me immediately.

This is the kind of reply that many scientists would give.

All scientific truth is provisional, subject to modification in light of new evidence. There is no alarm bell that goes off to tell scientists that they've finally hit on the ultimate, unchangeable truths about nature. As we'll see, it is possible that despite thousands of observations that support Darwinism, new data might show it to be wrong. I think this is unlikely, but scientists, unlike zealots, can't afford to become arrogant about what they accept as true.

—Jerry Coyne,
Why Evolution Is True

Those in the scientific community are used to working with facts that can be overturned at any time by new observations. It's a humbling position. You make a guess and, more often than not, your experiments fail to prove your hypothesis. If the experiment comes out right, you publish a paper and your peers review it and may see something you didn't and still prove you wrong. And even if the whole scientific community accepts your "truth," it may very well happen that the next generation makes a new observation and proves it wrong. In fact, many scientists cringe simply on hearing that word prove, *because it implies a certainty that is essentially unattainable.*

That approach to truth is such a contrast to ours. We believe that the only truth that exists is the truth established by God's Word. We believe that Word to be inerrant. It will never change. No new revelation or observation can prove wrong what God has already said, even if that new message somehow came from an apostle or an angel from heaven (Galatians 1:8). No number of fossils or radiocarbon data will ever convince us that what God says in Genesis is false!

Considering that's the opposite of the way so many evolutionists have been trained to think, you can understand why they might say:

"I wish creationists were more open-minded."

To really understand nature, we have to do more than glance, and we have to think beyond our knee-jerk reaction that insists that since we make things with intent, nature must also be made with intent. If we want to understand better than a child, we have to look harder, and think deeper. We can see that silt and sand, carried by streams of melting snow, piles up as orderly cones against mountainsides, and we can see that freezing ice crystals make geometrical snowflakes. We have to keep our minds open to the possibility that undirected, random processes can also generate order, even in the domain of living things.

—Cameron M. Smith and Charles Sullivan,
The Top Ten Myths About Evolution

Our interviewee said it more succinctly:

Q: Is there anything you want to say to Christians that might be reading this book?

A: I'd just say, "Keep an open mind to science."

—Elizabeth,
see above, "Listening to Elizabeth"

Our minds are open to learning more about God's world. They are not open to entertaining anything that contradicts what God says about his world. Does that make us the previously mentioned "zealots" that are "arrogant about what they accept as true"? Being zealous for the truth of God's Word is an accusation we can wear proudly, as did the writer of the longest psalm:

You are righteous, LORD,
and your laws are right.
The statutes you have laid down are righteous;
they are fully trustworthy.
My zeal wears me out,
for my enemies ignore your words.
Your promises have been thoroughly tested,
and your servant loves them.
(Psalm 119:137-140)

The Spirit has convinced us that the Word is trustworthy. It has passed the test of time. We know that it is truth. We can't stop someone from judging that confidence as arrogance.

*But do we sometimes come across as arrogant **unnecessarily?***

Of all people, we Christians should show humility in our dealings with others. We know that we are sinners who have fallen just as short as everyone else. We recognize that God gives different gifts to different people and that others may have abilities to observe and perceive what we do not. We acknowledge that we have no more right to the truth than anyone else. We concede that we don't know everything.

*In fact, we wouldn't know **anything** if God hadn't revealed it to us! Our senses can deceive us and our logic can betray us, so we must rely on Someone who cannot do either. We may think we know what's right. We may even wish that our hypothesis were true. But if it's proved wrong by God's Word, we stand corrected. In a way, that gives us something in common with every scientist.*

*We may still be labeled as closed-minded. But could it be that when that charge is leveled, what is really meant is that we are **closed-eared?** That's evidently how creationists come across to some:*

Oftentimes they're not willing to—they're not really open-minded. You can't even take a different interpretation of the Bible with them—like it isn't up for debate or discussion. Just, "No, it's this way.

You're wrong." So there's no point. Why even disagree at that point? I learned nothing; you learned nothing; thanks.

—Nate,
see above, "Listening to Nate"

Even outside observers have noticed this impasse.

A temptation [for evolutionists] has been to reply . . . that so-called scientific-creationism "is not science." Evolution on the other hand is "a fact." Such approaches, while compelling to secularists, are singularly compelling to fundamentalists, who are likely to respond by repeating their own well-worn contrast between "the theory of evolution" and "the facts of science," or by saying once again that "evolution does not even qualify as a scientific theory." . . . The gap and lack of communication between the two groups could hardly be greater.

—George Marsden,
Science and Creationism

What can we do to bridge the communication gap? How can we be appropriately open and humble? Perhaps we can begin by admitting that there is much that we don't know. We can listen and learn. We can accept, or at least entertain, anything that does not militate against God's revelation. [17]

Good scientists should be aware of the logical faults with what they're doing and the aspects in which our practice is based on faith. You should always be aware of these things, just as I think it would be good practice for any religious person to be aware of the science of the day.

—Nate,
see above, "Listening to Nate"

---

[17]As a cautionary tale, consider the story of Galileo, the 16th- and 17th-century Italian astronomer who insisted that the earth revolves around the sun. Some in the church believed that such a view was incompatible with Scripture, and the Inquisition tried him for heresy. It illustrates how important it is to open our ears and listen honestly to new ideas, and then to open our Bibles and study carefully to see what God's Word really says.

Yes, we can learn—and learn a lot—about how God's creation works, even from those who would not call it God's creation! This would be a good start.

We can also learn more about those on the "other side." They're not just evolutionists. They're people. People with backgrounds and stories that may be very different from ours, that have shaped their way of thinking, and that may provide surprisingly open opportunities to speak God's truth.

When you hear someone with a philosophy different from your own, it's easy to think, "Wow, that person must be stupid," and not realize that their experience is so different from your own, that unless you understand their experience first, you'll never understand why they live by that philosophy. So they definitely need to know each other better, but not necessarily philosophically. Just on a human level, there needs to be more connection.

—Nate

As we do that—as we get to know those people who are caught in evolution's snare—we can act as partners in a journey of discovery with them. Just as they might like to show us the "proof" that has persuaded them, we can show them the proof that has persuaded us—the Spirit-inspired, eyewitness accounts of a Savior who died for us and lives again. Through that proof, the Spirit can and will open minds and hearts to the truth.

7.

Have you been wondering how evolutionists feel about the whole origins issue?

The battle for evolution seems never-ending. And the battle is part of a wider war, a war between rationality and superstition. What is at stake is nothing less than science itself and all the benefits it offers to society.

—Jerry Coyne,
Why Evolution is True

Creationism strikes me as an astonishing waste of time and energy. I would love to be able to ignore it and focus on the real science, but creationists work very hard to disrupt science education and force their weird worldview on our students.

—Bill Nye,
Undeniable

Evolution doesn't care whether you believe in it or not, no more than gravity does. I want to rekindle excitement over what we've achieved as a species. . . . We can't afford to regress back to the days of superstition.

—Seth MacFarlane,
producer, filmmaker, actor, *Family Guy, Ted*

Where would we be in our understanding of the natural world today if the likes of Galileo, Newton, Einstein, and Darwin had given up explaining complex problems and instead simply lifted their hands in defeat, declaring an intelligent designer as the best and only explanation? We would be stuck back in the Dark Ages, that's where.

—Cameron M. Smith and Charles Sullivan,
The Top Ten Myths About Evolution

I am both angry at and amused by the creationists; but mostly I am deeply sad.

—Stephen Jay Gould,
paleontologist, evolutionary biologist,
historian of science

The problem with this argument is that evolution isn't "just a theory"; it's the glue that binds the biological sciences together, a common principle that links fields as diverse as development, genetics, and paleontology. In an age in which the flow of life science research has moved toward unification around evolution, taking Darwin out of the picture would send biology backward into an age of fragmentation. But the biggest problem posed by avoiding evolution is much greater than that. In a very important sense evolution is the canary in the mineshaft, an indicator whose presence signals the health or sickness of the entire scientific enterprise. That, ultimately, is the point of this book. The question of evolution is really a question of what will happen to the American soul.

—Kenneth R. Miller,
Only a Theory

It is absolutely safe to say that if you meet somebody who claims not to believe in evolution, that person is ignorant, stupid or insane (or wicked, but I'd rather not consider that).

—Richard Dawkins

These are the kinds of things you'll read in plenty of books on evolution. Prominent scientists, evolutionists, and educators are terribly distressed about the fact that there are many in this country and this world who believe that God created the earth in six days. They worry about what it means for the state of science and education and technology in our country. They write about it and debate about it and fight hard for their point of view.

*But here's something that's very important to understand: **Not all evolutionists are so concerned.** In fact, most of those who believe in evolution would say this:*

"I don't feel as strongly about this as you might think."

For every Bill Nye, there are untold numbers of people who accept evolution but would probably not even call themselves evolutionists. Evolution isn't a cause for them. It's not an argument they care to make. It's not something worth fighting about.

Who are they?

He's the typical American who attended public schools and learned that evolution is how things came to be. But ask him about it now that's he's an adult and he remembers as much—and cares as much—about evolutionary theory as he does about the causes of World War I or the way to diagram a prepositional phrase.

She's the young woman in a Bible class reading Genesis chapter 1 and hearing about a literal six-day creation seemingly for the first time, even though she had grown up in a Christian church. She furrows her brow and asks why we don't believe that God used evolution to make the world. "Because he says he made it in six days," the pastor replies. "Oh, that makes sense," she says, smiling and nodding and ready to move on to the next question, the Spirit having done his work.

She's the research biologist who uses many tenets of evolution in her day-to-day work. They come second nature to her, and she can see them at work in her lab—finding similarities between a human gene and a fruit fly gene, using "survival of the fittest" to choose the bacteria with the properties she wants. But she's much less concerned about the evolutionary principles as she is about finding a cure for Alzheimer's, and she doesn't seem bothered at all when a creationist shares his viewpoint. In fact, she readily admits that the origins of the world aren't fully understood, or can't be proven. She even welcomes hearing how different cultures have wrestled with the "Where did we come from?" question and is hesitant to say anyone's belief system is wrong—lest she offend.

He's a Christian and a scientist, struggling to match what he sees with what the Bible says:

It's hard when the fossil record doesn't match up exactly with what the Bible says. I guess I take it question by question. In the past, I've put more evidence in what I can see than what the Bible says, because the evidence is more tangible. Whether or not that's correct, I'm not sure. That's why I try not to make a big fight over it. I'm happy to say that I could easily be wrong, and God could have easily created the earth in six days. In fact, I could totally understand why someone would believe in a six-day creation. I think both ideas are miraculous and show his omnipotence.

—Joe,
behavioral biologist, personal interview

Don't let a vocal minority fool you. According to a 2014 poll, for every person who feels strongly that evolution is true, there are two who think it may be true but aren't so sure.[18] *Stauncher evolutionists actually lament this fact:*

It is easy and natural for those of us of a more secular bent to smile somewhat smugly at what we take to be the insecurities and failings of the religious. We do not reject evolution, even for humans, and we want no interventions from outside nature. But interestingly and depressingly, when it comes to Darwinism—natural selection as the chief causal process behind all organisms—large numbers of people stand virtually back to back with the religious critics. It is well known now that many students of literature and (particularly) those drawn to cultural studies have little but contempt for (and, one suspects, fear of) almost everything to do with science and technology. Notorious is their claim that there is no objective truth and that everything—science particularly—is a social construction.

—Michael Ruse,
Darwinism and Its Discontents

Interesting! The idea that there is no objective truth, so ingrained in our culture today, is lamented not only by Christian parents, pastors, and teachers but also by some evolutionists! "The enemy of my enemy is my friend"?

Not quite. There's no way to feel good about how all truth, especially God's truth, is attacked and questioned nowadays. But it does give us an open door. In an age when everyone is taught not to be too dogmatic about things, perhaps there will at least be a willingness on the part of those who subscribe to evolution to consider that it may not be the truth.

Remember, even scientists steeped in evolution are searching—searching for answers to specific problems or perhaps to life's big questions.

The problem of how and where life began is one of the great outstanding mysteries of science. But it is more than that. The story

---

[18] This and other interesting statistics on this topic can be found here: http://www.gallup.com/poll/21814/ evolution-creationism-intelligent-design.aspx.

of life's origin has ramifications for philosophy and even religion. Answers to such profound questions as whether we are the only sentient beings in the universe, whether life is the product of random accident or deeply rooted law, and whether there may be some sort of ultimate meaning to our existence, hinge on what science can reveal about the formation of life.

—Paul Davies,
physicist, professor at Arizona State University

Because its starting point excludes divine intervention, science cannot solve the "mystery" of life's origin or the ultimate meaning to our existence. But Scripture can—and has! We can confidently hold out its solution to those who are still searching, who may be readier to listen to its answers than we realize.

After all, it's human nature to long to be part of something bigger than ourselves.

Some part of our being knows this is where we came from. We long to return. And we can. Because the cosmos is also within us. We're made of star-stuff.

—Carl Sagan,
1980s narrator and co-writer of *Cosmos: A Personal Journey,*
the most widely watched series in the history of American public television

Though his facts are wrong, the yearning he describes is real. In fact, it is from God, who "set eternity in the human heart" (Ecclesiastes 3:11). And we can provide the answer for it! We can tell of a God whose eyes twinkled when he thought of us, even before he made those stars. A God who put us at the center of his grandest plans. A God who has joined us to himself and to all his people of all time as members of one body. A God who dwells within us as a guarantee that one day we will shine like stars in his heaven. These are God's answers to the longing that so many still feel.

True, some seem to have settled on a different set of answers. But even those who tell you they don't believe in God may not be so certain.

Ultimately, we believe in the scientific method entirely on faith— that this law of induction will not change tomorrow or any other day. And all of our best theories rely on that. So at the end of the day, there are logical holes in any belief system that you choose to live by, but I would still say that there's a lot more evidence for induction, however flawed and circular the underlying logic is. It's just a belief system I'm more comfortable with.

—Nate,
see above, "Listening to Nate"

*That doesn't sound like a brick wall. It sounds like a door that is open, at least a crack. An opportunity to share the Word of Truth, the living Word that has the power to convince the most skeptical minds and hearts that there **is** truth, that **it is** truth.*

The woman sits on the edge of the dune, her eyes wide and blue as the sky above her, taking in the breathtaking scene. She's not quite as young as she was when she sat on the canyon's rim. But the youthful wonder has not changed. In fact, now it's mirrored in the gaze of her daughter, who sits at her side and takes in the same sand and water and forest. The wind blowing in off the lake tosses their hair and reinforces the profound nature of their conversation. "Isn't it amazing how God made all of this? There's no way it could have been an accident," says mother to daughter, who nods in agreement. Her husband, listening from a distance, smiles again. The woman's faith is unfazed by trail signs and park literature touting the evolutionary process that was supposed to have created these great lakes. It is a faith that burns in the heart of the next generation beside her, something no less miraculous than the land and water that God had arranged so beautifully around them.

Down the dune, another mother and daughter are no doubt having a much different conversation. "Isn't it amazing how millions of years of natural forces could carve out such a beautiful landscape?" The wonder is there, sadly pointed in the wrong direction.

How can we help this mother and daughter see what they're missing? The same way the first pair were and remain convinced. Only by the Word, the same Word by which God called this marvelous creation into existence. God grant us boldness to speak it—and grace to listen.

quick to listen

ATHEISTS
TALKING TO CHRISTIANS

by Christopher Doerr

LISTENING TO EZRA

I grew up Presbyterian. And I was actually pretty active in the church when I was younger. I went to a lot of church camps and planning committees for youth conferences and things like that.

But I think, probably as I got to be 15 or 16, it all stopped making as much sense to me. I just found a lot of contradictory thinking in different things that I was supposed to believe. And when it came down to it, the more I studied how the Bible and various texts came to be, the less sense it made to me that God would trust so much to the accurate reproduction of his words through people. If monks copied these words over and over and there were all kinds of errors and there were various clerical decision-making processes that threw some texts away and kept some texts—and those were human decisions—it seemed to me pretty fraught with error, given all the human imperfections that are out there. It just required a lot of accurate transmission. In retrospect, it would've been a lot easier if he had had people invent cameras and video recorders and more accurately transmit things.

I think once I accepted that I really couldn't believe it anymore, there was a period of anger and grieving, just because it had been an important part of my life. I went through a little bit of an "angry atheist" phase. And I think a lot of the big, loud atheists that are out there, like Richard Dawkins and whoever, kind of got stuck there. I mean, at some point it's like, "Okay, guys, let it go. If you really don't believe it, you're really giving this stuff a lot more power over your life than you need to." So I don't have any particular ax to grind. I'm not one of those evangelical atheists out there, who wear it on their sleeve and are really ready to pick a fight and won't rest until they smash the church. That seems kind of pointless to me.

I don't think the church is horrible. It gives a lot of people comfort, and it gives a lot of people guidance in the many, many ways that you can walk through this life. So I don't have any particular problem with it. A lot of my favorite people are Christian or some manner of religious. I have a lot of Quaker and Unitarian friends—I wish I had their faith, even though it's a pretty open and nondogmatic kind of "faith."

That's kind of the broad arc of my story.

The two main things you mentioned are contradictory thinking and just the whole process of the transmission of the message.

Yeah. A lot of what gets passed down is sort of the philosophy around it and the interpretation, rather than the fragmentary texts that we actually have.

And, I don't know, but I feel there are a lot of things that would be sort of unfair for a supreme being to ask of people.

Did you want to give an example?

(Laughs.)

I kind of knew you were going to ask that. But I feel like I've gotten a little bit rusty and soft with thinking of examples, just because I haven't been as actively engaged mentally with it as I was when I was at the "angry atheist" stage. So I don't have these bulleted lists and point-by-point refutations of various Scriptures.

What did your family think at that time, when you told them what was going on inside of your head?

My family is very conflict-avoidant, so I never openly said it.

I think my parents sort of confronted me about it at some point, when they saw that I wasn't going to church or being actively involved anymore and it had been such a big part of my life. And I think when I got married to somebody who is not especially religious—though she is much more tolerant than I am and keeps a much more open mind—and when they found out we were getting married in a Unitarian church, they confronted me about it and said, "We always thought you might be a minister someday" or "We thought it was a much more important part of your life. What happened?" And I think they felt like they had gone wrong somewhere.

I said, "It just stopped making sense to me at some point, and I haven't really been a Christian for a long time."

So I didn't proactively volunteer the information. I just kind of went on with my life and didn't tell them about it.

But that's pretty par for the course with my family. We kind of don't volunteer information. I don't know, maybe it's a Presbyterian thing.

There wasn't any particular person that influenced you—your change or transition.

No, I don't think so.

Was there a certain moment that the dam started to crack? Or was it just cumulative and you can't remember how it all started?

I think there were probably a lot of little fissures along the way. I don't think the dam really cracked at any point. It just sort of slowly drained. I wish there was a more dramatic story for you.

No, that's alright. I should ask, what would be some misconceptions that you would think a lot of Christians have about atheists?

I think from the Christian point of view, there's this idea that "without God, anything goes," and I think that sort of the opposite is true. I think that if you don't believe that there's an afterlife or [if you believe] that there's nothing out there that can clean up your mistakes, you've got the responsibility to fix it and you've got to do it now. You can't wait for some apocalypse to just burn everything up and start over. You actually have to take a stand, and you have to be a responsible human being. I think the idea that morality suddenly goes off the table if you don't have a god to enforce it is kind of silly.

Any other misconceptions that come to mind?

I don't know if it's a misconception, but it's just an attitude of . . . I don't know. I haven't really been challenged by a lot of Christians, to be totally honest.

Does that surprise you?

Not really, because I'm not a confrontational person about it, I guess. I enjoy talking to people about ideas and having debates of various kinds, but I don't especially enjoy talking about this so much.

When you asked if there was anybody out there to interview and I volunteered, I thought it might be fun to talk about, just because I haven't put my ideas into words on the subject in a long time. But I don't normally engage in conversations about it.

Part of me also thinks it's . . . When at the end of any conversation the person that you're talking with has to depend on faith and has to depend on things that you can't prove or things that you have no evidence for, then it's somehow unsatisfying to me because you're just arguing or conversing or debating using two different standards of how you resolve things, really.

So it's like a dead end?

Yeah, to some extent.

This might not be a relevant question, but are there things that Christians have said to you, or maybe said about atheists, that you find hurtful or offensive? "Christians, you aren't doing yourselves any favors by talking that way"—that kind of thing?

Sure. It's hard. I think just culturally here in Boston or on the East Coast—nah, that's not true: religion is pretty big here; the Catholic Church certainly has a lot of influence and certainly there are a lot of very religious people, including people that I work with who are scientists. But it's also not as culturally embedded, and there's also more tolerance here than there is farther south. I mean, for example, we go to visit my wife's sister in Virginia. It's northern Virginia, D.C. suburbs. But really the first question people ask you is, What do you do, and where do you go to church? So it's a lot more assumed that you do. I think that probably the only times I've felt a little bit—I wouldn't say "hurt," because that's pretty traumatic—but the times when I've been surprised at someone's point of view is when they ask where you go to church and you say, "I don't go," and they're just kind of shocked.

The attitude is sort of like, "Wait a second. I thought you were a good person and you're telling me you don't go to church."

And it's like, "Well, yeah."

And I think there have been friends we've met through our son who have kind of given us the stink eye a little bit, just because—or I think have been a little bit more reluctant to let our kid play with theirs—because they know that we don't take him to church.

That's sad.

My son tends to be a lot more religious than I am. I mean, he asks a lot of questions. I try to give him a pretty neutral point of view, but he's told me that he believes in God and I'm like, "Oh, okay." I try not to do anything to discourage it. I try to keep his curiosity about it. I know his grandparents are happy to talk to him about it.

Yeah, I was meaning to ask you about being a parent, and you brought it up yourself. I appreciate that.

It certainly occurred to me . . . I think I got a lot out of being involved with the church as a young person, and I think there's so much history and context that it's pretty hard to understand if you don't have even the stories and the thinking as part of your upbringing—so I certainly wrestle with that a bit. Even my wife—her dad is Jewish and her mom is Presbyterian, so she sort of grew up going to neither and really feeling attached to neither—I'll make references to things or just certain cultural ideas and she's completely oblivious to them. I think that there's a richness that you miss if you're just not sensitized to growing up with that thinking.

That said, I think there's a lot of damage that happens in self-doubt and guilt and shame over things that I think are just human. So I think it's a trade-off. And I've opted for going the atheist route. I think some people make a decision that, even though they're atheist, they're going to take their kids to Sunday school and they're going to raise them in the church. I know one of my best friends from high school is in that boat. I just don't know that I would do that.

Changing channels a little bit. What about the frequency of how often it comes up in your head that you are an atheist? Do you know what I'm saying? For a religious person, I think maybe they would have a misconception that being an atheist is as central to your life as being a Christian is to my life, for example. But is that realistic? Or that's not really how it is?

I can't speak for everybody else, but it does not occupy a lot of my mental space at this point. It probably did when I was younger. But, again, you gravitate toward the things you are attracted to. Other parts of my life have sort of taken up the slack. You know, it's not that I have a meaningless life at all. That's probably another thing for the misconception bucket: the idea that you need religion to give your life meaning. I mean, things just have meaning. It's part of being human and your attention sort of gives it that.

But, yeah, I don't really think about that much. I think about it when it comes up in the news or culturally or when someone brings it up.

If you could say something to every Christian, or thousands of Christians, what would it be?

Gosh, I don't know. Like I said, I'm not really evangelical about it. I mean, there are certainly times when I envy people who have faith. They seem a little happier.

I have no interest in converting people. I don't want to say that they're wrong.

You mentioned self-doubt and things like that. Would you just give them a message like that?

Nah. Again, I think it's kind of a trade-off. There are good things that come out of it. I felt like I was freeing myself when I let go of a lot of that, but I don't really want to convert people. "The more people that think like me . . . ," is not really a goal of mine.

I don't know. I think that I would encourage Christians to see other points of view. That's probably one of the most damaging parts of Christianity, this idea of zero tolerance for other kinds of thinking.

Because it hurts the people they aren't understanding? Or it hurts the Christians themselves? Or . . .

Yeah, I think a little of both. I just think the world is big enough for more than one religion.

LISTENING TO REBECCA

I'm basically a cultural Jew. My parents are Jewish and grew up in Jewish families. My mom's family was more religious, for longer than my dad's. My mom's family was more working class. My dad's family was more upper-middle suburban. My parents were open to kind of letting me believe what I wanted to. They weren't enforcing it or anything. My mom says she's more of an agnostic. She kind of doesn't want to commit one way or the other. My dad's definitely an atheist.

I was definitely raised without any belief in an afterlife. There were no magical characters in my life (outside of being read to, and reading, a lot of fiction) like Santa Claus, references to reincarnation or coming back to life like Jesus. I think there was some Tooth Fairy action for a while, but I'm pretty sure it was presented as a ritual without any real belief that a Tooth Fairy really existed.

I actually decided kind of late that I wanted to be bat mitzvahed. So I had a bat mitzvah[19] and everything. I'm not sure why I decided I wanted to do it. I hadn't been going to temple. I had to go for a year and train with the rabbi to do it, and I went every Friday. I'm glad I did it. I liked learning the songs and I liked the history of it. And I actually chose the conservative shul[20] in our town rather than the reformed temple. I just liked [how it was] kind of darker and more sedate and the melodies were older. But I can't say that I felt I believed in the story. I don't remember what I was thinking about in terms of believing in God at that time, which is weird. I don't remember if I was consciously like, "I'm going to do this, but I just won't tell him that I don't believe."

---

[19] *Bat mitzvah* means "daughter of the commandment." A Jewish girl's bat mitzvah is a religious initiation ceremony that occurs when she is 12 years and 1 day old.

[20] A synagogue.

So you were learning all these prayers [to sing for the ceremony], but you weren't actually thinking of them as praying to anybody?

Maybe not.

I mean, we would go every Friday for services. And I really like that we had to kind of stop—this is something I appreciate about organized religion—you stop your regular life. You're mindful. You sit and focus on the music and think about what you're saying. You clear your mind. It was kind of like meditation.

I practiced for the bat mitzvah, but I didn't really pray outside of that. I mean, I loved it, but it felt more cultural to me than religious. Probably the rabbi would not be happy with me to hear that. Although he left soon after. Maybe I ruined it for him, I don't know.

I don't know if my parents were doing it out of culture or real belief. I'll have to ask them. But both of my parents are very active in social justice and left politics, and my dad's a Marxist scholar. He's a political scientist. So I think that's maybe the space that religion would fill—I don't know. I participated since I was a little kid. You know, go on marches and talk about class and race and gender and all of what feeds poverty and marginalization and stuff like that.

So almost everything flows through that lens, that social justice lens. For example, when I was very young I was aware of Catholics protesting the School of the Americas.[21] Where in other religions there's a parallel of my parents' social justice beliefs and those of religious organizations—that's something I have paid attention to. Wherever I had positive feelings toward organized religion, it was at those intersections.

But there's also the Crusades. There's a lot of violence done in the name of religion. Homophobia, a lot of things, very male-run—all of those things I would put in the negative column.

---

[21] "Originally established in Panama in 1946 to train Latin American military forces and subsequently named the U.S. Army School of Americas in 1963, the school has trained over 60,000 members of Central and South America militaries. . . . The school has been criticized for decades as a training ground for military leaders from Central and South America, many of whom subsequently became notorious human rights abusers." (Bill Quigley, "The Case for the Closing of the School of the Americas." Brigham Young University Journal of Public Law. Vol. 20, Issue 1, Article 2. Accessed online, Nov. 21, 2016 at http://digitalcommons.law.byu.edu/cgi/ viewcontent.cgi?article=1355&context=jpl).

There was a lot of evidence for me to support where my parents were coming from. So it wasn't just like, "There's no god, period." It was like, "Poor people, old people, struggling people should all be supported. Here's where our movement works toward that. Here's where organized religion works toward that. Here's where organized religion works counter to our belief." You know what I mean? At least as far as it can be in your perspective, it was an evidence-based belief system.

I think it's enviable to have faith in situations of grief or feeling lost. I feel like that's where I kind of see [faith] as easy, although I know it's not. But you have a go-to structure for feeling comforted, that some higher being is leading you. For example, I know somebody—she's not a friend, more a business acquaintance—who was recently just dumped by her boyfriend. She was expecting him to propose to her. For two days she was devastated, and on the third day she said, "I know God has a plan for me." And then like two weeks later she met somebody who's just perfect for her. Where I or my parents believe in human backup, she believed that a higher power is leading her however she needs to be led. So that's enviable to me. It sounds comforting.

You don't think that she's being weak, by leaning on a "crutch"? Some people talk that way.

I don't think she's being weak.

But because I don't believe, I find it surprising to find people who align in every other way—or most other ways: I like baseball, somebody else likes basketball, whatever—you don't have to align perfectly to be friends. But by the same token, my friends who are religious—I think I have three close ones—are all . . . they have a sense of humor. They walk their talk. So they volunteer. They're not homophobic, which to me is a big one. They don't—as far as I know—say, "My way of practicing is the only way and yours is wrong." I think my friends who are believers, who are religious, are the type of nonhypocritical believers that I appreciate.

So there are people who—and maybe this is you, that's up to you— who think that gay people are going to hell or that people who aren't baptized are going to hell. Maybe my friends believe that and I just don't know, but I don't think so. All three of them are very open . . .

Oh, that's the other thing I was going to say about religion. Besides feeling like you have backup, like you're being led in a way that's comforting, there is community. One thing my dad talks a lot about, in terms of being an organizer—he works with labor. He does a lot of political organizing work. One thing he says often, which I agree with, is that the only consistently present organized spots of support in the United States are religious. For example, if there's a flood or if you move somewhere and you don't know anyone—there might be clubs or whatever—but the most rooted, consistent community is around religion. So that's another thing that I think is a positive. If you can't afford cancer treatment, your church will raise money. You know, that kind of stuff. There may be pockets of it in other aspects of community life, but nothing as organized as religion. I wish there were secular spots like that that were as rooted. That's a positive.

There is one thing that bugs me a lot. In baseball, let's say a pitcher strikes out a batter. He thanks . . . You know, he looks up. He crosses himself. On the one hand, if you believe, you know that whatever happens is supported by the higher power. But on the other hand, is God or Jesus or a saint spending the time to allow pitcher number three in game number 50 of the St. Louis Cardinals to strike out one batter? I don't know. I find that very frustrating. It just seems unlikely. But if that's how that pitcher gets through . . . I mean, it's one thing to walk into the street and if a car misses you to say, "I was protected." That I buy more than these tiny things. They're not about life and death. They're not even about love. They're just sports. But that's just my judgment, and it's not very important.

I respect my friends' forms of involvement in religion, more than people who say something like, "That woman got cancer because she's a lesbian." You know, there are a lot of super-hateful groups—or heads of churches who use tax-exempt status for their own benefit, like a fancy house. But having said that, there are secular people who do crappy stuff too.

So it sounds like being an atheist wasn't so much a decision against religion, against God. It was just that social justice is important. That's what matters. It wasn't an active process where you rejected God. Is that accurate? It wasn't like you ever "broke up" with God?

Right. It was super interesting when I taught in Tennessee. A lot of my students were the first generation in their family to go to college and had super-super-conservative, fundamentally religious families. And a lot of them didn't necessarily reject God, but they started to have problems with their family's type of religion because they would make friends with people who were gay or not Christian.

And they found out they were nice people.

Yeah, good people. And I felt really proud of those students because they weren't just rejecting everything out of hand, but they started questioning and they didn't give up. And that's really scary, because losing your family—if they're really hard-core—is a possibility. It's really scary. It's sad.

Part of the reason for this book is to put a face on people such as atheists—this bogeyman—and to let Christians see that these people are a lot like themselves.

I get the feeling that a major belief of people who are conservatively religious and think atheists are hellions is that because we don't believe in a higher power or a monotheistic situation, we don't have morals and ethics. Morals don't only come from religion.

In your case, it's the opposite. Your "religion" is about ethics: social justice. And that's why there was never a pull toward organized religion. Is that accurate?

I think so, yeah. And it just was really hard to ignore all of the things that have come out of it, since the beginning of religion.

And still do.

Yeah, big time.

And for me—and I'm assuming for my dad too—there's a feeling like, if you can't see, if you can't walk up to God and shake his or her hand, or its hand, how do you know? That's just the super-basic, first-grade level question.

Have you had things that Christians have said to you—you've mentioned a few of them already—but that just . . . if you were advising Christians, you would say, "Don't say that!"

I don't know if this is exactly answering that, but if you have ever seen on Larry Wilmore's show on Comedy Central—he was just canceled, but he always had really interesting and super-diverse people on mini-panels to talk about stuff. He had on Neil deGrasse Tyson and a guy who—I don't know if he was a pastor, but he writes a lot: he's some form of Christian personality who philosophizes and writes and editorializes. And this guy was talking about how his perspective is to believe in God and believe in science together—however he did it, I don't remember—but to allow those two things to be together instead of giving up scientific fact. I think that's a big thing: How do you deny the science? That's hard for me. So, at least in my view, this guy makes more sense: to believe and weave in all of the science of how creatures and humans developed over time, big bang theory, all the stuff. Because to me, denying that is problematic.

And—I don't know if this is off-topic or not—I'm really, really a believer in the separation of church and state. To me it's a huge problem. Now, having said that, if you don't believe in the science, I understand where people are coming from who want to have their religion in school. When I was growing up, the school would spend money on Christmas decorations. There are Jews who marry Christians who have mixed Christmas and Hanukkah celebrations. My family wasn't like that, and it really pissed me off that any of my public school dollars would go toward Christmas decorations, that the county building had a crèche, and often the solution was just to put a Star of David next to it and that doesn't really cover me.

I don't know if this is something you can tell a believer: "Believe in science too." That's kind of up to them. I just don't understand people who deny the history of scientific discovery. That's hard for me.

I think one thing that's super important—not that people who are religious should teach their kids to go a different way, but I think it helps a lot to defuse bad feelings—is to teach kids, even in one class period, the range of religions and the fact that atheists exist. I think that's really important. The us-and-them mentality is just 100 percent damaging, even in terms of one religion against another, outside of atheism.

I was thinking Jesus was pretty welcoming to different kinds of people.

Yes!

Except for hypocrites. But otherwise he didn't have much of an us-and-them mentality.

Yeah, if everybody who called themselves a Christian would follow his—at least what we read of his—actions and teachings, so much would be solved. Take care of poor people and sick people. Love everybody. I would say that 99.9% of people who are involved in religion aren't operating that way.

In Chattanooga—which is known even within the Bible Belt for being particularly conservative—it was hard for me. I'm not going to lie. I was always respectful of my students. But, you know, if people have a car that's a huge gas-guzzling car and they don't have kids and then they have a silver fish [sticker] on the back, that's hypocrisy. It's a really interesting place. There were parts I loved. But it was hard because religion is in public life almost everywhere. At the doctor's office and where I got my car fixed, there would be Bibles and paintings of Jesus and crosses.

And what's hard about that? It's shoved in your face?

A little bit. And also it assumes that we all have the same beliefs. It's hard because if you have a business and you're Christian, you can do whatever you want in your business.

But they're assuming everyone will appreciate their picture of Jesus on the wall?

Yeah, the dentist, the eye doctor, everywhere. And certainly I'm coming from the exact wrong place to be comfortable in a scenario like that, because I wasn't even raised as some variety of Christian altogether.

What if it was a Jewish Chattanooga and everybody put up Moses and Abraham and the great rabbis of the past? Would that bother you as much?

That's a really great question. I think it would have bothered me seven-and-a-half percent less, just because I would be used to it and I wouldn't feel like . . . I mean, it felt threatening a little bit.

Like, "If these people knew who I was, they might not . . . " what?

I'd have to say, part of me was like, "I want my eye doctor and my doctor to believe in science first, heavily interested in science." So that was one thing.

I guess maybe [I thought they might] judge me or not give me the right care or really think ill of me instead of just thinking, "Well, she's not going the right way, but whatever."

It was fascinating, actually. I could talk to you for about ten hours about living in Chattanooga.

A serious Christian would try to think about Jesus every day. As an atheist, are you thinking multiple times a day about being an atheist? Something like, "I'm glad I don't believe in God today"? Or are you militant about it and talk to people about it?

I don't. I mean, I have no question that that's how I feel. And I'm happy to talk about it, but I don't proselytize necessarily, to borrow a term.

But with things that happen in the news and in the world, I meet the idea of religion—I meet that issue coming from where I come from. But, yeah, I don't think about it routinely.

Anything else you want to say to the Christians who are going to read this book?

I don't think so. I think the main thing is that morals and ethics are not only for people who believe in God. That's the big thing, I think, for me. One of the most insulting things is when it's suggested that if you don't believe in God you don't have those.

And then, contrarily, to say to Christians, "Be more like Jesus"?

Yeah, that's how I feel. At least based on reports, he seemed to have a pretty good . . . yeah, I really wish people were more like that.

LISTENING TO ROB

My story in a nutshell: I can't remember a time before I believed in God. It was a given in our house. We went to church. We took it seriously. When my parents split up, church became a second home, a safe place where I could get away from the fighting. My youth ministers didn't just teach me about the Bible, they encouraged and challenged me to grow in wisdom and stature, in favor with God and with my fellow human beings. Before I graduated, I knew in my bones that I wanted to do that for someone else.

I went off to Bible college, then youth ministry, and eventually a solo, small-town pastorate. Over 15 years in ministry, I moved further and further to the theological left as my faith confronted life in the real world. Free will. Suffering. Hell. These weren't theological concepts anymore, worthy of reasoned argument. They were questions from the hearts of people I deeply loved, and they deserved real answers. I would spend the week in study and prayer and then out in the community, always searching for a way to connect the Good Book to the real world. I'd condense that all down into a sermon and reinforce the message one-on-one in the mess and pain of real relationships.

Eventually, it wore on me. I only carried a tiny fraction of the pain and doubt of each individual, but there were many individuals and all those little fractions added up to a lot of hurt—which would have been bearable, if my fellow Christians weren't constantly making it worse.

I remember spending a week studying to bring something life-giving to God's people. Then after the sermon I went out to the car, turned on the radio, and listened to a fellow preacher use the exact same section of Scripture to support the divinely ordained subservience of women. I wanted to puke.

At the same time, Christians were becoming more and more annoying, and foul-mouthed comedians started making more and more sense. If you want some examples, go read Mark Twain's essay on the fly in *Fables of Man* or his thoughts on biblical slavery and witchcraft from *A Pen Warmed Up in Hell*. The highbrow venom of Hitchens or Dawkins never moved me, but comedians sure did: George Carlin, Louis C.K., Sarah Silverman, Ricky Gervais, Eddie Izzard, Tim Minchin; *Harry Potter and the Methods of Rationality* by Eliezer Yudkowsky. They carved out space in my head: room for new ideas, room for people who weren't believers like me yet somehow managed to be hilarious, intelligent people. How is it that so many of the scientists and comedians I respect so much are atheists?

My doubts began to nag at me as my patience and strength wore thin. It was all a very gradual process, but I do remember one turning point in particular. I was studying the scientific method, how tests have to discriminate between outcomes. To put that another way, you have to risk something to gain actual knowledge. If both test results prove the same idea, then it's not actually a test. I sat with that idea for at least a month before I started to notice I was doing it all the time.

Person was healed? God is good! Person was not healed? God is mysterious! Person's faith improves their morals? God is good! Person's faith makes no difference in their life at all? God is good enough to allow free will! If any evidence can be twisted to support your claim, you're not actually testing. You're just confirming.

Another turning point was morality. Which is better? To do good because someone told you or because it's good? Is theft wrong because it made the list of commandments, or did it make the list because it's wrong? Is murdering your child wrong? How about genocide? Is it still wrong if God tells you to do it?

I knew I could've spoken my doubts from the pulpit. The congregation members would have walked with me through that. They were amazing. But that would've inverted the relationship. My job was to shepherd the church, not dump my doubts on them. I chose to resign instead. When I was free of the responsibility, free to think my own thoughts without worrying how it might hurt the church, I came to accept that I don't believe anymore.

The thing I never expected, and my family still doesn't understand, is that it doesn't feel like a choice. When you deeply believe something, it never feels like a choice. I didn't wake up today and choose to believe it's Tuesday. I never woke up one day and decided, "Hey, I've got a fun idea. Let's deny God." I just looked at the world and accepted what my heart already believed. It feels as obvious as the sun. Atheism doesn't mean I'm actively choosing to deny God. That's anti-theism. Atheism just means I don't believe it.

One quick aside: When I was a believer, I didn't run around saying, "I think . . . maybe . . . probably God exists." It was obvious to me, so I said, "God is." If you cornered me about it, I'd admit that means, "I believe God is," but that's not how I talked day to day, and it's not how anyone else talks either. Now that I don't believe, it seems just as obvious to me, so I say, "There is no God." If you want to be pedantic about it, then yes, that's a statement of belief. But that's not how anyone talks, so get over it. Just because I don't believe a thing doesn't mean I'm trying to force my nonbelief on you. It doesn't mean I know, in any ultimate sense, the truth of the matter. All it means is that the evidence used to compel me and now it does not.

Since no one from my family or my old faith community seems to understand that, they all assume what I really need is a more compelling argument. Which means every conversation about faith begins and ends as a fight. Yay, God. Thanks for making your followers so loving.

"You never really believed anyway. Your faith was too shallow and built on your parents. You should've prayed more."

"You'll never take my faith from me."

"It's just a phase. You're just burnt out. It's just a midlife crisis. You'll get over it."

"How can you spit in the face of everyone who ever loved you or taught you, everyone who ever listened to you preach?"

"You're going to hell."

"You've had it so easy. You never had to rely on your faith. The first test comes, and you jump ship."

"You deserve to get your ass kicked."

If I was ever on the fence, I'm not anymore. And it's not because of the stupid things Christians do and say. I grew up in the church. I was used to that a long time ago. No, the difference is in how I see the world and how I feel in my own head. When I was a believer, I had to perform mental gymnastics to explain the Bible, suffering, unregenerate believers, prayer, and on and on. Now I don't have to explain any of it. A messed-up world is exactly what you would expect if there were no all-powerful, benevolent God intervening on behalf of his people. The world makes so much more sense now. It feels like I was holding a muscle in tension my entire life, and I can finally let it relax.

Does that mean I'm all happy now? No. I look back over my life and see all the choices I would have made differently, all the energy and sacrifice that might have been dedicated to some other cause. At the very least I would have gotten something other than a master of divinity degree. Who's going to hire someone with a master of divinity? Got any Greek participles that need conjugating? So, yes, I'm one of those angry atheists, grieving the loss of not just a career but an entire circle of friends who want nothing to do with me now, grieving the loss of any kind of "normal" relationship with my family.

It feels like I'm starting over from scratch. But the good news is, starting over is a doable thing. People do it all the time. The tiny fraction of people who stuck with me through it all are true friends, and the new ones I'm making now accept me for who I am, not what I believe.

Two brothers, Bob and George Conway, are among the five Westerners who end up in the legendary Himalayan valley of Shangri-La in the classic 1937 movie Lost Horizon. Bob, the older brother, a world-famous but world-weary diplomat about to reach the pinnacle of his career, finds Shangri-La to be a paradise. However, little brother George, Bob's loyal right-hand man, cannot rest. He is convinced they are being lied to. As much as Bob has been his hero all his life, George is sure that Bob has been fooled this time—and that if they don't take their first chance to escape, they'll be held there forever, against their will, cut off from civilization (and from all his hopes for his big brother's bright career).

Bob wonders that his little brother could be so blind to the beauty all around him in Shangri-La: the peace, kindness, learning, and human flourishing that the rest of the world so sadly lacked—as they both knew well from their diplomatic travels.

George is panic-stricken that the big brother he idolized could fall for the fantastical stories of Shangri-La. Hasn't Bob even considered that it could all be a lie? Where was the proof, the evidence? And what about Maria, who had been there longer than they and said it was little more than a prison, said she would rather die than stay there a minute longer?

I have watched this movie several times.

When I get to the part of the movie where the two brothers have their final argument—George's desperate final attempt to get Bob to leave Shangri-La with him—one of the things I wonder is this: What if Bob hadn't basically ignored his brother for the several weeks since their arrival? Bob was so busy being swept up in the beauty of Shangri-La—having ethereal conversations with the High Lama, falling in love with his new soul mate Sondra—he had pretty much zero time to listen to his panicking brother. Zero time to ask him basic questions like, "Why are you so desperate to leave? What is it, exactly, that you find so evil about this place? Could you tell me why it is so hard for you to relax here or let your guard down?" Of course, that may have dragged out the movie too much or made for a much less dramatic finish. And maybe, "realistically," there was nothing that could've been done for someone like George. But it seems like it would've been a good first step in addressing George's skepticism—besides just being a good way for Bob to show brotherly concern for his loyal companion.

I know that it is easy for me to be like Bob Conway, to get swept up in the beautiful treasures, wisdom, and people we have in Christianity. Meanwhile, I have pretty much zero time to listen to my neighbors who are blind to the goodness of God and who wonder how we Christians could fall for it all.

What if I made time? What would I hear?

"How can there be a God, with so much suffering in the world?"

I turned to speak to God
About the world's despair;
But to make bad matters worse
I found God wasn't there.

—Robert Frost,
winner of four Pulitzer Prizes for poetry

In other words, it would be something to at least have God tell us why he allows all the despair-worthy suffering in the world. But Robert Frost says we don't even have that.

As far as God being hard to find or hard to pin down for answers, many of the poets and prophets in the Bible have agreed with Mr. Frost.

Maybe the first person we would think of here is that suffering "blameless man" of the Old Testament: Job.

What does Job complain about, it seems, even more than his great suffering? The fact that he could not talk to God about his grief or question God as to why his life had become so sorrowful. "If only I knew where to find him," he says (Job 23:3). Not to mention that he's sure that even if he could find God, he knows God wouldn't let him get a word in: "Even if I summoned him and he responded, I do not believe he would give me a hearing" (Job 9:16).

In some ways, Job's frustrations are not too different from Mr. Frost's.

However, if our neighbors were to talk like Mr. Frost, I'm not so sure our first reaction to them would be too different from the reaction of Job's friends to him. Their reaction was basically chapter after chapter of, "How can you say that, Job?" They wanted to come to God's defense. Without realizing it, we quickly react the same way: How can you say God isn't there? How can you say God doesn't answer?

And we could pile answers one on top of another. God is never the cause of evil (James 1:13-17; 1 John 1:5). God created a world that had no suffering (Genesis 1:31). Suffering came into the world when human-kind abandoned God, not because God somehow abandoned human-kind (Romans 5:12). God takes no pleasure, not even the slightest, in the death of anyone (Ezekiel 18:23). In heaven, I will get to "know fully, even as I am fully known" (1 Corinthians 13:12), and surely that will include learning better how every pang, teardrop, and scar from this world's suffering had some perfectly good end and, then, glorifying God for this into all eternity.

*But we don't **know fully** now. What we know, if we're watching, is suffering, much of it apparently senseless. Much of it crushing chil-dren whose only "sin" seems to be they were born under the wrong parents, religion, weather pattern, or regime. What we see is, as Frost wrote, "the world's despair." And we see a God for whom—as his own Son in deathly sorrow reminded him—"everything is possible" (Mark 14:36) . . . not stopping the despair.*

Piling on answers is what Job's friends did.

This might be a kinder, more compassionate reaction when our neighbors are wrestling with why God doesn't ease up the world's despair: to say to them, "Several of the most godly men in the Bible struggled with just what you're talking about." (Although I suppose the book of Job would be much less dramatic if his friends had reacted to him that kindly.)

It is rather unfortunate that the Koran gives the example of the ele-ments as signs of God's munificence since they are as much a cause of misery as happiness. Rain, we are told in sura 7.56 is a harbinger of God's mercy. Yet floods claim the lives of thousands of people in, ironically, a Muslim country, namely Bangladesh. The cyclone of 1991, with winds of 200 kilometers per hour, resulted in floods that left 100,000 dead and 10,000,000 without shelter. Despite the omni-presence of water, Bangladesh goes through a period of drought from October to April. Thus, the wretched population, among the poorest in the world, is submitted to both periodic floods and drought. . . .

Indeed, all natural catastrophes from earthquakes to tornadoes seem hard to reconcile with a benevolent God, especially as they seem to be visited on particularly poor, and often Muslim, countries. During the Lisbon earthquake of 1755 literally thousands of people died, many in churches as they prayed, and these deaths had a profound effect on the eighteenth century, particularly on writers like Voltaire. Why were so many innocent people killed? Why were the brothels spared, while pious churchgoers were punished?

—Ibn Warraq,
founder, Institute for the
Secularisaton of Islamic Society

Rain is supposed to be evidence of God's mercy. But Ibn Warraq says, as it were, "How can rain tell you if God is merciful or not? Sometimes rain saves lives, but often enough it takes them."

We could look up online the verse that Mr. Warraq refers to here. (He seems to mean sura 7.57, not 7.56. Perhaps it was a typo.) We could discuss with him the verses that follow it. They talk about why Allah sometimes sends rain, but sometimes drought. They even talk about Noah, and how Allah spoke to the people through Noah, so that others besides Noah's family might be rescued from the flood. In other words, Mr. Warraq seems to have been oversimplifying the message of the Koran in his line of argument here.

Still, it isn't just one verse of the Koran that points to rain as evidence of God's goodness. The Bible does too. The psalmists, Jesus, and St. Paul all talk about how good God is to send rain, yes, "on the righteous and the unrighteous" (Matthew 5:45). These Bible people knew that rain isn't always welcome, that rain sometimes destroys and kills, or sometimes the rain stops and people die of drought. They knew that the rain of Noah's flood killed tens of millions, including infants and the handicapped. But they still assumed people would agree when they said things like this: "[God] has shown kindness by giving you rain" (Acts 14:17).

And I need not be embarrassed that the Bible talks this way. The fact is, our planet is not just a vast desert. I can walk through the northwoods of Wisconsin in July and eat black raspberries nobody planted and nobody watered, and I need not be embarrassed to think that God put them there for me and the deer and the red ants to enjoy their sweetness.

It is good for me to realize, however, that not every unbeliever will see the rain this way, as proof of God's kindness. The forces of nature also destroy. They show not only God's goodness but also his fearsome power.

Can he be both good and fearsome?

That's the trouble, isn't it? And not just for Mr. Warraq. And not just when it comes to rain and earthquakes.

I lost my faith in God when I lost my daughter to Cancer, the beast. I begged, I cried, I offered my life for hers, and day by day, I watched that beautiful little Angel slip off. So, excuse me for not taking my seat next to you on Sunday in Church, I feel too cheated to worship.

—Vince Neil,
lead singer of heavy metal band Mötley Crüe

*I too have lost a daughter to a terminal illness, despite many prayers. The loss changed my view of prayer, of God, and of church. Until then, I didn't really know God as a God who "takes away" (compare Job 1:21). I know that, personally, it is much easier to see how God was there to comfort my wife and me **after** our daughter's death[22] than to see how he was listening to any of our prayers for her health. I can see why Mr. Neil's feelings would keep him out of church.*

Again, our first reaction might be to come to God's defense, to say Mr. Neil is being too harsh with God, to remind him that God's ways are beyond our understanding.

I would suggest that a better, less trite-sounding, more caring reaction would be to join him in grieving over his daughter.

Perhaps Jesus described someone like Mr. Neil in his parable of the sower. He might be like the seeds that "fell on rocky ground," receiving "the word with joy . . . but they have no root. They believe for a while, but in the time of testing they fall away" (Luke 8:6,13). Tender little plants withered up by the harsh noonday sun—and a daughter's death to cancer or any other beastly tragedy is surely a "time of testing"— how can the parched, root-scorched plants be revived? The water of sympathetic tears might help. Harsh, withering accusations might only scorch further ("How could you say God has cheated you?"), even if

---

[22] Some comforts I remember: Genesis 28:16 reminding me that God is present when he seems not to be; an image from the funeral sermon of a thirsty sheep resenting the shepherd who won't let it drink from a mud puddle; loved ones joining us in our grief and listening to us talk about our daughter; songs like "I Know of a Sleep in Jesus' Name," "I Will Rise," and "My Baby Needs a Shepherd"; and a half-week at a grief-therapy lodge in the Northwoods with other bereaved parents.

only implied. Rather we need to pray like Moses, "Let . . . my words descend like dew . . . on tender plants" (Deuteronomy 32:2).

Silence slowly prevails and then, from my bunk on the top row, I see and hear old Kuhn praying aloud, with his beret on his head, swaying backwards and forwards violently. Kuhn is thanking God because he has not been chosen.

Kuhn is out of his senses. Does he not see Beppo the Greek in the bunk next to him, Beppo who is twenty years old and is going to the gas-chamber the day after tomorrow and knows it and lies there looking fixedly at the light without saying anything and without even thinking anymore? Can Kuhn fail to realize that next time it will be his turn? Does Kuhn not understand that what has happened today is an abomination, which no propitiary prayer, no pardon, no expiation by the guilty, which nothing at all in the power of man can ever clean again?

If I was God, I would spit at Kuhn's prayer.

—Primo Levi,
Auschwitz survivor, to whom Christopher Hitchens
dedicated *The Portable Atheist*

Can we agree with Mr. Levi? Did Mr. Kuhn's prayers show childlike faith or garish shallowness? Shallowness toward his neighbor Beppo, who had only two days to live; shallowness also toward how abominable his situation really was . . .

I have to confess that often enough my view of the world's suffering is pretty shallow. I wake up, and in my morning prayer I thank God for keeping my family and me safe through the night. I don't have time to think about those countless thousands—some in my own city, many more around the world—for whom every night is full of horrors.

God's ears are discerning enough that he could very well spit at my shallowness and still, for Jesus' sake, accept my sincere and simple thank-you prayers.

I should not assume my neighbors' ears are nearly that discerning. If I come to God's defense in any way that even seems to downplay the great suffering in the world, my neighbor may hear nothing besides my shallowness.

Far from suggesting infinite goodness, miracles—even ones that do great good—seem to suggest that the responsible party is *not* omnibenevolent.[23] Many miracles are presented as good: Jesus is alleged to have healed a crippled man so that he could walk again, Jesus cured a group of lepers, and he miraculously fed thousands of hungry people. Similarly, many people are alleged to have been miraculously healed at Lourdes, France. Muhammed is said to have supernaturally multiplied food and drink on several occasions in order to feed hungry masses. God is reported to have parted the Red Sea to save the Israelites.

The problem is that at any given moment on the planet, now and when these miracles are alleged to have happened, there are millions or even billions of other people who are not being cured, healed, or benefitted by miracles. So any miracle that we attribute to an infinitely good God is problematic because it would indicate that God is out there and, under *some* circumstances, will intervene in the course of nature to achieve some good end. But there are all of these other cases where he does not help. The occurrence of a miracle, particularly one in the midst of so many instances of unabated suffering, cannot easily be reconciled with an omnibenevolent source.

. . . On the contrary, if a doctor goes to a village with enough polio vaccine to inoculate one thousand children but gives only ten of them the shots, throws the rest of the vaccine away, and then watches the remaining 990 die or be crippled, we would conclude that doctor is a monster, not a saint.

—Matthew S. McCormick,
Atheism and the Case Against Christ

The Bible doesn't give us the complete answer to the question Mr. McCormick raises here, does it? That is, since Jesus could heal everyone, why doesn't he?

It is tempting to add to Mr. McCormick's brief parable. What if the doctor who only saved ten children, soon afterward very purposefully endured torturous suffering, giving his life to keep the entire country safe from a disease far worse than polio? We might, then, conclude

[23] That is, perfectly good in all things and toward all people.

that the doctor was more of a mystery than a monster. That is more like what Jesus did.

Yet there is still very much a mystery. Jesus has the power to heal everyone. "He does not willingly bring affliction or grief to anyone" (Lamentations 3:33). He feels compassion for every human being (Psalm 145:9). He still weeps with those who weep (John 11:35) and longs to hold the children in his arms (Luke 18:15,16), and he will never change (Hebrews 13:8). He says we can ask him for anything in prayer, he will hear his Spirit interceding with wordless groans on behalf of our prayers, and he will deliver his people from every trouble. Still, as Mr. McCormick says, there are "so many instances of unabated suffering." Why doesn't Jesus abate them, much less soothe or cure them? He surely, in every case, has his righteous, faithful reasons (Psalm 145:17). But he most often doesn't tell us what those reasons are.

If our neighbors bring up questions like these, will we have the humility and modesty to admit we don't know the answers? Ultimately, such modesty—displayed over the course of many sincere listening sessions—might only end up making our faith more impressive and attractive: "You look all of the world's suffering right in the face, you tear yourself up over it even more than I do, and still you are so sure that your God is good. I wish I could be sure like that . . ."

*We could help with that wish! One encouraging way to start might be to say, "Well, I don't always **feel** so sure, but Jesus has years of experience convincing doubtful people that he's good."*

I cannot see why we should expect an infinite God to do better in another world than he does in this.

—Robert G. Ingersoll,
nicknamed "The Great Agnostic"

Look where we end up. When we take a hard look at the suffering God allows in this world, we could question his goodness, then the value of going to his church (Vince Neil), then of saying prayers to him (Primo Levi), then of believing in his miracles (Matthew McCormick), and finally of spending eternity with him (Robert Ingersoll).

This line of logic starts with a very great and Christ-like virtue: deploring the world's suffering as it deserves to be deplored.

We can learn that virtue better. We can listen better to the way "the whole creation has been groaning . . . right up to the present time" (Romans 8:22).[24]

The better we learn that virtue, the more we see how God lets the whole world keep groaning. Yet Christianity tells us to hope that this same God will make a new world where all will be joy, where we'll understand perfectly and contentedly why he let all the groaning go on. Do we base such a hope on what we can see? Mr. Ingersoll says that if we don't, our hope is foolish. But that is to reject the very concept of hope. Only a few lines after writing about the world's groaning, St. Paul reminds us, "Hope that is seen is no hope at all" (Romans 8:24).

(By the way, the last half of that same Bible chapter, Romans 8, has plenty of comfort in it as far as where God is when suffering comes. It has glorious answers. The trick is that those answers are not meant to be comforting to those who refuse the love of Christ. But let us not forget their glorious comfort! This is why we want to have such conversations with unbelievers, so we can eventually lead **them** to this glory and to the immovable conviction that they're loved in Christ.)

In college, I could have shared my faith a lot more than I did—God, please forgive me! But I remember sharing it with Nikki, a girl I had a crush on. When we first met, she said she wasn't sure there was a God. I asked her why. She said because of all the suffering in the world, including in her own family life. I wish I could remember how our conversations went. (That would probably make this a much better story!) I remember trying to be a good listener. I remember she eventually was ready to try church again, and praying again.

With a little listening, we can get the chance to help our neighbors find hope again, despite all the suffering they see.

Christian apologist Sean McDowell talks about how he replies when people ask him why a good God would allow so much suffering in the world. He too emphasizes listening:

> I typically turn the question back on the questioner. I just say, "Wow, that is such an important question. Of all the questions you could ask about God, why that one?" And I regularly hear stories of

---

[24] Joining the creation in its groaning can be a sign that we have "the firstfruits of the Spirit" (Romans 8:23). That would be an attention-getting thing to say to someone bemoaning all the suffering in the world: "You sound like someone with the Holy Spirit." This could lead into a conversation about Romans 8:22,23 and perhaps a chance to talk about some of your other favorite verses in Romans chapter 8.

abuse, abandonment, pain, and suffering. With that said, we have to be careful not to read meaning into a question that isn't there. Sometimes people ask that question in the abstract. (AFA Journal, interview, January 2016)

In other words, be ready to listen and sympathize. But at the same time, don't think that all atheists are miserable and hopeless and deeply scarred by suffering. . . .

"You say that life is meaningless without God, but you are wrong."

Well I don't think we're *for* anything. We're just products of evolution. You can say "Gee, your life must be pretty bleak if you don't think there's a purpose." But I'm anticipating having a good lunch.

—James Watson,
co-discoverer of the structure of DNA

It may be hard for some Christians to believe Dr. Watson. He doesn't want Christians like us to feel sorry for him. He says his life is not bleak. He says it is full of simple pleasures like a good lunch. Our knee-jerk reaction might be to assume that he is just trying to cover up the "God-shaped vacuum" in his heart that's secretly tearing him apart.

Turning again to the words of righteous Job in the Old Testament, Job would say we should believe Dr. Watson, that Dr. Watson is just one of many. He says there are many unbelievers who "spend their years in prosperity and go down to the grave in peace" (Job 21:13), and he says his three friends are naive to think any different.

We don't want to be naive about how unbelievers think. Do we assume their lives are all bleak and joyless? Then we aren't any wiser about that than Job's friends.

Like many people, I have no religion, and I am just sitting in a small boat drifting with the tide. I live in the thoughts of my duty. . . . I think there is dignity in this, just to go on working.

—Federico Fellini,
four-time Oscar winning film director

It is commendable to find dignity and meaning in one's daily duties and work. We could commend Mr. Fellini, and other unbelievers like him, at least for that.

Wise Solomon teaches us that "it is appropriate for a person to eat, to drink and to find satisfaction in their toilsome labor under the sun during the few days of life God has given them—for this is their lot" (Ecclesiastes 5:18). It is unfair of us not to recognize when our unbelieving neighbors have tapped in to a little of the wisdom that Solomon discovered.

So I be written in the Book of Love,
I have no care about that book above;
Erase my name, or write it, as you please—
So I be written in the Book of Love.

—Omar Khayyám,
influential Medieval Persian scientist,
mathematician, and poet

"So long as I find love on earth, what should I care for heaven?" How should we respond to such a sentiment?

Our first reaction might be to speak up in defense of heaven: "How can you compare the eternal joys of heaven to the short-lived joys of love or sex?" Even to attempt such a comparison might seem like idol worship, a sinful and serious confusion of priorities.

But it is a tremendous blessing from God to be loved by a good and affectionate spouse. "He who finds a wife finds what is good and receives favor from the Lord" (Proverbs 18:22). We don't have to downplay that blessing or call it a sinful idol. We could instead join our neighbors in their joy over that blessing. And then we could draw special attention to how that joy is evidence of God's favor in their lives. (And if he's so good at writing "the Book of Love," then "that book above" must be—wow!)

I can very well do without God both in my life and in my painting, but I cannot, ill as I am, do without something which is greater than I, which is my life—the power to create.

—Vincent van Gogh,
Dutch post-impressionist painter

We can't necessarily say that van Gogh was wrong to find meaning and life in using his artistic abilities. Now his paintings sell for tens of millions of dollars. Others have found great meaning just in looking at them.

Life's too short to believe in another.
She don't have no time for heavy Jesus in her life.
The only religion that she's known is rock and roll.

—Honus Honus,
from their song "Heavy Jesus"

*We could tell the girl in this song that there is nothing "religious" about rock music. We could tell her that all the pleasures of rock and roll are worthless in the end. But I wonder if it would be more appealing to a girl like that to show her how Jesus can make her rock and roll even **more** meaningful. (And I don't mean by just putting his name into every song.)*

You know, it's not that I have a meaningless life at all. That's probably another thing for the misconception bucket: the idea that you need religion to give your life meaning. I mean, things just have meaning. It's part of being human and your attention sort of gives it that.

—Ezra,
see above, "Listening to Ezra"

It is sometimes argued that disbelief in a fearful and tempting heavenly despotism makes life into something arid and tedious and cynical. . . .What nonsense this is. There are the beauties of science and the extraordinary marvels of nature. There is the consolation and irony of philosophy. There are the infinite splendors of literature and poetry, not excluding the liturgical and devotional aspects of these, such as those found in John Donne or George Herbert. There is the grand resource of art and music and architecture, again not excluding those elements that aspire to the sublime. In all of these pursuits, any one of them enough to absorb a lifetime, there may be found a sense of awe and magnificence that does not depend at all on any invocation of the supernatural.

—Christopher Hitchens,
The Portable Atheist

It's not just meaning in life. Unbelievers can also find awe and magnificence, without finding God. What are the lessons here?

One is that God is good to all. Just because people refuse to believe in him or thank him for their blessings doesn't keep him from showering their lives with pleasures, both small and magnificent.

Another lesson: Notice the contrast between this section and the previous. In the previous section, how did the atheists complain? "Look how messed up the world is: there can't be a God." But in this section it's a different tune: "Why do I need God? My life is very meaningful and good the way it is." I'm not sure how helpful it would be to point this contrast (one might even call it a contradiction) out to an atheist. But perhaps we could be ready so that when they kind of wish they had someone to thank for all that meaning and goodness they've found in their lives, we could introduce them to that "someone," saying, "I know just who you mean."[25]

A third lesson: We should not despise the unbelievers' quality of life. We should not assume, as Mr. Hitchens wrote here, that they have only an "arid and tedious" existence. Talking that way will just give the unbelievers more reason to think we are out of touch with reality.

And it is insulting to them.

All of this is not to ignore the fact that, with their claims to meaningful lives, religion-less people are contradicting something very basic about our faith. Yes, in his generous goodness, God keeps both the godless and the godly "occupied with gladness of heart" so that "they seldom reflect on the days of their life" (Ecclesiastes 5:20). But gladness isn't the same as meaning. Death and the often tragic uncertainty of tomorrow make this life "Meaningless! Meaningless! . . . Utterly meaningless!" unless we have hope in Christ (1:2). The Bible doesn't

---

[25] Ch. P. Arand and Erik H. Herrmann tell of an unbelieving couple who started going to church because one afternoon the wife said to her husband, "We've got it so good right now. This house, our family, our health, your work . . . Everything is just so very . . . good. I just feel like I need to give thanks to someone." ("Living in the Promises and Places of God: A Theology of the World," *Concordia Journal*, Spring 2015.)

just say we have been saved from sin, death, and the devil, but also from empty lives. Notice the words of the apostle Peter:

> Since you call on a Father who judges each person's work impartially, live out your time as foreigners here in reverent fear. For you know that it was not with perishable things such as silver or gold that **you were redeemed from the empty way of life** handed down to you from your ancestors, but with the precious blood of Christ, a lamb without blemish or defect. He was chosen before the creation of the world, but was revealed in these last times for your sake. Through him you believe in God, who raised him from the dead and glorified him, and so your faith and hope are in God (1 Peter 1:17-21).

Christ poured out his precious blood and was sacrificed like a blemishless lamb so your days in this world could be what? Not an empty life but a life of joy and purpose and lasting hope. When unbelievers say, "We already have meaning," they devalue Christ's great payment.

And Peter piles up the reasons why, with Christ, your life isn't empty anymore.

- Like a small child is proud to be able to say, "Dad, watch what I can do," you have the privilege of prayer. Anytime, anywhere, you can "call on a Father" who loves to hear your voice and help you. A life where you can talk to God that way every minute is not empty.

- Yes, and he does watch everything you try to do for him—your Father "judges" your "work impartially." Whoever you are—however lowly or dirty your work seems, however pointless or thankless or repetitive or behind schedule—your Father smiles to watch what you do for him. That's no empty life.

- Yours is not an empty life, because your religion has a real Savior, not an idol made of silver or gold, which could never hear your prayers or cover up the bad you've done. You face each day with a clean slate, a clean conscience—clean like the Lamb who died for you "without blemish or defect"—knowing that the Lamb is now your glorious King.

- Yours is not an empty life, because it is part of an eternal plan, a story without beginning or end. Your Savior "was chosen before the creation of the world" and your "faith and hope" reach beyond death into all eternity, for Easter shows how your Father raises his sons and daughters from the dead.

Such costly gifts of meaning and purpose call for cautious, careful "reverent fear," Peter says. Alert thinking. Constantly asking yourself, How are you living this hour, this moment? Carelessly forgetting prayer and eternity? Finding meaning in whatever flits past your eyeballs? in the perishable pleasures of today? As if you agree with the unbelievers who say life is just as meaningful when you forget about your Father and the precious blood? Or are you living the life that finds all its fullness in the Father and the Lamb? Despite what the world says, that life, and that life alone, is not empty.

"Having religion does not make people good or moral."

I refuse to be labeled immoral merely because I'm godless.

—fb.com/wflscience,
posted on the "think before you preach"
Pinterest board

I think that probably the only times I've felt a little bit—I wouldn't say "hurt," because that's pretty traumatic—but the times when I've been surprised at someone's point of view is when they ask where you go to church and you say, "I don't go," and they're just kind of shocked.

The attitude is sort of like, "Wait a second. I thought you were a good person, and you're telling me you don't go to church."

And it's like, "Well, yeah."

And I think there have been friends we've met through our son who have kind of given us the stink eye a little bit, just because—or I think have been a little bit more reluctant to let our kid play with theirs—because they know that we don't take him to church.

That's sad.

—Ezra,
see above, "Listening to Ezra"

I think the main thing is that morals and ethics are not only for people who believe in God. That's the big thing, for me. One of the most insulting things is when it's suggested that if you don't believe in God you don't have those.

—Rebecca,
see above, "Listening to Rebecca"

Have you ever had someone insult not just you but your character and the character of your whole family? Perhaps you could try to imagine it, at least. Imagine what it would feel like.

"Immoral" would be such an insult.

Now this seems like a tricky subject.

*Who are the sources of temptation in a Christian's life? There are three of them: the devil, **the world**, and our sinful flesh. That's what I learned from my pastor as a young boy, in memory passages from Luther's* Small Catechism *that I still say to myself as part of my prayers almost every morning. That's what I taught my students and still teach my own children. And what does that mean, **the world**? That's the unbelievers.*

In other words, it's a pretty basic teaching of the church that unbelievers are not only themselves immoral, but they are also a great danger to those who want to be upright and moral. The Bible warns us quite stringently against toying around with that danger. For example, "Do not love the world or anything in the world," says the apostle John. "If anyone loves the world, love for the Father is not in them" (1 John 2:15). The apostle James agrees: "Anyone who chooses to be a friend of the world becomes an enemy of God" (James 4:4).

But the world doesn't appreciate being seen that way or talked about that way, as a great moral danger. Is there any room for us here to "tone down our rhetoric"? It seems wrong even to ask such a question. It seems to imply that the rhetoric of Scripture must be toned down somehow. Well, let's listen more first. Maybe the real problem is that, at least to some extent, we are talking past one another, using different definitions of moral.

I have come to accept that this alignment of moral goodness with "spirituality" and moral evil with "materialism" is just a frustrating fact of life. . . . We materialists are the bad guys, and those who believe in anything supernatural, however goofy and gullible the particular belief, have at least this much going for them: they're "on the side of the angels."

... There is *no reason at all* why a disbelief in the immateriality or immorality of the soul should make a person less caring, less moral, less committed to the well-being of everybody on Earth than somebody who believes in "the spirit." But won't such a materialist care only about the *material* well-being of the people? If that means only their housing, their car, their food, their "physical" as opposed to "mental" health, no. After all, a good scientific materialist believes that mental health—spiritual health, if you like—is just as physical, just as material, as "physical" health. A good scientific materialist can be just as concerned about whether there is plenty of justice, love, joy, beauty, political freedom, and, yes, even religious freedom as about whether there is plenty of food and clothing, for instance, since *all* of these are material benefits, and some are more important than others. (But for goodness' sake, let's try to get food and clothing to everybody who needs them as soon as possible, since without them justice and art and music and civil rights and the rest are something of a mockery.)

... plenty of "deeply spiritual" people—and everybody knows this—are cruel, arrogant, self-centered, and utterly unconcerned about the moral problems of the world. Indeed, one of the truly nauseating side effects of the common confusion of moral goodness with "spirituality" is that ... [t]here are many people who quite innocently and sincerely believe that if they are earnest in attending to their own personal "spiritual" needs, this amounts to living a morally good life. I know many activists, both religious and secular, who agree with me: these people are deluding themselves.

—Daniel C. Dennett,
Breaking the Spell

*What does Dr. Dennett mean when he says that a person who denies the soul and denies God can still be moral? He uses phrases like **caring for others** and **concern for the world's problems**.*

A recent psychological experiment involving 1,170 children ages 5 to 12 from six countries tested which children would be more gener-

ous in sharing stickers with their playmates: children from religious homes or nonreligious homes. Its findings were reported on many mainstream news websites: "Our findings robustly demonstrate that children from households identifying as either of the two major world religions (Christianity and Islam) were less altruistic than children from non-religious households."[26]

Does the Bible teach that unbelievers cannot care for others?

*In fact, in what is perhaps the Bible's most famous story about caring for others, Jesus' parable of the good Samaritan, the **only** person who cares is the Samaritan, and in the minds of Jesus' Jewish listeners, a Samaritan was the **worst kind** of unbeliever. Could the famous atheist Dr. Dennett and our Savior Jesus be making the same point? It seems they might be. Both of them are saying to the "religious people," **Maybe you could learn a thing or two about good old-fashioned caring by looking at the unbelievers**.*

It would be good for us to be humble enough to listen to a "lecture" like that, not just from our Savior but also from our unbelieving neighbors.

More than listening, it would be helpful for us to be more careful in how we talk about the "sinful world" so that we don't come across as saying people who don't go to church don't care about anybody, can't be trusted in anything, and so on.

The biblical authors do not define wickedness and sin in terms of moral and ethical conduct. Indeed, they are far more concerned with the purity of religion than with the pursuit of justice. The very worst sin of all, as they see it, is not lust or greed, but rather the offering of worship to gods and goddesses other than the True God.

—Jonathan Kirsch,
God Against the Gods

There is some truth in what Dr. Kirsch says here about "the very worst sin of all." It is unbelief, contempt for God. It is failure to love the Lord with heart, soul, mind, and strength. In order for the atheists to say, "We are moral; really we are," they have set aside the most important

---

[26] Brad Tuttle, "Study Shows Non-Religious Kids Are More Altruistic and Generous Than Religious Ones," time.com, Nov. 6, 2015.

commandment. It is valuable for us to realize that and to not fall for their faulty line of thought.

It is a line of thought that doesn't just set aside the highest commandment. It also sets aside God's highest grace: making us alive when our hearts were dead in sin (Ephesians 2:1-5). This grace tells us that faith in Jesus' love and gratitude for that love are the oxygen of the soul. Meanwhile, souls that put their faith in themselves are suffocated and dead, no matter how alive they might look on the outside. We need to pray that God would help us take him at his word on this (and help us keep rejoicing in our oxygen).

But from the atheists' point of view, we Christians give the appearance that we don't care so much about "the pursuit of justice," so long as people will come to our churches and sing a few Jesus songs. What are some specific things we do or say that would give that appearance? Could you make a list?

An atheist believes that a hospital should be built instead of a church. An atheist believes that a deed must be done instead of a prayer said. An atheist strives for involvement in life and not escape into death. He wants disease conquered, poverty vanquished, war eliminated.

—Madalyn Murray O'Hair,
founder of American Atheists,
"most hated woman in America"
according to *Life* magazine in 1964

I think from the Christian point of view, there's this idea that "without God, anything goes," and I think that sort of the opposite is true. I think that if you don't believe that there's an afterlife or [if you believe] that there's nothing out there that can clean up your mistakes, you've got the responsibility to fix it and you've got to do it now. You can't wait for some apocalypse to just burn everything up and start over. You actually have to take a stand, and you have to be a responsible human being. I think the idea that morality suddenly goes off the table if you don't have a God to enforce it is kind of silly.

—Ezra,
see above, "Listening to Ezra"

*I mentioned this Madalyn Murray O'Hair quote to another Christian at lunch the other day, someone very thoughtful about a lot of things, someone who has spent years living in a third-world country. His response? **The atheists aren't always so interested in building hospitals either.** I suppose that's right. He would know. He has lived in the places where nobody has a hospital, where disease is far from vanquished, etc.*

Atheism might give someone reasons to help their neighbors more, like Ezra said it does for him. And for someone else it might not. Same with churchgoing: It makes some people into great neighbors; some it doesn't.

Maybe the atheists have a stereotype of us Christians. "So heavenly minded, you're no earthly good," sang Johnny Cash, using that atheist stereotype to scold his fellow Christians.

We don't like to be stereotyped or scolded like that. But we might stereotype others. We might assume too much about the morals of unbelievers, about their priorities, motives, and behavior. Or we might talk like everything about them is evil. Not every atheist is building hospitals, but neither should we talk as if they're all just one Darth Vader after another. We will sound "kind of silly," kind of not worth listening to.

Many, I know, will not abandon their cherished religious beliefs. It took me years to break free from mine, and in the end I was compelled by logic, reason, and a growing sense of cognitive disconnect with how my religion treated reality and how reality actually seemed to be. I know I cannot get other believers to go through the same experience and turn them into fellow Atheists. The thing is, I quit caring about doing that the moment I realized it wouldn't work. Instead, I focus more on getting religious folks to understand that all Atheists aren't selfish, greedy, mean, incapable of devotion and love, unimpressed by nature, or merely "in rebellion" against God. In this I find much more success and, to be honest, far greater value in my life as an active, passionate Atheist.

—Brandon from Johnson County, Missouri,
commenting on an article at nytimes.com;
his comment got 334 "thumbs-up"

The doctrinal statements of my church give high praise to the out-wardly righteous acts of unbelievers, calling these acts "righteousness of reason," that is, righteous things that people can do only by the power of their own human reason, without the Holy Spirit working in their hearts:

> *We cheerfully assign this righteousness of reason the praises that are due it (for this corrupt nature has no greater good, and Aristotle says aright: **Neither the evening star nor the morning star is more beautiful than righteousness**, and God also honors it with bodily rewards).[27]*

But rarely do I take time to appreciate the righteousness of unbelievers. Much less do I make a consistent effort to praise them cheerfully for it.

Wait a minute. Praising unbelievers for what righteousness they do have—that seems like it would be counterproductive. That won't draw them to the Savior who had to leave heaven and hang on a cross and die in order to atone for the tremendous amount of righteousness they are lacking. They need Jesus' words, "No one is good—except God alone" (Luke 18:19). They need to hear how evil they are, how much guilt they bear before the utterly holy God. Praising them will just feed into their self-delusions of goodness.

I'm not sure that it has to feed their self-delusions.

It could help them see that we Christians are not self-deluded, not thinking all the good in the world is done by us and our fellow church-goers.

Time and again, I met people like myself, who'd been raised with religion and long since walked away. I found in many of them the deep kindness, strong values, and commitment to charity so often attributed to the best of the religious.

—Katherine Ozment,
Grace Without God

Don't those sound like nice people? Kind, principled, and charitable as the best of the churched or religious, Mrs. Ozment says. We could make an effort to notice such people in our communities. We could say to them, "I know you aren't so sure about God. But here are some things

---

[27] *Apology of the Augsburg Confession,* Article IV, paragraph 24.

I'm sure of. I'm sure God sees the way you _____. I'm sure he wants you to keep at it. I'm sure God wants me to honor you for the good you're doing. And I'm sure God is at work through you—he uses people like you to keep our community from falling all to pieces." Those would be noble things to say. The kind, principled unbelievers would probably like it very much. While you have not said that their good works have any spiritual or saving value—that would dishonor Christ— you have begun a conversation about God in a way that is appealing and attractive. That's alright, really.

You might continue the conversation by sharing a saying or story of Jesus that shows that his kindness and charity go far beyond ours. (Loving enemies, touching lepers, sparing the adulteress, calling Judas his friend . . .) If you tell someone, "You remind me of Jesus," most people would probably want to hear why. And you never know what a story of Jesus' goodness might do in a listener's heart.

Since you don't believe in our god, what stops you from stealing and lying and raping and killing to your heart's content? . . . self-respect and the desire for the respect of others.

—Christopher Hitchens,
Hitch-22

My own text [to read at my father's funeral] was from that same Paul of Tarsus, and from his Epistle to the Philippians, which I selected for its non-religious yet high moral character:

Finally, brethren, whatsoever things are true, whatsoever things are honest, whatsoever things are just, whatsoever things are pure, whatsoever things are lovely, whatsoever things are of good report; if there be any virtue, and if there be any praise, think on these things.

—Christopher Hitchens

Regarding the first quote, Mr. Hitchens wrote how, at his public speaking events and debates, Christians often would ask him that "what stops you" question. What does such a question show about those Christians? They just couldn't imagine any reason for being good besides the Ten Commandments. Some Christians are too wrapped up in their own little worlds to realize that there are actually billions of people in this world who barely know the difference between the Ten Commandments and a No Parking sign but who still find reasons not to be murderers, adulterers, child molesters, or highway bandits.

Then you go on to the second quote from Mr. Hitchens. This internationally known atheist could even find something to admire in some of the moral statements of the Bible, something he could read with all sincerity at his father's Christian funeral. That suggests a fine opening for a Bible conversation with an atheist: "Is there anything you could think of that's worth admiring about the morals that Christianity teaches?"

A friend of mine is a senior in college. She went to Christian schools from kindergarten through 12th grade and says that at those schools, "it was easy to nod and smile and regurgitate the correct answers on worksheets about what God says about atheists." (In other words, that they're bad and dangerous and so on.) But now at a public university, her roommate "is an atheist, strong feminist and pro-choice, and sleeps with her boyfriend every night." The people she spends most of her time with are the kinds of people her Christian schoolteachers had warned her about, but now they "aren't arbitrary, hypothetical people on my worksheets, but they are my best friends, and they are really kind people." Why should she have been surprised at how kind unbelievers can be, what good friends they can be?

It seems to have been because, at least in her experience, the Christian grown-ups commonly (and we assume, unintentionally) stereotyped unbelievers as incurably wicked in every way.

*Read again the way my friend explained what damage such stereotyping does. Note how it leaves our young people unprepared to make the **most** of their friendships with religionless people.*

*In some ways, yes, the most important ways, it is impossible to exaggerate how evil people are without the Holy Spirit in their hearts. At the same time, we must not talk about this carelessly. The billions of people who don't have the Holy Spirit still **do** have the conscience God gave them.[28] Plenty of them "do by nature things required by the law" (Romans 2:14) and, sadly, Scripture itself has to use the outwardly good example of such unbelievers to condemn hypocritical churchgoers (2:27).*

---

[28] Imagine how awful this world would be if God didn't make sure of that!

May our righteous Savior help us not speak carelessly about morality,
so we do not get in the way of our own outreach to such kind, friendly,
lost and condemned sinners.

"Religion is responsible for a whole lot of pain in people's lives."

Our world is fast succumbing to the activities of men and women who would stake the future of our species on beliefs that should not survive an elementary school education. That so many of us are still dying on account of ancient myths is as bewildering as it is horrible, and our own attachment to these myths, whether moderate or extreme, has kept us silent in the face of developments that could ultimately destroy us. Indeed, religion is as much a living spring of violence today as it was at any time in the past. The recent conflicts in Palestine (Jews v. Muslims), the Balkans (Orthodox Serbians v. Catholic Croatians; Orthodox Serbians v. Bosnian and Albanian Muslims), Northern Ireland (Protestants v. Catholics), Kashmir (Muslims v. Hindus), Sudan (Muslims v. Christians and animists), Nigeria (Muslims v. Christians), Ethiopia and Eritrea (Muslims v. Christians), Sri Lanka (Sinhalese Buddhists v. Tamil Hindus), Indonesia (Muslims v. Timorese Christians), and the Caucasus (Orthodox Russians v. Chechen Muslims; Muslim Azerbaijanis v. Catholic and Orthodox Armenians) are merely a few cases in point. In these places religion has been the *explicit* cause of literally millions of deaths in the last ten years. These events should strike us like psychological experiments run amok, for that is what they are. Give people divergent, irreconcilable, and untestable notions about what happens after death, and then oblige them to live together with limited resources. The result is what we see: an unending cycle of murder and cease-fire. If history reveals any categorical truth, it is that an insufficient taste for evidence regularly brings out the worst in us. Add weapons of mass destruction to this diabolical clockwork, and you have found a recipe for the fall of civilization.

—Sam Harris,
The End of Faith

Some of my closest Christian friends have trouble understanding why atheists don't just leave Christians to enjoy their beliefs, the same way the atheists want to be left to enjoy their unbelief. And not all atheists are militant about spreading their unbelief to others. Not at all. But if you blame religion for "millions of deaths in the last ten years" and you consider religion a key ingredient in the "recipe for the fall of civilization," why wouldn't you be eager to see religion made extinct?

Notice how this connects to the previous section's misguided thinking about human goodness. Once you have decided that religion is not necessary to help people be kind and noble-hearted or, through prayers or offerings, to persuade the unseen spirits to shower favor upon the nations—yes, once you're convinced that religion isn't doing society much good, you feel like you have free rein to start noticing and protesting all the harm religion does in society.

Why would blacks consider a book as deplorable as the Bible sacred? It was the primary justification of the slavery of many of their ancestors and continues to be used as the primary justification for white supremacy in the United States. Why would Hispanics continue to participate in the religion of the empire builders who often enslaved their ancestors and oppressed them, destroying their culture in the process? And why would Native Americans convert to or remain Christians once they realize that Christianity was used to justify the extermination of their ancestors and was the primary tool used to attempt to assimilate them into white Anglo-Saxon Protestant culture?

—Ryan T. Cragun,
How to Defeat Religion in 10 Easy Steps

Human trafficking, genocide, racism—those are some big ugly crimes Christianity is accused of. How should we respond to such accusations? We could start by pleading guilty, at least on behalf of institutionalized "Christianity." We could say that just because wicked men try to hide behind holy words, that doesn't make the words any less holy. We could point to the Christians who spent their whole lives trying to better the circumstances of these mistreated peoples. Which response would better show caring and sympathy?

Anti-theism reached its peak in the writings of the German philosophers Karl Marx and Friedrich Engels. Marx famously viewed religion as the "opium of the people" and sought to eradicate it from society. "The abolition of religion as the illusory happiness of the people is the demand for their real happiness," Marx wrote in his celebrated critique of Hegel.

In truth, Marx's views on religion and atheism were far more complex than these much-abused sound bites project. Nevertheless, Marx's vision of a religion-less society was spectacularly realized with the establishment of the Soviet Union and the People's Republic of China—two nations that actively promoted "state atheism" by violently suppressing religious expression and persecuting faith communities.

Atheists often respond that atheism should not be held responsible for the actions of these authoritarian regimes, and they are absolutely right. It wasn't atheism that motivated Stalin and Mao to demolish or expropriate houses of worship, to slaughter tens of thousands of priests, nuns and monks, and to prohibit the publication and dissemination of religious material. It was anti-theism that motivated them to do so. After all, if you truly believe that religion is "one of the world's great evils"—as bad as smallpox and worse than rape; if you believe religion is a form of child abuse; that it is "violent, irrational, intolerant, allied to racism and tribalism and bigotry, invested in ignorance and hostile to free inquiry, contemptuous of women and coercive toward children"—if you honestly believed this about religion, then what lengths would you not go through to rid society of it?

—Reza Aslan,
scholar, author, and TV host, in a Salon.com
article criticizing the so-called New Atheists

We might be tempted to point to the evil atheistic (or anti-theistic) regimes of the 20th century and say, "Stalin and Mao committed far worse crimes against humanity in the name of godlessness than anything the old-time, churchgoing white conquistadors, slave traders, and Indian killers ever tried to justify with the Bible." Yet we would be mistaken to think that all atheists are as violently opposed to religion as Stalin and Mao. Making a caricature of all atheists isn't going to help us reach any of them with the gospel.

Being oblivious to what even the milder atheists claim to be as the evil excesses of religion isn't going to help us reach them either.

I have been into many of the ancient cathedrals—grand, wonderful, mysterious. But I always leave them with a feeling of indignation because of the generations of human beings who have struggled in poverty to build these altars to an unknown god.

—Elizabeth Cady Stanton,
American suffragist, 1815–1902

We can try to imagine how history would have been different if the backbreaking labor invested in those cathedrals had instead been invested in improving the health, sanitation, nutrition, and education of medieval Europe's millions of dirt-poor peasants. (At the same time, it isn't as though cathedrals were the only civic projects built on the tired backs of peasants.) Mrs. Stanton wants us to admit that religion causes pain by diverting energies and monies away from alleviating the very real suffering of all those generations of people living under the poverty line, whom we'd rather not think about much. In fact, the Bible says that any religion that ignores the poor and helpless is a deformed religion: "Religion that God our Father accepts as pure and faultless is this: to look after orphans and widows in their distress and to keep oneself from being polluted by the world" (James 1:27).

We might be wise to challenge the assumption that religion causes people to ignore the poor even more than they would otherwise. As Solomon writes, the poor are usually shunned by all, even their own relatives and friends (Proverbs 19:7). But we could agree with Mrs. Stanton that many practitioners of "religion" (even we ourselves?) have been far from "pure and faultless."

In Italy, the Inquisition was condemning people to death until the end of the eighteenth century, and inquisitional torture was not abolished in the Catholic Church until 1816.

—Carl Sagan,
1980s narrator and co-writer of *Cosmos: A Personal Journey*, the most widely watched series in the history of American public television

The debate about how many thousands (or even tens of thousands?) of people were executed by the Inquisition will perhaps never be resolved. Some would quibble and say, "None of these people were put to death by the church, but by their local governments." Others would say, "You can't blame all Christians for the bad things that the Church of Rome dreamt up." Or even, more dramatically, "Don't blame Christ for the bloody crimes of Antichrist" (see Revelation chapters 17 and 18).

On the other hand, before we go too far down that line of reasoning, we might want to remember what the penalty was for being a false prophet in Old Testament times. It was death. Why? Because it is so evil to lead someone away from God's truth: it harms an immortal soul made in God's image. If we say to the atheist, "The Inquisition, the 'thought police,' death sentences, and torture—that isn't how Jesus wants his church to treat people," an informed atheist could point to the Old Testament and say, "Well, really, your God **did** want people treated that way sometimes." Then what? (We could explain how the civil laws of the Old Testament are no longer in effect and so on, but that might just sound like we're making excuses, or even like we're embarrassed that God put death sentences in the Bible.)

Perhaps the best path forward on such a topic would be to bring the conversation around to Jesus, without entirely changing the subject. "Yes, when I think of religious law-courts putting people to death for their beliefs, I think of how that is what they did to Jesus. An ugly business! Have you ever read about the court-trials of Jesus?"

Putting the fear of god in children is the worst bullying.

> —attributed to Dwight Schrute,
> a fictional character on the TV show
> *The Office,* in an internet meme

Where I live in New York there's a lot of the orthodox Jewish community, and there were in L.A. when I was living there. And I watch these guys. You know, it's 96 degrees out. It's completely humid. It's nasty. It's brutally hot. It's sticky. It's muggy. And they're walking around in their, like, seven layers of medieval costumery. They've got the big furry hats and everything. And they just look miserable, as they should. And I look at them, and I think, "Wow, there but for the grace of God go I." (Looking up to heaven,) "Thank you. Thank you so much for not letting me believe in you like those people who *really* believe in you. And they look f***ing miserable and I'm in shorts and I'm eating a sausage, so everything's good." (Giving God a thumbs up,) "Thank you for that." Man, whenever I see an Orthodox family walking down the street and they're pushing a stroller and there's a kid crying in the stroller, I think, "(Gasp) It just found out what the rest of its life is gonna be like." Oh, it's so sad. (Pretending to talk to the child,) "No choices. No choices. None. Zero choices. You can't make any choices."

—David Cross,
atheist stand-up comedian,
from his show *Bigger and Blacker-er*

How does religion cause pain? It isn't just the crimes of organized religion from history books. These atheists say it is the "crimes" against tender children every day: filling them with guilt and fear over even small decisions (not to mention big lifestyle choices or feelings and desires they have no control over) that don't hurt anyone else.

Compare the sentiment here with the quotes from our previous section about how people do not need religion in order to be moral. Some atheists say that not only is religion not needed to help people be ethical, but, in fact, it is cruel and abusive to use religion (that is, the terror of hell and of a deity's anger) to get people to behave well. (Of course, the same people may say that any deity who gets angry or has a hell is himself cruel and abusive.)

Does that mean I'm all happy now? No. I look back over my life and see all the choices I would have made differently, all the energy and sacrifice that might have been dedicated to some other cause. At the very least I would have gotten something other than a master of divinity degree. Who's going to hire someone with a master of divinity? Got any Greek participles that need conjugating? So, yes, I'm one of those angry atheists, grieving the loss of not just a career but an entire circle of friends who want nothing to do with me now, grieving the loss of any kind of "normal" relationship with my family.

—Rob,
see above, "Listening to Rob"

When Mark outed himself as an atheist to their church community, he lost both his marriage and most of his friends. . . . "My wife is leaving me for her invisible friend," he said, meaning God.

—as told to Katherine Ozment,
Grace Without God

How does religion cause pain? The religious people persecute or abandon those who have lost their faith.
  I feel some embarrassment on this point.
  I can think of times, as a cocky young pastor, when I was not nearly as patient or loving as I should have been toward church members who were "straying away" from the faith they had been raised in. I caused pain, where my calling was to bring encouragement to the doubting.

In the United States, for example, public policies driven by people who pretend to know things they don't know [that is, people of faith] continue to hurt people: abstinence-only sex education, prohibitions against gay marriage, bans on death with dignity, corporal punishment in schools, failure to fund international family planning organizations, and promoting the teaching of Creationism and other pseudosciences are but a few of the many misguided conclusions wrought by irrationality.

—Peter Boghossian,
A Manual for Creating Atheists

Most British people think religion causes more harm than good according to a survey commissioned by the *Huffington Post*. Surprisingly, even among those who describe themselves as "very religious," 20 percent say that religion is harmful to society. For that we can probably thank the internet, which broadcasts everything from Isis beheadings, to stories about Catholic hospitals denying care to miscarrying women, to lists of wild and weird religious beliefs, to articles about psychological harms from Bible-believing Christianity. . . . Here are six ways religions make peaceful prosperity harder to achieve.

1. Religion promotes tribalism. *Infidel, heathen, heretic. . . .*

2. Religion anchors believers to the iron age. *Concubines, magical incantations, chosen people, stonings . . .*

3. Religion makes a virtue out of faith. . . . To stay strong, religion trains believers to practice self-deception, shut out contradictory evidence, and trust authorities rather than their own capacity to think. . . .

4. Religion diverts generous impulses and good intentions. *Feeling sad about Haiti? Give to our mega-church. . . .*

5. Religion teaches helplessness. . . . In the most conservative sects of Judaism, Christianity and Islam, women are seen as more virtuous if they let God manage their family planning. Droughts, poverty and cancer get attributed to the will of God rather than bad decisions or bad systems; believers wait for God to solve problems they could solve themselves.

6. Religions seek power. . . . And just like for-profit behemoths, they are willing to wield their power and wealth in the service of self-perpetuation, even it harms society at large. . . .

—Valerie Tarico,
salon.com article, "6 reasons religion
may do more harm than good"

How does religion cause pain in people's lives? We see that atheists can make long lists of the answers. The lists are kind of scary, aren't they? To some extent, it is like reading a list of "Reasons why we think the world would be a better place without you Christians."

How can we respond to these lists?

Perhaps we could help such list-makers notice or recall that the words of our dear Jesus also strengthen a whole lot of people's hearts.

Remember Ezra's words? "I don't think the church is horrible. It gives a lot of people comfort."

Remember Rebecca talking about her friend? "For two days she was devastated, and on the third day she said, 'I know God has a plan for me.' . . . she believed that a higher power is leading her however she needs to be led. So that's enviable to me. It sounds comforting."

Yes, some atheists will reply, "How does it help these people to find comfort in the words of an imaginary friend like Jesus?" But others would even be willing to have you share with them some of the sayings of Jesus you find most comforting of all.

*St. Peter has another rather straightforward and dramatic answer to these accusations: be good yourself, so good that you personally give Christians a good name again. "Live such good lives among the pagans that, though they accuse you of doing wrong, they may see your good deeds and glorify God on the day he visits us. For it is God's will that by doing good you should silence the ignorant talk of foolish people" (1 Peter 2:12,15). What good are **you** doing to silence those list-makers?*

Where in other religions there's a parallel of my parents' social justice beliefs and those of religious organizations, that's something I have paid attention to. Wherever I had positive feelings toward organized religion, it was at those intersections.

But there's also the Crusades. There's a lot of violence done in the name of religion. Homophobia, a lot of things, very male-run—all of those things I would put in the negative column.

There was a lot of evidence for me to support where my parents were coming from. So it wasn't just like, "There's no god, period." It was like, "Poor people, old people, struggling people, should all be supported. Here's where our movement works toward that. Here's where organized religion works toward that. Here's where organized religion works counter to our belief."

—Rebecca,
see above, "Listening to Rebecca"

"Also the Crusades"—yet another black mark on the church's record. Should we try to make excuses for it? Some do. It isn't hard to find justifications like these online: "The Christians were only trying to take back lands the Muslims had taken from them. The worst massacres were done by groups of soldiers acting on their own, as in any war."

Or should we speak up for Jesus and how he never would have condoned the Crusades or "violence done in the name of religion"? Jesus told Peter to put his sword away (Matthew 26:52). He told Pilate, "My kingdom is not of this world" (John 18:36), emphasizing that it could not be advanced by means of physical violence. Jesus' words about turning *"the other cheek" (Matthew 5:39) inspired Mahatma Gandhi, who said they delighted him "beyond measure" and gave him "comfort and boundless joy."[29] I'm sure such words of Jesus would resonate with someone like Rebecca.*

*But could it be that **actions** might resonate with her even more? Notice the word "works" when Rebecca says, "Here's where organized religion works toward [social justice]." This is what resonates with God's heart too:*

> *He has shown you, O mortal, what is good.*
> *And what does the Lord require of you?*
> *To **act** justly and to love mercy*
> *and to walk humbly with your God.*
> *(Micah 6:8, emphasis added)*

When we show with our actions that we care about people who are hurting, some atheists will pay attention. We will gain their positive feelings. We will "make the teaching about God our Savior attractive" (Titus 2:10). And besides all that, the people who are hurting (as well as God our Savior) will appreciate our caring actions a lot too.

"Faith is an excuse to stop looking for the real answers, for the truth."

I think, therefore I'm not religious.

—on a t-shirt,
from a photo on the Tumblr blog
"Atheism: We-Think-More"

"The single greatest cause of atheism in the world today is Christians, who acknowledge Jesus with their lips and walk out the door and deny him by their lifestyle. That is what an unbelieving world simply finds unbelievable."—Brennan Manning

---

[29] https://www.mkgandhi.org/articles/mahatma-gandhi-and-sermon-on-the-mount.html.

. . . Or, and this is a wacky idea, the complete and total lack of evidence to support the claim that a god exists . . . and specifically, their god.

—Redditor bipolar_sky_fairy,
top-voted comment in response to this
Christian quote on the r/atheism subreddit

Despite our conclusions in the previous section, we must be careful not to think, **If we Christians just live more like Jesus, everybody will be so bowled over by our goodness that they'll all come back to the church.** *That is an oversimplification. For many atheists, the roadblocks to faith are more about intellect and answers than kindness and social justice. There are plenty of atheists on bipolar_sky_fairy's side, who would disagree with Christian author Brennan Manning about "the single greatest cause of atheism." It isn't the hypocrisy of God's people, they would say. It's the lack of evidence for God.*

Do you know what they call a Pentecostal with a PhD? A miracle!

—Ryan T. Cragun,
How to Defeat Religion in 10 Easy Steps

To paraphrase, no well-educated person would still believe in faith-healing or tongues-speaking or prayer-miracles (or a literal reading of an ancient religious text): their education would show them that these things are made up, imaginary. And there are studies that show that more educated countries tend to have less religious people. We may question how conclusive such studies are, but atheists would say those study results are because strong faith is a plant that only grows in the soil of ignorance.

We know there is another explanation: we human beings are so sinful that the kind of education we apply ourselves to most fervently is the kind that teaches us the least about humility before our Creator.

It may be helpful to ask the question, Is higher education the only path to wisdom? One of the things that astonished the earliest enemies of Jesus' followers was their great eloquence despite being "unschooled, ordinary men" (Acts 4:13). It should have been no surprise, since their Teacher—accredited by his Father in heaven—was the one "greater than Solomon" (Matthew 12:42), with wisdom for both mind and soul.

"If you aren't ready to follow Jesus as some kind of Savior or God-Man," you could say to your atheist friend, *"maybe you could just follow him for his wisdom for now."* You want to give Jesus' wisdom a chance to make your friend *"wise for salvation"* (2 Timothy 3:15).

But for now, we practice the wisdom of listening some more.

When I was a believer, I had to perform mental gymnastics to explain the Bible, suffering, un-regenerate believers, prayer, and on and on. Now I don't have to explain any of it. A messed-up world is exactly what you would expect if there were no all-powerful, benevolent God intervening on behalf of his people. The world makes so much more sense now. It feels like I was holding a muscle in tension my entire life, and I can finally let it relax.

—Rob,
see above, "Listening to Rob"

Atheists like Rob say that faith is just another word for "mental gymnastics." Faith is constantly explaining away all the evidence that seems to say that God's Word and your prayers don't really have any power. Faith has to explain away the evidence that seems to say that God's promises only "come true" by coincidence and that only rarely.

Does faith ignore and explain away the evidence?

Certainly we can say that the claims of our faith are backed up by trustworthy evidence. For example, there is the eyewitness testimony of Jesus' first followers. There are also secular historians writing close to the time of Christ who mention him. The Roman historian Tacitus verifies in his Annals, *ca. A.D. 116, that Christ had indeed been crucified under Pontius Pilate. The Rome-sponsored historian of the Jews, Josephus, writing A.D. 92–93, testifies that Jesus, Jesus' brother James, and John the Baptist were historical figures well known in Palestine (and religious martyrs).[30]*

But the atheists might say our claims for evidence are hypocritical. They say our faith is selective as far as what evidence it accepts and what it dismisses.

---

[30] All of this evidence, biblical and secular, has its detractors, who question its authenticity. But it is still evidence.

When inventing a god, the most important thing is to claim it is invisible, inaudible, and imperceptible in every way. Otherwise, people will become skeptical when it appears to no one, is silent, and does nothing.

—Anonymous

Religion is like a blind man looking in a black room for a black cat that isn't there, and finding it.

—Source unknown
(falsely attributed to Oscar Wilde,
Charles Darwin, and others)

A blind man, because our five senses cannot tell us what's beyond this material world. A black room, because this world is full of grief and evil, just the opposite of what you would expect from a loving, good God. A black cat, because God is supposed to be invisible, unapproachable, and beyond understanding—all of which would seem to make him pretty hard to find.

You say you have found the cat.

Your atheist neighbor says, "Then let me pet it."

You say, "The cat won't let you pet it."

"Then hold it next to my ear so I can hear it purring."

"It doesn't purr anymore, and it won't let me pick it up. But I have a book here written by four men who love cats and who all said they heard this cat purring in this room, and they even petted him, and they know the cat will never leave here. It is a very convincing book."

This is how our faith appears to some atheists.

*Perhaps part of the reason why it is hard for us to understand their point-of-view is that we get used to taking for granted both our faith and the things God says. We forget how impossible it is that stubborn sinners like us would believe God's Word **at all** in the first place. On top of that, failing to consider how enormous God's historical claims and his present promises are, we rarely recognize how far they go beyond the expectations of human reason.*

God's Word is right no matter what our brains say or our senses. God's love and protection and answers are real even if imperceptible and silent, even when all the evidence tells us he hates and destroys and ignores. This clinging to God's Word, even at its least "reason-

able," is called faith. *Long before the Age of Reason, people needed to be reminded of this. Back in the 1500s, for example, this was one of Martin Luther's most insistent themes.*

> *Luther did not want men to believe that God answers prayer because they could point to a thousand instances in which it was manifest that prayer had been answered. He knew it was possible to find just as many instances in which it appeared that prayers had not been answered. He said that we must learn to put out of our sight whatever the flesh is able to comprehend, and, believing the Word, "hold just the opposite of what we know and feel and see." This is what he meant when he said that faith is "against philosophy and human reason." Faith, he said, would continue to believe that God is good even if he were to damn all men. (Siegbert W. Becker,* The Foolishness of God, *p. 98)*

> *If we insist on rejecting "what we know and feel and see"—and faith does have to do that, every time God's plan differs from ours—then we should expect to be ridiculed and/or pitied by our neighbors, who value their own independent thinking as one of their greatest freedoms and treasures. And we are.*

I have talked to many who have left religious belief behind, and it turns out that a willingness to think critically and independently has almost always played a pivotal role.

—Stephen Law,
author and philosopher

Philosophy is questions that may never be answered.
Religion is answers that may never be questioned.

—Anonymous

Blasphemy
is speech that has been outlawed to prevent your religion from losing arguments.

—Godless Mom,
meme shared by a Canadian blogger

Many atheists come from religious traditions and have found those teachings to be intolerable, irrational, insubstantial, divisive, abusive, meaningless, and worse. Most atheists know the fear and disparagement that the religions teach and project onto people who live lives of reason and free thought. We know exactly how difficult it is to move beyond the brainwashing of the church and how powerful the propaganda. We know how well-meaning and how good-hearted most believers are. We understand that the teachings of the churches have taught you to fear knowledge, disbelief, doubt, and all things different from you. We know how desperately the various religious institutions seek to keep you enslaved and fearful of losing an afterlife of various mythologies. *For we have been you.* We who have left the religions of our upbringing recall the teachings that discourage questions, doubts, exploration, and freethought ... for most of us had to work hard to escape it. It is for this reason and this reason alone that your beloved family and friends who are atheists tend to avoid confrontation or debate with you. We recognize the fear in your hearts and we know that you mean well. We also know that you cannot see the same truth that we can see.

—Karen Loethen,
blogger, "Homeschool Atheist Momma"

"It isn't just that you religious people don't think. It's that you are taught to be afraid to think, afraid you might think something heretical or even blasphemous. You are discouraged from asking questions because that too easily turns into questioning or doubting God's Word."

How much truth is there to these descriptions of religion?

I know that as both a pastor and a parent, I don't discourage questions. I long for my students and children to ask questions. I love to know that they are trying to think spiritual things through. But this isn't the kind of questioning the atheists have in mind.

They might say the only real questions are the ones that don't accept "because it says so" as an answer.

It is true that I teach that "because it says so" is practically the best answer of all. I pray that I can teach my children that we are to tremble at the Bible, not second-guess it. "These are the ones I look on with favor: those who are humble and contrite in spirit, and who tremble at my word" (Isaiah 66:2).

It is also true that the Bible sets before us mysteries (some would say contradictions), and we are to submit our human reason to those mysteries, not try to explain them: a three-in-one Trinity, a Savior who is both imperishable God and crucified man, a judge who calls us sinners before we are even born . . .

We are encouraged to have the faith of a child. We are told that the wisdom of this world is utter foolishness. We are told that our own thinking about God is blind and ignorant, that any "independent thinking" we can muster in matters of religion will be wrong and unsound.

This seemingly close-minded embrace of a two-thousand-year-old book is quite distasteful to those whose "gods" are human learning, human achievement, human innovation, and unbridled self-expression. Can we see just how distasteful it is to them?

What can we say to them?

There were parts I loved. But it was hard because religion is in public life almost everywhere. At the doctor's office and where I got my car fixed there would be Bibles and paintings of Jesus and crosses. . . . I'd have to say, part of me was like, "I want my eye doctor and my doctor to really believe in science first, heavily interested in science."

—Rebecca,
see above, "Listening to Rebecca"

But even if one were to argue that believing and being a Christian would have an overall positive impact on a person's life, it would be to miss an important point about the truth. The truth and being reasonable matter. All of your goals, projects, and aspirations directly depend on the truth. Humanity's welfare depends on the extent to which we attend to the truth, among other things. We have a moral and personal responsibility to be honest and accurate with ourselves and with others. In order to have intellectual and moral integrity, we must avoid self-deception. . . . Humans cannot achieve fulfillment in an environment that obscures, rejects, or belittles the truth. We cannot give due respect to human rationality and moral autonomy without striving to be as reasonable as possible in all things. . . . Immersing yourself in an environment that discourages curiosity and skepticism stifles the intellectual dissent that is essential to scientific and human advancement. . . . In fact, since access to new information is vital to our making informed political, social, and moral decisions, we may legitimately worry that religious environments, particularly those with a more evangelical or fundamentalist bent, are antithetical to the foundations of a democratic society.

—Matthew S. McCormick,
Atheism and the Case Against Christ

People who pride themselves on being able to ignore scientific evidence and "hard facts" in the name of religion are a danger to themselves, to their customers or patients, to society, to democracy, and to the advancement of humankind. Is this our reputation as conservative Christians? With a growing number of people, this may be the case.

One thing we could possibly say to such people is that although we distrust human reason when it comes to spiritual matters, we believe that human reason is a great tool that God certainly wants us to use when it comes to nonspiritual matters. Martin Luther once said,

> *In temporal things and human relations man is rational enough; there he needs no other light than reason. So God does not teach us in Scripture how to build houses, make clothing, marry, wage wars, sail on the seas, and the like; for there our natural light is sufficient. But in divine things, that is, in those which pertain to God and which must be so performed as to be acceptable to Him and obtain salvation for us, our nature is so stark- and stone-blind, so utterly blind, as to be unable to recognize them at all.[31]*

Maybe we need to be more vocal about this distinction, about our gratitude for God's gift of the human mind. Maybe we need to put a painting of a great scientist or two on the wall to go with our paintings of Christ and our crucifixes. Or maybe we just put it out there: "Just because I believe in the Bible doesn't mean I want to avoid having my ideas challenged or avoid being forced to think things through. What do you want to talk about? I'm all ears."

Or maybe none of that will help . . .

When at the end of any conversation the person that you're talking with has to depend on faith and has to depend on things that you can't prove or things that you have no evidence for, then it's some-

---

[31] *What Luther Says*, 3705.

how unsatisfying to me because you're just arguing or conversing or debating using two different standards of how you resolve things, really.

—Ezra,

see above, "Listening to Ezra"

My three-and-a-half-year-old son has lately been working through an "I'm always right" stage, with bits of "Let me correct everything you say" thrown in there too. I am generally not okay with being corrected by him, although he is very cute in his unintentional impudence. "I am 43. You are 3 1/2," I tell him. "I know more about football than you do. I know more about what colors are on the Chinese flag than you do. I know if it's snowing outside or not." Sometimes I will show him proof that I am right, in an encyclopedia, out the window, etc. Often enough, I will not. I expect him to trust me and be humble enough to take me at my word.

It really is God's prerogative to treat us like I treat my three-and-a-half-year-old. To say, "I expect you to humbly take me at my word."

*The atheists say, "That isn't good enough for us. **Why** should we take him at his word? How do we even know whose word it is? If there were a God, wouldn't he prefer me to use the brain he has given me?"*

In that old movie, Lost Horizon, *after Bob Conway tells his younger brother George everything he has learned about Shangri-La, George asks him, "How do you know the things they told you are true? Did they show you any proof?"*

Bob replies, "I don't need any proof."

George, getting angrier, asks him again, "How do you know the things they told you are true? Did they show you any proof?"

Is this the way all our conversations with atheists have to turn out?

No, it isn't.

Again, there is evidence. In archaeology. In the wondrous complexity of God's creation. In secular history. In eyewitness accounts. In a religion that spread across the Roman Empire with miraculous speed and still spreads today. In changed lives. In consciences given peace.

But we are optimistic about sharing faith not so much because of the evidence that backs it up but more so because we have a God who convinces the unconvincible. We must not give up the hope that the apostle Paul reminded his spiritual son Timothy of in this regard:

*The Lord's servant must not be quarrelsome but must be kind to everyone, able to teach, not resentful. Opponents must be gently instructed, **in the hope** that God will grant them repentance leading them to a knowledge of the truth, and that they will come to their senses and escape from the trap of the devil, who has taken them captive to do his will. (2 Timothy 2:24-26)*

Gentle and *kind* instruction means patient listening, giving others a chance to explain themselves, showing interest in them and in the ideas that matter to them, showing them that we do not consider them scary because they ask hard or even borderline-blasphemous questions. We give thoughtful answers to the "How do you know?" questions. We make an effort to be sensitive to perceptions that faith talk is a cop-out from using our brain. But we still talk about Jesus' goodness when these patient, thoughtful, caring conversations lead to teaching or sharing opportunities.

Ultimately, knowing Jesus' goodness is how we know his words are true. The atheists in this section say that isn't enough for them. But they don't know just how good Jesus is. "I know you aren't ready to acknowledge Jesus yet as good with science, but maybe we could just agree for now that he was very good to people." You could even offer: "How about this? I'll read some reasonable science with you. Then you read some good Jesus with me." The message of Jesus' generous, unfailing goodness is what God will use to bring his opponents "to their senses." His truth is stronger than the devil's entrapping lies. That is our hope.

"All 'believers' use the same reasoning that atheists use when it comes to denying the gods of other religions."

Ironically, the word "atheist" was first used by *pagans* to describe *Christians* because they denied the very existence of the gods and goddesses whom the pagans so revered. . . . Nor did the pagans seek from their many gods and goddesses anything different from what Christians, Jews and Muslims seek from the deity that they regard as the one and only god. Pagans prayed for health and happiness, safety and security, a good life here on earth and some kind of salvation in the afterlife. They embraced the values of justice and mercy, and, by and large, they sought to live decent and moral lives.

—Jonathan Kirsch,
God Against the Gods

Notice that we are atheists as far as all the other gods that have ever been worshiped. "But our God is different. He is real." The pagans who taught their children to say their bedtime prayers to those gods would ask, "How is he different?" There are many similarities, as Dr. Kirsch points out here. And if the pagans asked us Christians, "How do you know our gods and goddesses are not real?" what would we say? How would we explain away their beliefs? And are we hypocritical if we get upset at unbelievers for trying to explain our beliefs away using the very same reasoning against us that we use against the pagans?

The hell of dead gods is as crowded as the Presbyterian hell for babies. Damona is there, and Esus, and Drunemeton, and Silvana, and Dervones, and Adsalluta, and Deva, and Belisama, and Axona, and Vintios, and Taranuous, and Sulis, and Cocidius, and Adsmerius, and Dumiatis, and Caletos, and Moccus, and Ollovidius, and Albiorix, and Leucitius, and Vitucadrus, and Ogmios, and Uxellimus, and Borvo, and Grannos, and Mogons. All mighty gods in their day, worshiped by millions, full of demands and impositions, able to bind and loose—all gods of the first class, not dilettanti. Men labored for generations to build vast temples to them—temples with stones as large as hay-wagons. The business of interpreting their whims occupied thousands of priests, wizards, archdeacons, evangelists, haruspices,[32] bishops, archbishops. To doubt them was to die, usually at the stake. Armies took to the field to defend them against infidels: Villages were burned, women and children were butchered, cattle were driven off. Yet in the end they all withered and died, and today there is none so poor to do them reverence. Worse, the very tombs in which they lie are lost, and so even a respectful stranger is debarred from paying them the slightest and politest homage.... [After listing many more names, he continues.] You may think I spoof. That

---

[32] A religious official who used animal innards to tell the future or interpret omens.

I invent the names. I do not. Ask the rector[33] to lend you any good treatise on comparative religion: You will find them all listed. They were gods of the highest standing and dignity—gods of civilized peoples—worshiped and believed in by millions. All were theoretically omnipotent, omniscient, and immortal. And all are dead.

—H. L. Mencken,
Time magazine in 1943 called him the nation's "outstanding village atheist"

All those millions were wrong about their religions, for surely if their deities were real they would have used their power to keep somebody worshiping them to this day. All those millions—who made their religions a matter of life and death for themselves and others (too bad for the others!), who invested countless hours and monies and goods in pleasing their gods—were wrong. How do we Christians know that we aren't wrong about our religion too?

I think I have a good answer to that question. I will share it with you at the end of this section. But right here I think there is something worth noticing.

It is this: When the atheists point to how very many gods humankind has believed in over the centuries, they are admitting they are the odd ducks. The prevalence of belief, of theism and not atheism, is evidence of God's love for humankind. God did not let sin so corrupt the human heart that atheism would become natural. God has implanted in the human brain a tendency to ask questions like, "Who put all this here? Who made the sun come up today?"

Deb Kelemen, a professor of psychology at Boston University, looks at how children develop what she calls teleological thinking—the belief that things happen for a reason, or that objects or behaviors exist for a purpose. . . . Her work has shown that children differ from adults in that they have a "promiscuous teleological tendency," as she put it. . . .

Kelemen was born in England and describes herself as an atheist. One day she and her son were playing outside when he noticed some flowers and asked her where they'd come from. She and her hus-

---

[33] The pastor in charge of an entire parish.

band were raising their son to have a clear grasp of science, so she was intrigued to see that he was so attracted to finding a teleological answer to his questions. "He certainly hasn't been going to church or anything like that," she said. "And he gets these physical explanations from me and my husband for why things are as they are. So I was like, 'Oh, they come from the seeds. They got germinated when the rain falls.' And he said, 'But who made the seeds?'"

—Katherine Ozment,
Grace Without God

Isn't that wonderful? God put into that little boy a "promiscuous teleological tendency." We could even call it a theo-logical tendency. Despite the spiritual handicap of growing up with parents who disdain to teach him about God and won't take him to church, he still asks the right questions: "Who made the seeds?"

All the dead gods are not evidence that our God is dead too. Rather, they are evidence that he lives and he won't let humankind become a race entirely made up of atheists. In his love he has placed in the brain of every human child a promiscuous theological curiosity "so that they would seek him and perhaps reach out for him and find him, though he is not far from any one of us" (Acts 17:27).

PB: That's really interesting. But I have a question. How do you know the thing you felt was caused by Jesus?

YM basically went on to say he "just knew" it was Jesus and he felt it was true in his heart.

PB: That's interesting. But a lot of people feel some religious belief in their hearts, Buddhists, Muslims, Mormons, people who think the Emperor of Japan is divine. But they can't all be correct. Right?

The conversation went back and forth a few times, with YM reiterating that he just felt it to be true.

PB: So what do you think accounts for the fact that different people have religious experiences that they're convinced are true?

YM: I don't know.

PB: Yeah, I don't know either.

(Long pause.)

PB: So people who deeply and genuinely feel these experiences—these religious experiences—do you think they understand that they might not be caused by what they think they're caused by?

YM: Some probably do. Some don't.

PB: Yeah, that's probably right. But you've thought about the feelings you had not being caused by Jesus. Right?

(Long pause.)

YM: No.

PB: So is it possible that the feelings you had were not caused by Jesus?

(Long pause.)

I repeated the question.

YM: I don't know.

Jackpot! He went from certainty to uncertainty—from absolute confidence to doubt; . . . from thinking he experienced Jesus to being unsure.

—Peter Boghossian,
describing his conversation
with a young man (YM), abridged,
A Manual for Creating Atheists

I have had Bible class groups discuss this dialogue between Dr. Boghossian and the young man. I ask the groups, "Where did the young man go wrong?" A common answer has been, "He based his faith on his feelings instead of on God's Word." That is an important topic: Basing our faith on our feelings can be dangerous, because our feelings change so much. But Dr. Boghossian could have had a very similar conversation with the young man even if the young man talked more about the Bible than about his feelings. Imagine it:

> *YM: I know Jesus is for real because the Bible says so.*

> *PB: But a lot of people in other religions have their own holy books. Their books say things that contradict what the Bible says. But they can't all be correct. Right?*

PB: The people who believe in holy books that are all made up, just myth and fiction—do you think they understand that their holy books might not be as true and reliable as they've been taught to believe?

(Pause.)

YM: Some probably do. Some probably don't.

PB: But you've thought about the Bible not really being God's Word. Right?

(Long pause.)

Should we be able to give an answer to this line of questioning? Should we be able to explain how we know that all other religions' holy books are lies but ours is true? There are beautiful answers. I have referred a couple times to our good evidence. I have another answer coming soon, which I think is most beautiful of all.

Father in heaven, show us how to help all Christians make these answers their own!

The "God" and the "Jesus" that Christians worship today are actually amalgams formed out of ancient pagan gods. The idea of a "virgin birth", "burial in a rock tomb", "resurrection after 3 days" and "eating of body and drinking of blood" had nothing to do with Jesus. All of the rituals in Christianity are completely man-made. Christianity is a snowball that rolled over a dozen pagan religions. As the snowball grew, it freely attached pagan rituals and beliefs in order to be more palatable to converts. . . .

It is extremely hard for a Christian believer to process this data, but nonetheless it is true. . . .

Obviously the pagan believers, from whom Christianity derived its myths, worshiped gods that were imaginary—If gods such as Horus, Ra, Mithras, etc. were real, we would have proof of their existence and everyone would be following those gods. Our "God" and "Jesus" today are simply extensions of these imaginary forerunners. Therefore God is imaginary.

—Marshall Brain,
godisimaginary.com

We could (and should) dispute claims like those of Mr. Brain that Christianity's chief doctrines have been plagiarized from other ancient superstitions and sects.[34] For example, a study of the deadly struggle the Maccabees fought (167–160 B.C., not all that long before Christ) to keep Judaism pure from the religions of the surrounding nations should go a long way to convince us how repulsive the New Testament gospels would have been to the Jews of Christ's day if they had given off even a whiff of being an "amalgam" of a dozen pagan mythologies. And yet the New Testament was written by conservative Jews (including Paul, the strictest of Pharisees), and for at least the first two decades of the early church, the vast majority of Christians were Jews.

Here, then, is the dilemma for the believer. If she acknowledges that there are so many more erroneous religions with natural explanations that have at least some nominal similarity to her own, then on what grounds can she think that hers is different? On the basis of what differences can she assert both that "the majority of human religions spring from mistakes," and that "mine is not a mistake"?

—Matthew S. McCormick,
Atheism and the Case Against Christ

Not that I am an expert on world religions. My college roommate for two years was the Imam of the campus Muslim group. I have taken non-Christian college-level classes on the religions of China. I have an eight hundred–page book, Man's Religions *(written from a secular perspective), and I have spent several hours reading it and skimming it. I have double-checked Hinduism's* kripa *and Islam's* fadl. *And I can say I still haven't found any exception to this fact: Christianity is qualitatively and essentially different from all the other religions, because Christianity has real grace.*

---

[34] See, for example, "Is the New Testament Filled with Myths?" chapter 14 of Josh McDowell's *A Ready Defense* (Here's Life Publishers, 1990). Or more thorough and more recent is "Christianity's Beliefs about Jesus Were Copied from Pagan Religions," challenge #4 in Lee Strobel's *The Case for the Real Jesus* (Zondervan, 2007).

Another way to respond to such claims is to point out that, while authors like Joseph Campbell in his famous book *The Hero with a Thousand Faces* could show some striking similarities in the myths of cultures around the world, "Christians realize these different narratives are 'all drawing on the One True Story'" (video game developer Chris Skaggs, quoted in Kevin Schut's *Of Games and God*, Brazos Press, 2013).

Or to put it another way, Christianity has a Matthew.

Do you remember Matthew from the Bible? What was his job before he met Jesus? A tax collector. Back then, the tax collectors among the Jews were generally godless, loveless men, living off of the poor, outcast spiritually along with the town prostitutes. But Matthew went on to write one of the four gospels! One of the main eyewitnesses of Christianity, one of our main authorities and authors, was a tax collector, an outcast. Christianity proclaims salvation even for the godless, the cheats, the spiritual failures: the tax collectors.

The other religions don't have that, and you don't have to read an eight hundred–page comparative religions book to see that. The other religions (even the ones that have concepts sometimes translated as "grace") are about what you have to do for Allah or Krishna or your ancestors or to be as pure as Buddha or to keep the spirits happy— and if you do enough, think enough, eat the right things, give the right offerings, you'll probably be okay. Their "grace" is only for the good, the prayerful, and the observant.

Our religion condemns the Pharisees and befriends the prostitutes. It scorns the Bible-scribes and embraces the Samaritans, the demoniacs, and the deserters. Our religion is about what the Lord did to save even a Matthew, a tax collector whose greed had ruined families and lives, a man reviled and defiled.

Dr. McCormick's "religion" doesn't save Matthews either. It doesn't have grace either. The 1.1 billion people on earth who worship themselves—and some days we join their "religion" too—they very much need to hear just how unique Matthew's Savior is.

"If you grew up in a different culture, you would have different beliefs."

In countries where the government provides extensive social welfare—health benefits, unemployment benefits, disability benefits, and retirement benefits—people tend to be less religious. Where governments don't offer such benefits, people tend to be more religious. Religion, for many people, serves a compensatory function. When life is challenging, when resources are limited, when your future is bleak, when you are deep in the throes of fear, the promises religion makes are very attractive because they are comforting.

—Ryan T. Cragun,
How to Defeat Religion in 10 Easy Steps

Large groups of like-minded people who come together often undergo a euphoric experience through the release of·oxytocin in the brain, much like a drug. This is what you are feeling in church, not God.

—atheistic.darwinists
(an Instagram page for poking fun at religion)

In other words, religion is something human beings turn to for comfort, for security, for answers to life's scary questions, and for large-group oxytocin. Most any religion provides those benefits, to a greater or lesser extent. Whatever religion you grow up in is the one you are most likely to turn to, to find those benefits. It is not about what religion is true: it is about what religion you are used to getting good feelings from.

Does that mean no religion is true? Or that we have no objective way of telling which religion is true?

Or does it just mean that the devil knows his surest way to lead sinners away from God's beautiful religion of grace is to offer them attractive substitute religions?

(To keep these serious charges against your religion from rattling you, it may also be helpful to remember people like Elijah, Jeremiah, or John the Baptist, who clung to their religion even when it was the greatest danger to their comfort, it meant life suddenly had a lot scarier questions, and it brought them long-term, oxytocin-starving isolation.)

Q: As Christians, you (were probably raised to) believe that every other religion is wrong. But if you were born in the Middle East (and were raised) as a Muslim or in India (and were raised) as a Hindu, would you still have such faith in Christianity?

A: I'm not a Christian (though I was born and raised as one), but I have to answer. You have really hit the nail on the head. Coming to see the truth of what you're saying is one of the major reasons that I ultimately rejected Christianity. I can't believe that so many people don't see this. I guess the reason is some combination of: (1) religious brainwashing; (2) lack of a really broad education; (3) lack of exposure to people from diverse backgrounds, cultures, etc.; (4) an unwillingness to question things, to critically examine certain claims and so on. Don't people realize that they believe the way they do largely because of where they were born and raised, who their parents are, and so on, and not because what they believe is "The Truth" or better in some sense than what other religions believe?

I would put this question to followers of all religions. These days, I especially wish the Muslims (and especially fundamentalist Muslims) would consider this.

PS: I should add that there is a lot of wisdom in a lot of religious teachings and practices, but one doesn't have to accept the mythology associated with some religion to believe and follow them. The good ones, the ones worth following, stand on their own.

—pollux,
level 4 Yahoo! Answers user,
voted best answer to this question

I suppose the natural response would be, "I believe in Christianity because it's true, not just because that's how I was raised." And we have already talked about some ways in which Christianity is qualitatively different from all other religions.

We can also point to the fact that not all Christians were raised Christian:

I've long been fascinated how many Christians came to faith in Jesus Christ as adults, not because they were brainwashed into it by their parents. I often ask Christian audiences, "Who here became a Christian after the age of 15?" and frequently more than half the hands shoot up. . . . As the West becomes increasingly secular, fewer and fewer people are being raised in Christian homes. But that doesn't stop them finding faith—often in surprising ways. (Andy Bannister, Director of the Solas Centre for Public Christianity, Life Light Magazine, December 2016)

There is another point to keep in mind here, however. It is okay for us to base our beliefs on our parents' beliefs. All by itself, "I was raised that way" is not a valid reason to believe just anything and everything, or even to condemn others for not believing it. But it can be vaild. "Continue in what you have learned and have become convinced of, because you know those from whom you learned it, and how from infancy you have known the Holy Scriptures" (2 Timothy 3:14,15).

It is right to say, "One of the reasons I have not given up my religion is that I know my parents and my pastor are trustworthy, thoughtful people." It should also be something we have personally "become convinced of" and we should be ready to explain why we have found it convincing. But I don't need to be embarrassed of God's gracious gift to me of Christian parents who taught me that Jesus is worth praying to and trusting in. If anything, I need to appreciate that gift a hundred times more than I do.

People most often follow a religion not because of personal reve-lation or transcendent truths, but because the religion is culturally familiar, taught at an early age, and linked to where and by whom one is raised.

—David G. McAfee,
atheist author, quoted on the Tumblr blog
"Confronting Babble-On"

Behind this observation about the religions of different cultures is a sorrowful truth, a truth that the heart of God cries over: the truth that in the course of centuries past, many entire nations have rejected him, not only for themselves but also for their children. What a heavy bur-den of guilt it will forever be on the parents in those various lands who originally, generations ago, failed to tell their children God's Word! The doctrinal statements of my church talk about this:

> *Thus in the history of some nations and some persons God shows his own people what all of us would rightfully have deserved, earned, and merited because we misbehave over against God's Word and often sorely grieve the Holy Spirit. This will lead us to live in the fear of God and to recognize and glorify God's goodness to us. . . . God permits us to behold his righteous and well deserved judgment over certain lands, nations, and people so that, as we compare ourselves with them and find ourselves in the same con-demnation, we may learn the more diligently to recognize God's pure and unmerited grace.[35]*

---

[35] The Formula of Concord, Solid Declaration, Article XI, paragraph 59,60.

How would that be, for a humble response to this argument of the athe-
ists?—"Yes, it is a frightening fact I think about often, that for the many
times I have despised God's Word, I deserve to lose it forever and never
be able to teach it to my children, just like the people of so many other
nations have. I am no better than any of them."

But we do not think about this often. We do not "compare ourselves"
with the other nations and "diligently . . . recognize God's pure and
unmerited grace" to us. Sadly, we may need the atheists to remind
us that there are many other religions in the world and that most
people don't know Jesus. Could we simply, sincerely thank them for
the reminder? In some cases we could sincerely compliment them, "I
honestly admire the way you are so often thinking about the people of
other religions and cultures: I wish I were more like you that way."

Your religious beliefs typically depend on the community in which
you were raised or live. The spiritual experiences of people in ancient
Greece, medieval Japan or 21st-century Saudi Arabia do not lead to
belief in Christianity. It seems, therefore, that religious belief very
likely tracks not truth but social conditioning. This "cultural relativ-
ism" argument is an old one.

—Gary Gutting,
professor of philosophy,
University of Notre Dame

So many people, both now and in the course of history, have been
socially conditioned to believe something besides the promises and
message of Jesus. Many of them have claimed spiritual experiences
to back up their beliefs. We are told that this is evidence that human
spiritual experiences are based not on truth but only on culture. We are
told we should realize that we think about God the way we do because
that's what we have learned from our community, not because that is
how God really is or how he has miraculously revealed himself to us.

Except that the gospel transcends culture. Hop on the internet and
Google "where is Christianity growing the fastest" and be amazed at
the search results. Again, God is too loving to leave all the nations in
the ignorance their ancestors have bequeathed to them. There is, in
fact, no culture that will be able to completely resist the power of the
gospel. Heaven will be "a great multitude that no one [can] count, from

every nation, tribe, people and language, standing before the throne and before the Lamb" (Revelation 7:9).

Perhaps we could have our atheist friends do that same Google search and listen to their thoughts about the continuing rapid spread of the gospel. What are all those people finding so appealing about the news of Jesus? We could prompt our friends to wonder what is drawing all these people from all these other cultures to find the true freedom of repentance and grace.

We are not told why our resurrected Savior had his disciples meet him on a mountain (Matthew 28:16). I think it was to show their eyes just how transcendent and how high above culture his gospel really is. A mountain gives you a panoramic view. The Savior's plan to get his saving news into the world and his saving faith into human hearts throughout the world might seem like a horribly flawed plan. Why use selfish Christians, fumbling pastors, and untrained parents to "make disciples of all nations"? Why not give the world more dramatic proof, something more objective and undeniable than the secondhand words of such commonplace, fallible people? But the resurrected Savior's power is so great, it doesn't matter how weak his messengers are: the job will be done. "All authority in heaven and on earth has been given to me," he says (28:18). Jesus ruled over all that the disciples could see from that high mountain—and far more. And with that authority behind them, his messengers would indeed reach all the nations on the earth (28:19): as far as the disciples could see from that tall mountain—and much farther. Disciples are being made, by the hundreds of thousands, in even the unlikeliest lands, where it simply can't be just the result of "social conditioning."

There is a scene toward the end of that old movie Lost Horizon where a character is asked if he believes in Shangri-La—someone who hasn't actually been there, someone who hasn't even seen the high Himalayan mountains where it was supposed to be hidden. After a dramatic pause, the character replies, "I believe it . . . because I want to believe it."

It seems like the atheists have that impression of us: we **want** heaven and guardian angels and Jesus' love to all be true, so we try to convince ourselves it really is and we teach our children too. We want that because of the culture we were raised in. And we want it so much we ignore all the counterevidence.

With God's help, we can start disproving that last sentence by being kind and gracious listeners to the atheists themselves. Jesus wants *them as his disciples too. We can be for them living examples of how patiently Jesus listened to the stubborn questions of those he was training to be his own. He is used to turning doubters into devotees.*

quick to listen

BIBLE SKEPTICS
TALKING TO CHRISTIANS

by Luke Thompson

LISTENING TO DAVID

When we read about controversial subjects that interest us, we usually read material written by people with similar opinions as ourselves. Even if we study material from different perspectives, most of us fail to identify and overcome our hidden biases. However, we should not be discouraged by complex problems.

Science now understands that the human brain creates false memories, and history has shown that people invent and exaggerate stories in order to gain respect, attention, power, wealth, fame, and affection. These are important facts to acknowledge when examining supernatural stories that are told to influence and persuade.

Consider the following: Jesus was a charismatic preacher who convinced his disciples that he was the Messiah because of the depth of his messages. Jesus proclaimed himself to be the Messiah in Jerusalem, which ultimately led to his crucifixion. After Jesus' death, his disciples still believed that he was the Messiah and exaggerated and invented stories about him in order to convert people.

This is a more plausible account of the life of Jesus than the biblical account because it doesn't make any claims about the supernatural and relies only on scientific/natural presuppositions.

Although there are many supernatural stories in the Bible, I will focus on only one because I think that one example is all that is required to make my point. The resurrection story was likely developed between A.D. 30 (the approximate year of Jesus' death) and A.D. 70 (the approximate year that the gospel of Mark was written). Stories about Jesus were being told and retold to convert people for approximately 40 years between the time Jesus died and the time that the first account of Jesus' life was recorded. Forty years of oral tradition is a long time, and it is conceivable that stories about Jesus were being exaggerated or misinterpreted in order to convert people.

Many Christians think that *if* the majority of the disciples were martyred for their beliefs, *then* the disciples must have known that Jesus was resurrected. There are several problems with this reasoning. It is possible that Jesus' disciples believed that he was the Son of God *without* believing that he was resurrected. Miracles aren't required for people to give divine status to charismatic preachers; a study of contemporary cults proves this to be true. Also, the disciples' acts of martyrdom should not lead us to conclude that the resurrection story is true, because people don't need to witness miracles to be martyred. Thousands of people were martyred throughout history without reporting to have witnessed any miracles. For example, in England, in the 1500s, over one thousand Christians were martyred for their beliefs without having witnessed any miracles at all. It is wrong to assume that acts of martyrdom prove the truth of miracle stories because that assumes that people are infallible. Historians agree that in the first century, most people believed in magic and spirits and that there was probably not much distinction made between what writers actually believed and the religious propaganda that they wrote (Worrall, 2016). It's more likely that the gospels, as products of first-century oral tradition, are part fact and part fiction.

Some of the supernatural stories in the Bible claim to be firsthand, eyewitness testimonies. Even if the Bible included several firsthand, eyewitness testimonies about supernatural events, the problem is that eyewitness testimony is no longer considered to be as reliable a type of evidence as it once was. Cognitive psychologists now have an understanding of how the human brain creates false memories. James Coan, clinical psychologist and Director of the Virginia Affective Neuroscience Laboratory at the University of Virginia, showed that a person can be led to believe that an entire event had occurred in the past when, in fact, it had not. In 1992, Coan prepared four booklets containing recollections of events from his childhood and gave one booklet to each member of his family. All of the stories were true except for the story given to Coan's brother. The story given to Coan's brother was a description of him being lost in a shopping mall as a child and an older man finding him and then reuniting him with his family. Each family member was asked to read through the booklets and familiarize themselves with their contents. Then they were asked to recall the stories. Coan's brother "remembered" the events and even added additional details that he invented himself. This technique of implanting false memories has since been tested in various formal experiments, and it has been found that it is very easy to implant false memories of events that are entirely fictional (Coan, 1997). Scientists have also learned that eyewitness' confidence in their memories of events often do not diminish, even when they are provided with evidence that their memories of the events are false. False memory research has started to impact our legal processes, specifically in regards to witness and victim questioning. We know that people often "reconstruct" their memories to confirm their personal beliefs about the world (Shermer, 2011). When we consider what we know about false memories, the agenda of the early church leaders, and the unreliability of stories transmitted through oral tradition, we have a natural explanation of how the supernatural stories in the Bible could have developed.

The Bible's supernatural stories are probably not true because they lack reliable historical evidence and make claims about the universe that are unsupported by science. Furthermore, more plausible explanations for the supernatural stories have been presented by both historians and scientists. Supernatural stories should only be believed if there is strong evidence or if the storyteller has earned trust, or if the storyteller asks for trust tentatively with the promise of forthcoming evidence. The Bible gives us none of that. Rather than believing supernatural stories, it is more reasonable to admit that people in the past were probably just as fallible as we are today.

SOURCES

Bissell, Tom. *Apostle: Travels Among the Tombs of the Twelve*. Pantheon, 2016.

Coan, J. A. "Lost in a Shopping Mall: An Experience with Controversial Research." *Ethics & Behavior* 7(3) (1997): 271-284.

Ehrman, Bart D. *Jesus Before the Gospels: How the Earliest Christians Remembered, Changed, and Invented Their Stories of the Savior*. Harper Collins, 2016.

Shermer, Michael. *The Believing Brain*. St. Martin's Griffin, 2011.

Worrall, Simon. "These 12 Men Shaped Christianity—But Were They Real?" *National Geographic*, March 6, 2016, news.nationalgeographic.com/2016/03/160306-bible-apostle-jesus-christian-religion-ngbooktalk.

"False Memories: How false memories are created and can affect our ability to recall events". *Psychologist World*, www.psychologistworld.com/memory/false-memories-questioning-eyewitness-testimony.php.

LISTENING TO JOSH

It was in my second year of university that I began exploring my atheistic side. I suppose it had been there for several years, rearing its head briefly at weddings and funerals, but the day-to-day perversions and guilty pleasures of one's teenage years do not lend themselves to introspection or contemplating one's beliefs. As I transitioned from the couch-surfing apathy of my teen years to the budding mind of an early twenties undergrad, I became eager to dissect my atheism and the beliefs of others. I took advantage of any opportunity that presented itself to engage my peers on this topic. Being enrolled in the sciences, I found myself in the presence of atheists more often than I would outside the university walls (which was almost never). I was curious about what it was that had led others to atheism, so this was always among the first questions I would ask. I was surprised to learn that some of those who I surveyed had based their beliefs, or lack thereof, on reasoning that was just plain bad. For example, some expressed a discomfort with being told how to live their life as a factor in their atheism, while others offered that the cruelty of the god of the old testament influenced their movement toward nonbelief. Not liking what is in the bible says nothing to whether it is true or not.

An individual's reasons for becoming an atheist can be well-thought-out, based on logic and rational thought, or they can be illogical, off the mark and/or impulsive. Being an atheist means that you have rejected the claims of every religion that you are aware of. The rejection of Christianity is but one doctrine of many that I have determined to be unmerited with respect to truthfulness, but it is perhaps the most significant rejection as it is the doctrine I was brought up to believe. In the remainder of this short essay, I will attempt to present a logical explanation for why I have become a bible skeptic, and thus a nonbeliever of the Christian faith.

In my opinion, there are two primary academic arguments against the legitimacy of the bible: the historicity argument and the contradiction argument. I will not focus significant attention to either because they are not my thoughts and because I believe that a personal approach would prove more compelling in this context, compared to an academic one. However, I do think it important to dedicate some time to covering these bases, albeit at the highest level. Following this terse sampling of the historical literature, I will provide a more thorough and personal explanation of the experiences, knowledge, and decision-making that has informed my own beliefs.

Historicity Argument

To my knowledge, the most comprehensive and convincing assessment of bible historicity comes from Bart Ehrman (see *Jesus Interrupted*, for example). For purposes of brevity, I will focus on one particular line of argumentation of his that I find especially compelling. Ehrman purports that in assessing the historical accuracy of the bible, it fails on all essential measures generally agreed upon by historians in determining the probability of an event having occurred: primary sources, multiple sources, contemporary sources, and unbiased (corroborating but not collaborating) sources.

It is widely agreed that historical confirmation of the resurrection of Jesus and his ascension into heaven is necessary for the validity of the bible and thus for belief in Christianity. Simply put, if Jesus did not resurrect, the sins of humanity would not have been absolved, the case for his divinity would be weakened significantly, if not lost all together, and his relevance as a historical figure would be greatly diminished. Therefore, this biblical event is ripe for historical analysis.

The gospel of Mark reports that there were two women and one man who were present at Jesus's tomb following his ascension into heaven three days after his crucifixion. It is important here to note that while these three people ostensibly witnessed the empty tomb from where Jesus is said to have resurrected, none of them recorded it. It is likely that none of these people would have had the ability to write, so this is not all that surprising.

The four gospel writers who wrote of this event did not claim to have witnessed the resurrection or the empty tomb and did not write of the event for decades after its alleged occurrence. In fact, it is generally believed by biblical historians that the four gospels were written by unknown authors who had no direct association with Jesus. So in terms of having a primary source, the gospels fail quite badly. On the measure of multiple sources, the resurrection story seems to fare better at first glance. After all, it was reported by four different authors: Mark, Mathew, Luke, and John. But a more granular look presents a significant problem. It is widely agreed, again by biblical historians, that the writings of Mathew and Luke were influenced by those of Mark, which weakens the corroboration measure by way of collaboration. In addition, the gospel writers were themselves early Christians and so cannot be considered unbiased in their claims. Finally, the gospel accounts are estimated to have been written 20 to 60 years after the death of Jesus, approximately two thousand years ago, thus scoring poorly in providing a contemporary timeframe.

Contradiction Argument

Building on the same example as above, contradictions between the four gospels present a major problem in demonstrating a high probability that the resurrection actually occurred. Depending on which gospel you read, the resurrection was either witnessed by two women (Matthew), two women and a man (Mark), many women (Luke) or a single woman (John). Obviously, all reports cannot be true. So at best, one or multiple women provided a personal and accurate account of Jesus's resurrection to one of the gospel writers or to someone who told the gospel writers (or someone who told someone who told the writers, and so on), while similar but wrong accounts were provided by someone else to the other three gospel writers (or the other writers took liberties). This is problematic on its own, but is confused further by the fact that the reports also differ in the details of what was discovered at the tomb. Matthew depicts a violent earthquake followed by the arrival of an angel who rolled away the stone. Mark describes a man dressed in white waiting for the witnesses at the tomb, with the stone already rolled away. Luke explains that the witnesses found the tomb empty, the stone already rolled away, followed by the arrival of two men whose clothes "gleamed like lightning." John simply states that the witness found the stone removed and the tomb empty. Again, the writers of the gospels were not firsthand witnesses to the resurrection, which creates a major problem in and of itself. Even if the four gospel writers spoke directly to the woman (or women) who witnessed the empty tomb, we must ask what is the most likely explanation? That a miracle happened? Or that the woman (or women) lied, was mistaken, or never existed at all: that is, the presence of the woman (or women) and the story of the crucifixion were manufactured by the authors. The answer should be obvious. If your neighbor came to your door in a panic, explaining that he had just witnessed a man die, rise from the dead, and ascend into heaven, you simply would not believe him. No, you would assume that this person was lying, mistaken, or had experienced some sort of hallucination.

A Personal Experience

I was born an atheist and raised catholic. I remained catholic until somewhere between the ages of 15 and 20. Like most atheists, I presume, I did not convert overnight. It was an accumulation of information and thoughts, over time, that patiently led me astray. I'm not quite sure if it was my unbelief in god that caused me to question the legitimacy of the bible or my discomfort with the bible that led to my unbelief. The answer to this is not all that relevant as I have dedicated many hours contemplating the validity of the bible since losing my faith.

It was only recently that I became interested in the academic arguments against the legitimacy of the bible. As compelling as they are, the sculpted arguments produced by academics from a wide range of disciplines (history, philosophy, theology, biology, and physics) were not required for the formation of my own beliefs. However, they have helped validate my own conclusions and, from time to time, have provided leverage in discussions with pious relatives or unwelcome door-to-door zealots pitching their spiritual wares.

My first steps in the direction of unbelief came at a young age, during a time when I was at my most pious, perhaps eight or nine years old. I prayed to god regularly, and even spoke to him casually from time to time, not out loud but with the voice in my head. I asked him for things, like most people do, be it advice, comfort, actions, rewards—the usual wish list. Initially, it was okay that my voice was left unanswered; after all, *god is a busy guy, right?* and he works in mysterious ways, ways a mere child might not recognize. Well, it was only a matter of time before I started wondering if there was, in fact, anyone out there. According to the bible, god was listening, waiting to answer my prayers because I believed in him, but while I kept my end of the bargain, he did not keep his. Looking back on this time in my life, now I blush, both in recognizing my willingness to believe whatever I wanted to be true and in remembering my unrelenting desire to live in a world that wasn't real and, in retrospect, was not even all that appealing.

My next movements in the direction of atheism, and toward a stronger skepticism of the bible's proclamations, came while studying the sciences in high school. The beauty I had once seen as a child in the bible was quickly and thunderously replaced by the awe I felt when learning about the mechanics of the universe and the workings of the living cell. If you have not already taken the opportunity to situate yourself as a tiny speck, looking out at a broad, unending sky, or a giant looking down into the depths of a microscopic wonderland of perfectly synchronized parts, I urge you emphatically to do so. It will bring you great joy and contentment. But I have digressed. Learning of the vastness of the universe, in both time and space, and the relative smallness of one's own life requires the student to take on a new perspective of life. To refrain from doing so would be an invitation for cognitive dissonance to set up shop in one's head. Understanding Einstein's theories of special and general relativity is empowering, unlike anything I've experienced. To look at space and time and gravity and to understand how they actually behave is proof that the human mind can achieve wonderful things, understandings that were once unimaginable. To close one's eyes and envisage DNA being read inside the nucleus of a cell and protein being assembled a small distance away is to understand life itself; its mechanics, but also its meaning.

So what does this have to do with the bible and my skepticism of its validity? It's quite simple, really. For me, a book that is said to be the greatest and most enlightening of all time in terms of explaining life and the universe fails with unfathomable severity if it says nothing of the laws of physics, trivializes the formation of the universe and planets, is wrong about the arrangement of celestial bodies, or does not make reference to biological workings at the cellular level or the levels below. However, this is, in fact, what the old testament offers in terms of explaining the world in which we find ourselves: nothing. While the new testament attempts to explain little, if anything at all, about our physical environment, it does provide a moral code. However, this code, to treat others kindly and as you expect to be treated yourself, is one that was not uncommon at the time it was written and had, in fact, predated it by many years—see the works of Aristotle, for example.

It can be said that the teachings of the bible are not concerned with the workings of the physical world and that any propositions in this regard should be read as metaphor. On the former, I would ask why on earth would you (god) think that we would not be interested in questions of this sort? It is these very questions that had occupied the minds of leading thinkers for many centuries before you sent down your son. And on the latter, the fact that biblical answers to empirical questions are explained as metaphors only after being proven wrong by scientific investigations should be viewed with suspicion, if not incredulity.

Finally, in university my eyes were opened to the world of evolutionary theory. If my religious belief was not already dead at this time, it was surely now being given its last rites. The wonder and beauty of evolutionary theory is revealed through its far-reaching explanatory power juxtaposed against its surprising simplicity. In the words of the Eastern Orthodox Christian Theodosius Dobzhansky, "Nothing in biology makes sense except in the light of evolution." In my opinion, it is the single most significant finding in the history of mankind, as it answers the single most important question that has ever been asked: Where did we come from? The bible's rib and clay explanation is majestic, albeit incestuous, but it has not been supported by a single piece of evidence or even a rational guess at how this could be physically possible. It is clear that the cashing out of this explanation is not meant to be found in the physical world; rather it is meant to be drawn out of faith and imagination. While this might be an approach that brings great comfort at a low cost, it is my contention that it is not at all effective in discovering truth.

LISTENING TO RICHARD

Doubting Thomas Had It Easy

It will be easier for me to discuss my thoughts and feelings about the Bible after I describe my long road from believer to nonbeliever, so I ask for your indulgence.

I had the good fortune to be born right into the correct religion, or so I believed—just like millions of other kids in countless other religions. I was certain that my particular god and holy book were true and that all other gods and holy books were Satan's clever deceptions.

My first brush with doubt came when I was six. I came down with the flu, so my mother stayed with me Sunday morning while my dad went to church. I asked my mom why God would let me get so sick if he was all-powerful and all-loving. (I probably didn't use exactly those words.) My normally patient, kind, and loving mother got angry and told me it was wrong to ask such questions. And that was that. She had effectively nipped in the bud any armchair philosophizing I was going to do for about ten more years.

As I got older, I slowly realized that certainty comes easy but proper doubt takes hard, honest work.

At 17, after a decade of keeping my doubts chained to the floor in the basement of my mind, I realized something: If God is all-knowing, then he knows the future. If he knows the future, then he knows that I would have my doubts and eventually lose my faith, leading me to eternal damnation. Now, if he knew that I was going to end up in hell for eternity, then why would he let me be born in the first place? Not bad for a teenager who had never heard of Spinoza, Hume, Russell, Paine, or Dawkins. Still, it wasn't enough to make me *seriously* doubt my faith. Too much was at stake, and I wasn't about to fritter away eternal life (and perhaps even the love of my own family!) just on a silly little hunch. But, like a faintly flashing firefly in a dark field, the thought persisted, off and on.

It wasn't until university that my doubt began to properly crystallize. I was studying engineering, which allowed for only one elective in first year. I took a course called Problems in Philosophy. It was there that I read Bertrand Russell's "Why I Am Not A Christian" and realized that I wasn't alone. There was at least one other person on earth who had doubts, and he was able to state them clearly and reasonably. That was as close to a eureka moment as I ever got. It did not cause an instant deconversion, but it was the single biggest step in that direction. A few years later I read Richard Dawkins' *The Selfish Gene* and *The Blind Watchmaker* and learned that over a century earlier Charles Darwin pulled the rug out from under the argument from design for God's existence. I had no idea!

That's the shortest version of the story of how a Canadian lower-middle-class boy went from devout Christian to devout none-of-the-abover. My sense of morality remained intact—arguably it was now on a firmer foundation—but my willingness to sweep hard questions under a supernatural rug had gone. I wasn't afraid to ask hard questions, and I wasn't going to be bullied by threats of an unsavory afterlife.

The most interesting thing to come out of all this is my acceptance of the thought that *I could be wrong*. I am comfortable with this possibility. I don't deny it. *I could be wrong.* It is possible that I've not considered some important piece of evidence, or I've misunderstood something, or I've not heard a certain persuasive argument. Maybe Saint Anselm's ontological argument is flawless and I am just too blind to see it. It could be that the Gospel is inerrant and I've just been misled by some arrogant jerks.

All of this is possible, but after a couple of decades of thinking about it, I have concluded that it is very unlikely. Yes, I could be wrong about Jesus' existence and divinity, just like I could be wrong about the hundreds (if not thousands) of other gods who have been the objects of sincere devotion over the millennia. I've heard it said that atheists and Christians disbelieve in *almost exactly* the same number of gods. If you're not losing any sleep over your doubts about Osiris, then you know exactly how I feel!

My religious belief was never predicated on the careful weighing of all the bits and pieces of the Bible, so its dismantling did not require refutation of every verse in every chapter. My position today is that the Bible is a diverse collection of books written by diverse and anonymous authors across several centuries. Some of it is historical, some is not; some of it is wise and timeless, some of it is cruel and barbaric. Some of it can be inspiring, but some of it is embarrassing to all but the most faith-imbued mind.

In short, it is a kind of Rorschach inkblot test. It can appear to be whatever the beholder wants it to be. If you want to own slaves, the Bible can support you; if you want to emancipate slaves, the Bible can support you; if you want to persecute homosexuals, the Bible can support you; if you want to fight for gay equality, the Bible can support you. Are you looking for guidance regarding abortion? gun control? women's rights? democracy? how to deal with a witch? Whatever your position on whatever topic, the Bible can support you. That could be one of the secrets of its success, if numbers of copies is a measure of success.

As a former Christian, I know that Christians place a great emphasis on the good news of the New Testament. If you had to boil the whole thing down to one verse, then John 3:16 usually does the trick, or at least this was the case in what was my denomination of Christianity.

I can still recite that verse from heart: "For God so loved the world that He gave His only begotten Son, that whosoever believeth in Him shall not perish but have everlasting life."

How did I do? I'm probably off by a word or two, but that is exactly what I was able to remember (without any help from Google) after over 30 years of dormancy. I guess that means it was probably the King James Version (KJV) of the Bible that I used to study.

I've learned since then that the King James Version of the Bible was translated and updated from earlier texts by some of the greatest English writers of the day, possibly even Shakespeare himself was among them. So the beauty and poetry of the KJV is no mere coincidence. By that same token, we can infer that pre-KJV Bibles did not have quite the same oomph, which might make one wonder: How many layers and how many languages have the books of the Bible gone through to get to us in their current form? What forces shaped each iteration? At what point was God involved?

It seems to me to be too much of a coincidence that the God of the Bible so much resembled the people He was speaking to. These people knew nothing about atoms, viruses, quasars, electricity, etc., and so neither did their god. These people were concerned about livestock, adultery, property, wars, and filial responsibility, and therefore, so was their god. This is either an odd coincidence, or it is exactly what it looks like: the Bible is a book written by humans, with the same brilliances and shortcomings that humans have—much like the Book of Mormon, the Koran, and any other holy book that has ever been written.

I could be wrong.

The sisters sit in silence. They've just been talking about the past, about their childhood. About the darkest parts of their childhood. About how a father could treat his daughters the way he did, and how a mother could sit idly by and do nothing. Worst part of all, both agreed, was that their family was so well known in the community as exemplary Christians. And these "exemplary" Christian parents taught their kids Scripture, especially the parts about God creating Adam in charge and Eve as a silent helper, about Paul commanding women to be silent and submissive, about women that ought to do their duty.

After the two sisters had moved out of their parents' house, each took off in an opposite trajectory.

One hated her parents, hated God, and hated religion. Most of all, she hated the Bible. At the end of the day, the Bible was used to justify all these dark things from her past. And it was used not only to justify what she had suffered but the sufferings of millions of women throughout history. As she went through university, she found out so much more about the so-called Word of God. This Bible is old! The newest parts were written 2,000 years ago and then copied by hand for 1,500 years. That's 1,500 years for thousands of copyist errors, 1,500 years for misogynist men to slip in their own words, 1,500 years for pure myth to turn into something people today actually take seriously. She hates the Bible. In it she finds nothing but foolishness and despair.

Her sister couldn't have felt more different. During university, she began spending time with Christians who actually read the whole Bible, using clear passages to make sense of the unclear ones. And these Christians loved history and manuscripts, showing her that the Bible had an unparalleled number of manuscripts for scholars to study, and so an unparalleled integrity compared to every other ancient book. But most of all, they showed her a Jesus who began to bring light to her dark past, a Jesus who began to heal wounds to her self-identity that she never thought would be healed. She found a Jesus who loved her, died for her, and now cares for her. She found a Jesus who condemned men for treating her like an object or toy or lesser person. She found a Jesus who championed her and called for the men in her life to champion her. She loves the Bible. In it she finds nothing but joy and hope.

How can two people see the Bible so differently, feel so differently about it, and find such opposite things within it? But more important, what can they do about the silence? How can they begin talking about this book that has so polarized them from each other? And most important, who knows the real Jesus best, and how can she start to share him so that the healing might begin anew?

"I can't trust what's survived from old books."

We don't have the originals of the New Testament. What we have are thousands of copies of the New Testament that were made in most cases centuries later. We don't have the originals. We have copies made centuries later. These copies that were made centuries later contain numerous mistakes. Thousands of mistakes. Tens of thousands of mistakes. Hundreds of thousands of mistakes . . . At some point I came to the realization that my belief in the inerrancy of the autographs did not make sense. If God inspired the Bible without error, why hadn't he preserved the Bible without error?

—Bart Ehrman,
New Testament scholar

Are old books, like the Bible, trustworthy enough to build religions on? Bart Ehrman suggests no, and Ehrman is no slouch. He was at the top of his class while studying at Princeton under Bruce Metzger, one of the world's most influential New Testament scholars (and a Christian). He has written over 30 books, including college and seminary textbooks on the history of the New Testament. Almost single-handedly, he made reading about the historicity of the New Testament in vogue, writing five New York Times Best-sellers *on the life of Jesus, most recently* How Jesus Became God. *Again, he's no slouch. He's done his homework. He's put in his time. In fact, I once heard Bart Ehrman speaking at a professional conference of biblical scholars, and he said to the room of scholars, "You ought to be ashamed of yourselves," for not having a better handle on their Greek! And now this recognized leader in the field of textual criticism (the study of differences between the handwritten copies of ancient documents, especially the Bible) tells us these surviving manuscript copies of the Bible contain hundreds of thousands of mistakes (often referred to as "variants"). And he's right. God did not preserve the Bible without copying errors. And this has led to a general impression that the Bible is so old, there's no way today's translations reflect the original documents, since the Bible has evolved so much throughout history. Consider comedians Bill Hicks and David Cross:*

They believe the Bible is the exact word of God. Then they change the Bible! Pretty presumptuous, huh? "I think what God meant to say . . ."

—Bill Hicks

Back when the Bible was written, then edited, then rewritten, then rewritten, then re-edited, then translated from dead languages, then re-translated, then edited, then rewritten, then given to kings for them to take their favorite parts, then re-written, then translated again, then given to the pope for him to approve, then rewritten, then edited again, then re-re-re-re-re-re-rewritten again . . . all based on stories that were told orally 30 to 90 years after they happened . . . to people who didn't know how to write . . . SO, I guess what I'm saying is, the Bible is literally the world's oldest game of Telephone.

—David Cross

Here's another layer of the discussion: Besides all the differences between surviving manuscript copies, there is a gap of time between when the original documents were written and our earliest copies, and we don't know entirely what was happening to the document in that gap of time. For example, Paul wrote his Letter to the Galatians sometime around A.D. 48. That letter was then copied, the copies were circulated around the Mediterranean, and those copies were copied, and so forth. Over time, the original letter Paul wrote disintegrated and passed into oblivion, but some of the copies still exist. One of the earliest copies of that letter we have dates from 175 to 225 (Papyrus 46). This means between 120 and 180 years passed between when Paul wrote Galatians and our earliest copy of that letter. We don't have the original letter, and we don't have any copies that were made in that 120–180 year gap. This is all meant to stress the point: We don't have Paul's original letter to the Galatians, and we don't have any copies of that letter for at least 120 years. What we do have are copies after 120 years have passed, and they don't all agree 100 percent on what Paul wrote.

When we combine these two facts, that, on the one hand, there are hundreds of thousands of variants among our New Testament manuscripts and that, on the other hand, there is a gap of around 100–200 years between our earliest surviving manuscripts and the original letters, we might be tempted to speak like Bishop John Shelby Spong, an Episcopal theologian who, because of the perceived unreliability of the Scriptures coupled with a belief in evolution, gave up entirely on defining his faith in Trinitarian or orthodox Christological terms.

The question must also be raised as to whether we have the actual words of Jesus in any Gospel.

—Bishop John Shelby Spong

Given what top scholars like Ehrman are writing, we can begin to understand why Spong might reach his conclusions. The reality of a vast amount of variants and the gap between the documents we have and the originals is fact, and so it's taught in university classrooms around the world. In fact, all of the pastors in my own church body study these facts in seminary, and every week we use critical editions of the Greek New Testament when we prepare our sermons, and in those critical editions we can compare the differences between some of these manuscripts. What Ehrman said above is technically correct, and so he asks a very legitimate question: Nothing is more important to the Christian than a reliable Bible, because to be a Christian is to take what the Bible says about Jesus Christ and believe that it is, in fact, historically and objectively true. But if the historical integrity of the manuscripts can't be trusted (if we can't know for sure if what we're reading is what the original authors wrote), how can we be certain that what we teach is true?

*A Christian's immediate response to Ehrman or someone who has just read one of his books might be something along the lines of "You've just gotta have faith." In other words, we'll let the textual critics do whatever they want and have whatever conversations they want, but that's a sphere of life that I'm going to avoid and not address, and I'm going to live my Christian life as if Ehrman's research and conclusions don't exist. But we need to realize that if that's the only response we give to our skeptical friends, it may simply reinforce their skepticism. After all, if we believe that the Bible we have is, in fact, what was written by the original authors, shouldn't we be aware of at least **some** evidence that would back that up? Shouldn't a love that rejoices in the truth (1 Corinthians 13:6) have at least a little bit more to say about the truth?*

169

The truth is, there is plenty of evidence that the Bible remains reliable. Here are a few things worth researching so that you can have a respectful yet productive conversation.

First off, determining how reliable a manuscript might be is an issue not only for the New Testament but for every other ancient document that we have. Before the printing press, all ancient documents were hand-copied and so have scribal variants (differences in words or spelling between copies) that historians must consider when determining what the original manuscripts of any ancient document might have been. The more manuscript copies historians find, the better the historians can reconstruct the family trees of copied manuscripts, and so the more confidence historians have of their ability to reconstruct the precise wording of the original texts.

Most famous works of antiquity have very few surviving manuscripts. And very few of these surviving manuscripts are early copies. For example, at the end of the first century A.D., the Roman historian Tacitus wrote the Annals, one of our most important histories of ancient Rome. Of the Annals' 16 books, we have one manuscript from A.D. 850 of books 1–6, books 7–10 are entirely lost; and 30 manuscript copies of books 11–16 were all copied from one manuscript from A.D. 1050.

In contrast, one of the reasons we have so many variant readings of the New Testament is because we have so **many** ancient copies of God's Word. God has preserved over five thousand manuscript copies of the New Testament in ancient Greek alone (and many more if we include translations). This is a staggering amount. Many of these copies are fragmentary with only parts of the original document surviving, but many are complete copies of entire books or collections of books. Manuscript fragments survive that have been dated from as early as A.D. 117, possibly only 20 years after those specific books of the Bible were written. We have complete copies of the entire New Testament in one manuscript collection from the early 300s, only two hundred years after the New Testament was completed. This means the New Testament has considerably more and earlier copies of manuscripts than any other work of antiquity. In fact, no other ancient document comes close.

And there are certainly hundreds of thousands of variants between the more than five thousand Greek manuscripts we have. But if we subtract the variants that are repeated in two or more manuscripts (in other words, if we are counting only unique variants), then the number is reduced to around ten thousand variants. Most of these ten thousand variants are simply differences in spelling or word order. This leaves *only a very small number where the original is debated (compared to the 138,000 words in the New Testament). And not one variant changes a single Bible teaching. We can be certain that the original message of the authors of the New Testament is preserved. No other book from Western antiquity comes near the amount of manuscript evidence that has been preserved, and so we can be confident that we are reading the New Testament as it has been written.*

Most Bible scholars do not talk about the biblical text in the same foreboding tone of voice of Ehrman. For example, Craig Blomberg, a Bible scholar and one of the editors of the world's best-selling English translation of the Bible, the New International Version (NIV), writes,

The vast majority of textual variants are wholly uninteresting except to specialists. . . . Less than 3 percent of them are significant enough to be presented in one of the two standard critical editions of the Greek New Testament. Only about a tenth of 1 percent of them are interesting enough to make their way into footnotes in most English translations. It cannot be emphasized strongly enough that no orthodox doctrine or ethical practice of Christianity depends solely on any disputed wording. There are always undisputed passages one can consult that teach the same truths.

—Craig Blomberg,
Can We Still Believe the Bible?

And so, interestingly, the more you join in with Ehrman and take a look at the manuscript history of the New Testament, the more blown away you'll be with how exceptional and unique our Bible is compared to any other book. God promised that he would preserve the gospel for us and that the Bible would remain trustworthy and dependable. Jesus himself even says, "Heaven and earth will pass away, but my words will never pass away" (Mark 13:31). And this is ultimately why we believe the Bible is reliable: God tells us it is. We don't need professional Bible scholars to prove this for us. Yet knowing how God has preserved it can be extremely useful for Christians. Despite God using imperfect humans that can make mistakes when they copy the Bible, the clear message of Jesus stands unshaken for two thousand years now. Being able to demonstrate that Jesus' words have indeed not passed away gives Christians the ability to have conversations they might not oth-erwise have, to address criticisms raised within the historical commu-nity, and to reject and replace caricatures of how the Bible has come to us. God has done something truly amazing in how he has preserved his Word, and so it's worth taking the time to let the Word amaze us.

"I can't believe a book full of such absurd things."

Religion easily is the greatest bull***t story ever told. Think about it. Religion has actually convinced people that there's an invisible man, living in the sky, who watches everything you do, every minute of every day.

—George Carlin,
comedian

The late George Carlin's observations are not unique but represent a worldview in our culture that has been growing since the 1800s—that all belief in the supernatural is absurd. In our firmly grounded scientific age, we hesitate to call anything true that hasn't been rigorously tested and approved by the scientific community. Carlin and other non-Christians would point out that we are usually quick to question the existence of other supernatural claims in our culture today, such as the majority of the claims of miraculous healings, visions of or from saints, visits from angels, or people claiming to be modern-day prophets. For example, James Randi states in his introduction to his book The Faith Healers, *which reports his travels throughout North America exposing faith healers as frauds,*

As you read these pages, it may seem to you that you have been whisked back to the Dark Ages.

—James Randi,
magician

In his essay "The Fine Art of Baloney Detection," Carl Sagan questions mediums claiming to channel the spirits of the dead:

How is it, I ask myself, that channelers never give us verifiable information otherwise unavailable? Why does Alexander the Great never tell us about the exact location of his tomb, Fermat about his Last Theorem, John Wilkes Booth about the Lincoln assassination conspiracy, Hermann Goring about the Reichstag fire? Why don't Sophocles, Democritus, and Aristarchus dictate their lost books? Don't they wish future generations to have access to their masterpieces?

—Carl Sagan,
1980s narrator and cowriter of
Cosmos: A Personal Journey, the most
widely watched series in the history
of American public television

Put succinctly from one commenter on Quora.com,

[T]o say that "miracles" are happening in churches without being able to substantiate such a claim with verifiable evidence is not going to get you anywhere.

—Anonymous

What kind of claims are these folks, and so many of us as well, rejecting? From 1940 to 1960, the Indian guru Sathya Sai Baba claimed to materialize objects, including soot, that healed those on whom he applied it. In 1996 an image resembling the Virgin Mary appeared on the windows of a bank building in Clearwater, Florida. Kim Jong-il, the supreme leader of North Korea from 1994 to 2011, is said to have shot a 38-under-par golf game, including 11 holes in one, the first and only time he ever golfed. Many people would reject all three stories, we may find some people that believe one out of the three stories, and it would be incredibly difficult to find even one person that would accept all three. If we're so skeptical of these claims, shouldn't we be just as skeptical of the Bible's claims? Based on the way the average Westerner thinks today, we ought to be entirely sympathetic toward people who speak like Carlin. You would think the same thing if cut from the same contemporary cloth.

Add to this the fact that religious folk, including Christians, have adopted what we might call postmodern religious language. Postmodernism is a philosophy that teaches, among other things, that religious statements can never have the status of real truth. It effectively relegates religious language to personal opinion. This has affected how many of us Christians talk about our own beliefs, such as when we're talking with a person of another religion. They share their faith, and we in turn share our faith, and we're left with two faith systems suspended up in the clouds of the unprovable among other things of faith that can never be tested, empirically experienced, or treated as historical. Our faith essentially becomes another relative personal point of view compared to things that can be scientifically tested. And if this is how we talk about our faith, as detached entirely from history or verification, no wonder Carlin and others take issue. One frustrated person in a Reddit thread put it this way:

My gf's friend is trying to convince my agnostic/atheist friends to becoming Christian. If his argument had merit, I would not be here. His argument is:

"You just got to believe you cannot ask whys. Either you believe or you do not. For me, there are certain things that has happened to me that I cannot explain. Its a leap of faith."

I kept my mouth shut last night, as I know I tend to get angry when people preach ignorance.

—Redditor name deleted

If the most our friends are able to hear when we speak is, "You just got to believe," we shouldn't be surprised when we're called ignorant. In today's day and age, "You just got to believe," without any qualification or explanation rightly sounds absurd.

For many intelligent and concerned persons there is a legitimate question about whether God exists at all—a question arising from the lack of evidence for God. Surely God could, if God wished, settle this question for us by making God's existence sufficiently obvious to us.

—C. Robert Mesle,

philosopher

Add to this the final fact that the Bible clearly describes a God who hides himself. Whenever figures in Scripture ask to see God face-to-face, God concludes that it's not possible for humanity to experience God's glory and live. (For an example, see Exodus 33:20.) Convenient, Carlin might say! So much of what we Christians hold dear cannot be verified: there is no way to put God under a microscope or to find his body and blood in the Sacrament or to prove there's a providential hand working through history. So comments like Carlin's make sense given our culture (which includes us, Christians) that is becoming more and more suspicious of claims of supernatural events occurring, given the Christian's penchant for talking about her faith like a relative personal point of view, and given Scripture's clear claim that God hides himself.

As offensive as Carlin's statement might feel, this is a perfect opportunity to take Peter's words to heart when he tells us to respond to the probing of unbelievers with respect (1 Peter 3:15). There is no room here for bullying a skeptic like Carlin with labels of ignorance or idiocy. Rather, respect the fact that our culture has largely shaped his worldview and that this is an expected response to a religious person sharing a faith that involves supernatural events that we ourselves would be skeptical of if they were reported today, conducted by a God who hides himself. From Carlin's point of view, the Christian God makes perfect sense as fairy tale, along with all the Bible's stories of supernatural events. And it has made perfect sense this way to many others.

You believe in a book that has talking animals, wizards, witches, demons, sticks turning into snakes, food falling from the sky, people walking on water, and all sorts of magical, absurd and primitive stories, and you say that we are the ones that need help?

—Dan Barker,
copresident, Freedom From Religion Foundation

You can point to the alleged miracles of the Bible, or any other religious text, but they are nothing but old stories fabricated by man and then exaggerated over time.

—Dan Brown,
The Lost Symbol

Supernatural stories should only be believed if there is strong evidence or if the storyteller has earned trust or if the storyteller asks for trust tentatively with the promise of forthcoming evidence. The Bible gives us none of that. Rather than believing supernatural stories, it is more reasonable to admit that people in the past were probably just as fallible as we are today.

—David,
see above, "Listening to David"

If your neighbor came to your door in a panic, explaining that he had just witnessed a man die, rise from the dead, and ascend into heaven, you simply would not believe him. No, you would assume that this person was lying, mistaken, or had experienced some sort of hallucination.

—Josh,
see above, "Listening to Josh"

*So perhaps the best way to have a conversation with someone like Carlin (or Dan Barker, Dan Brown, David, or Josh) is not to revert to postmodern religious language of personal faith, but rather to talk like Paul did to the skeptics of his day (Acts 26). When Paul stood on trial before a Roman governor and local king, both unbelievers, Paul reminded them that what he held to be true was based on his actual experiences with a God who entered time and space hidden behind the visible flesh of Jesus. Instead of saying, "You've just got to believe," and nothing more, Paul said, "I saw." And Paul reminded them that all the events surrounding Jesus were not done in a corner. Instead of saying, "You've just got to have faith," and leave it at that, Paul said, "What I am saying is true and reasonable. . . . None of this has escaped [the king's] notice, because it was not done in a corner" (Acts 26:25,26). Paul's faith did not float in the clouds of the unprovable and relative but, rather, was rooted in observable history. It was not based on events that only occurred in some fanatical believers' minds, but on very public happenings, matters of public record. We might not be able to say with Paul, "I saw" and "none of this has escaped your notice." But we can say with confidence, "**They saw**" and "none of this escaped **their** notice." Listen to and take seriously the skeptic's critique of the man in the sky, and so talk instead about the Son of Man who very publicly walked the earth.*

Even if the Bible included several firsthand, eyewitness testimonies about supernatural events, the problem is that eyewitness testimony is no longer considered to be as reliable a type of evidence as it once was. Cognitive psychologists now have an understanding of how the human brain creates false memories.

—David,
see above, "Listening to David"

While many apologists seem to think that this alleged eyewitness testimony is the strongsuit of evangelical Christianity, to me it seems
more like an achilles heel. . . . Eyewitness accounts are always a subjective experience and involve not only perception but also emotions.

—Former_Fundy,
"Eyewitness Testimony and Apologetics,"
debunking-christianity.com

What if "they saw" isn't good enough?

*Some Bible skeptics would like us to know that they are not impressed
with our claims that the New Testament gospels are based on eyewitness testimony. That testimony not only would have first been written
down only several decades after the events were witnessed. But also,
how could we know that the eyewitnesses remembered things correctly?*

*One thing that helps us here, in general, is the way that archaeology
and non-Christian accounts written in the first few centuries confirm
many of the nonreligious claims made by the four gospels and the
book of Acts. Now it is important to remember and be clear: The reason
Christians believe that the gospels are correct is not because we can
prove from **archaeology** or **secular history** that they are correct. The
reason we believe is because the message itself convinces us. Jesus'
words simply persuade us. The resurrection eyewitnesses' claims persuade us. **Then** we look at archaeological digs and ancient Roman and
Jewish historians, and we're not surprised when we find the data lining
up with the New Testament's account of the politics, customs, geogra-
phy, and events in that time period.*

*Something else to note, in order to be clear: Of the four gospels,
none of them directly name their author (we have names on them on
the basis of widespread, ancient church tradition) and only one of
them (John's gospel) claims in the text itself to have been written by
an eyewitness. Now, in the case of the gospel of Luke, his not being
an eyewitness himself is counterbalanced by his claims to extensive
research, that is, verifying claims made from as many witnesses and
sources as possible, just as nonfiction authors would do today if they
were writing a book on events 30 years ago. In other words, he says
he's fact-checking:*

> *Many have undertaken to draw up an account of the things that
> have been fulfilled among us, just as they were handed down to us
> by those who from the first were eyewitnesses and servants of the*

word. With this in mind, since I myself have carefully investigated everything from the beginning, I too decided to write an orderly account for you, most excellent Theophilus, so that you may know the certainty of the things you have been taught (Luke 1:1-4).

If you picked up a book this weekend at the bookstore on the life of Martin Luther King Jr., as you started reading you wouldn't question every sentence written by the biographer, assuming most of it was fabricated myth and you needed to find what few kernels of fact there might be behind it all. Similarly, there's no reason to question every sentence written by Luke, especially if many other sources corroborate his biography, which the other gospels and letters do (not to mention the writings of the church fathers of the early second century).

One more general point: Although the specific biographical works gathered in the Bible were completed and disseminated 30 to 60 years after the events, there is no reason to believe that they are only based on independent verbal accounts from memory. The apostles could very well have used other written sources created much closer to the events to help them with their works or were relying on communally preserved oral traditions. Most historians believe this is the case, for example, with Paul's creedal statements. (See page 185.)

But more specifically regarding the reliability of eyewitness testimony:

Memories **have** *proven to be quite unreliable at times, since memories by their nature are influenced by the subjectivity, interpretation, and faculties of the viewer. We can be ready to admit that to the skeptics.*

On the other hand, we know that memories are much of the time quite dependable, civilization and human life depending tremendously on them. Psychologists have carried out considerable studies to determine in what different circumstances and settings memories tend to be more reliable. Recollective memories of specific events (such as those found in the gospels) will be more likely to be reliable based on several factors. For example, "Emotion acts like a highlighter pen that emphasizes certain aspects of experiences to make them more memorable" (psychologytoday.com, "Why Do We Remember Certain Things but Forget Others?" October 8, 2015). Richard Bauckham, in his book Jesus and the Eyewitnesses, *sketches out many of these factors that psychologists believe help make events more memorable and accurately remembered. Some of the factors include that the event is unique (that is, not a habitual event the viewer does often) and that the event is considered* **important** *by the viewer.*

For anyone familiar with the gospel accounts, it is clear that the data preserved, which could have come from eyewitness testimony, falls into these categories. The events were largely unique, stirred strong emotions, and were of great importance to the viewers. Besides miracles, trials, and executions, Jesus' message was revolutionary for its time, publicly calling the religious elite into question, claiming to be the Messiah but in a way that no one expected, and often teaching things seemingly contrary to hundreds of years of established Jewish lifestyle and morality. One could easily argue it's an understatement to call the events during the life of Jesus simply unique. They were epic for his disciples, the pinnacle of human history. And think of the emotions they felt: awe, friendship, betrayal, grief, fear, and unbelievable joy. Truly, nothing in the world was of greater importance to them than the work of their master Jesus.

And we know this because multiple historical accounts tell us that they were willing to die for what they claimed they had witnessed. Certainly people are willing to die for a religious cause that they have been convinced is true based on the testimony of others. Today's terrorist suicide bombers are willing to do horrendous actions at the cost of their own lives because they have been convinced by others that Islam's message is genuine. But the disciples of Jesus who were martyred were not taking other people at their word; they were not being persuaded by people who claimed to have known Jesus. **The disciples themselves** *claimed to be the eyewitnesses and were willing to die for what they believed they witnessed. This strongly suggests the disciples believed to be true what they told others about the events and message they preserved, that Jesus was, in fact, God's Son come to earth to help us.*

Frequent rehearsal from retelling the event to others is also paramount. Bauckham writes,

> *This aspect is crucial for any assessment of the likely reliability of the eyewitness testimony of the Gospels. In the first place, we can be sure that the eyewitnesses of events in the history of Jesus would have first told their stories very soon after the event. After a healing or exorcism, for example, the recipient of the miracle would be telling the story to friends and neighbors (as the Gospels themselves indicate)—after all, this is how Jesus became well-known throughout Palestine as a miracle worker—but Jesus' disciples who had been present would also be telling the story to other disciples. They certainly would have gone on doing so. The nature of such reporting indicates that an eyewitness's story would acquire*

a fairly fixed form quite soon. Some key words of Jesus might be remembered precisely, and the story line or structure would be stabilized. It would have been in such stereotyped forms that the stories of the eyewitnesses would also have become, through a natural process of sharing memories within groups of disciples, part of a store of shared memories among those closest to Jesus. As a general rule, frequent rehearsal would have the effect of preserving an eyewitness's story very much as he or she first remembered and reported it. (Richard Bauckham, Jesus and the Eyewitnesses. *Wm. B. Eerdmans Publishing Co.: Grand Rapids, MI, 2006. pp. 345,346)*

Bauckham concludes:

The memories of eyewitnesses of the history of Jesus score highly by the criteria for likely reliability that have been established by the psychological study of recollective memory. (p. 346)

It may be difficult to share your faith when someone asks you to produce evidence for the events in Jesus' life and then when you do, they respond that it's irrelevant, since eyewitness testimony is unreliable. But just remember that if we used that tack in regards to every other area of historical inquiry, we wouldn't be able to trust anything in history.

The fact remains that the New Testament has far more manuscripts to study than any other ancient document, ancient manuscripts of the same Scripture portions from various locations all around the Mediterranean world confirm one another's accuracy, and the original documents were either produced by eyewitnesses (such as John's and Matthew's gospels, or even Mark's gospel, which the unanimous testimony of the early church says was crafted under the eye of Peter) or based on careful research of oral traditions and eyewitness interviews (such as Luke's gospel).

And on top of this, all the documents within the New Testament work together to produce a rich tapestry of the life, death, and resurrection of Jesus and how his life radically changes ours.

What more could you ask for from a collection of ancient papyrus scraps and parchments?

"I might not even believe Jesus ever existed."

It is only in comparatively modern times that the possibility was considered that Jesus does not belong to history at all.

—J. M. Robertson,
theologian, 1911

It's insulting to anybody who is rational, reasonable, and intellectually honest with themselves. . . . As far as Jesus is concerned, they have no historical evidence whatsoever.

—Dusty Smith,
CultOfDusty YouTube channel

I stopped and I thought, "What would Jesus do?" So I didn't exist.

—Bo Burnham,
comedian

For days, even weeks, I waited for the perfect opportunity. This was graduate philosophy, Hegelian studies. The topic was German philosopher G. F. W. Hegel and his interpretation of history, particularly how Christianity fit into world history and movements. Class after class, the professor drilled into us that Christian belief was just one more step in an evolving spiral of thought toward some ultimate end. Finally, I raised my hand and said, "I think Hegel's being quite unfair to the real historical Christianity. I don't think Hegel knew Jesus very well." The professor quipped back, "Jesus didn't even exist, so I'm not sure we ought to be too concerned about his opinion." And that was that. For the rest of the semester, I didn't utter one more word about Jesus. How could I? Here was a well-published philosopher, considered brilliant by his colleagues, who wrote books about this and that and was invited to present papers at conferences on religion and philosophy. And I was just a student.

There is nothing more negative than the results of the critical study of the Life of Jesus. The Jesus of Nazareth who came forward publicly as the Messiah, who preached the ethic of the Kingdom of God, who founded the Kingdom of Heaven upon earth, and died to give His work its final consecration, never had any existence. He is a figure designed by rationalism, endowed with life by liberalism, and clothed by modern theology in an historical garb.

—Albert Schweitzer,
The Quest for the Historical Jesus

Many history scholars, including scholars that specialize in biblical history or the New Testament, teach that Jesus was not the Son of God. They believe there may have been a real person in history named Jesus, a first-century Jew from Palestine who made his reputation as a wise teacher. But after his execution, over time, myths were created around the events of his life and eventually the core beliefs of Christianity (Jesus' divinity, his resurrection, etc.). In attempting to rediscover the **historical** *Jesus behind the myth, these skeptical scholars have undertaken several "quests for the historical Jesus." The first quest for the historical Jesus was famously concluded by theologian and historian Albert Schweitzer, who ended the quest believing that close to nothing concerning the actual life of the historical Jesus could be known and that all attempts thus far to reveal the historical Jesus tell us more about the researchers than Jesus! Liberal theologians discover a liberal Jesus, fundamentalist theologians discover a fundamentalist Jesus, etc.*

We can now know almost nothing concerning the life and personality of Jesus.

—Rudolf Bultmann,
influential New Testament
professor and theologian

Rudolf Bultmann, quoted above, was a professor and theologian in the wake of this first quest. Beginning in the 1950s, there was a second quest that began with promise, establishing criteria for determining what the probability of the stories in the gospels being historical might be. But due to the continuing skepticism of the New Testament as a trustworthy document, the second quest ended with as much disillusionment as the first. The Bible remained a collection of stories historians didn't quite know what to do with. A good deal of 20th-century scholarship on the life of Jesus leaves the impression that we can't know much of anything about the historical Jesus.

It's time to ponder whether a Jesus really existed.

—Jerry Coyne,
biologist and atheism advocate

Raised by these theologians of the first (like Robertson above) and second quest for the historical Jesus, my agnostic professor, along with a small group of other atheists and agnostics from various fields (like biologist Jerry Coyne, historian and blogger Richard Carrier, New Testament scholar Robert Price, the late journalist Christopher Hitchens) believe not only that Jesus was not the Son of God but that there was also no historical figure that the myths were based on. In other words, there is a contingency of thinkers today who think there was no Jesus at all, let alone one claiming to be the Son of God.

Jesus is a mythical figure in the tradition of pagan mythology and almost nothing in all of ancient literature would lead one to believe otherwise. Anyone wanting to believe Jesus lived and walked as a real live human being must do so despite the evidence, not because of it.

—C. Dennis McKinsey,
atheism advocate, publisher of the
monthly magazine *Biblical Errancy*, 1982–1999

*Beyond this, our world is littered with historical or mythical figures that have too often been put on the same level as Jesus, figures that may or may not have been historical but that most Westerners believe there is a good deal of mythology surrounding: Siddhartha Gautama, Socrates, Muhammed, etc. Atheists and agnostics like McKinsey ask, **Why should we treat Jesus differently?** Above, McKinsey reduces the history of Jesus to simply another "pagan mythology." If we have little trouble rejecting other pagan myths, isn't it about time we did the same with the Jesus myth? As Coyne concludes in his article, "It's time to ponder whether a Jesus really existed."*

Remember that eleven historical Americans signed statements at the beginning of the Book of Mormon testifying that they either saw the Angel Moroni point out the golden plates that became the Book, or saw the plates themselves. Yet nearly all of us reject that signed, dated, eyewitness testimony as total fabrication. Why are we so unwilling to take a similar stand about Jesus?

—Jerry Coyne

If, during conversation, one of your friends tells you she does not believe Jesus exists, mythically or historically, consider what might be influencing this view. The 20th-century quests for the historical Jesus look like a mess of scholarship in which no conclusions about Jesus were reached. One walk through a bookstore's religion and philosophy section reveals several titles like Carrier's On the Historicity of Jesus: Why We Might Have Reason for Doubt. *And on top of this, we have many other examples of historical figures that have become mythologized over time.*

Paul tells us, "Be wise in the way you act toward outsiders; make the most of every opportunity. Let your conversation be always full of grace, seasoned with salt, so that you may know how to answer everyone" (Colossians 4:5,6).

As daunting as it may be to hear someone question whether or not there was even a Jesus, consider the opportunity God gave you. This topic gives us the setting and chance to talk about what we really want to talk about: the historicity of Jesus! What does it mean to be "full of grace"? It at least means that you're as charitable as possible to your friend, showing sympathy for someone who has been raised in a culture that treats Jesus like fairy tale. And what does it mean to be "seasoned with salt"? It at least means that you have a spirit of celebration over the opportunity God has given you. With a flavorful demeanor, join in the search with your friend to find the truth behind this Jesus figure.

And some of the topics that you'll want to explore can include the following:

First, the quests for the historical Jesus didn't stop in the 1970s. We're right now in the midst of what some are calling the third quest, and this one is very different. Many of the leading figures in it believe that the Jesus of history is far closer to the Jesus we Christians know, love, and count on every day. N. T. Wright, considered by many the scholar at the forefront of the third quest, openly writes that the historical Jesus claimed to be the Messiah, performed miracles, was crucified as described in the gospels, and rose from the dead three days later. He makes these claims not only as a Christian but as a scholar with an Oxford doctorate, concluding that this is where the first-century evidence leads.

Second, some of the reasons N. T. Wright and others feel their faith is supported by the historical evidence is because of the early dating of important creedal statements declaring that Jesus physically rose from the dead. The most important of these statements is Paul's catalog of witnesses in his first letter to a church in Corinth (in what is now present-day Greece): "What I received I passed on to you as of first importance: that Christ died for our sins according to the Scriptures, that he was buried, that he was raised on the third day according to the Scriptures, and that he appeared to Cephas, and then to the Twelve" (1 Corinthians 15:3-5).

This catalog is almost certainly a quote from a creedal statement that Christians had been speaking in their weekly church services well before Paul wrote this letter. That's what he said: He received it and passed it on. If Paul wrote 1 Corinthians around A.D. 56–57 (the widely accepted date), then this statement Paul received must have been created at an earlier time. Paul records eyewitnesses to the resurrection who are still alive, and after the creed (verses 6,7), Paul writes there are many other witnesses still alive. The idea that a myth was created and spread throughout large regions of Europe and the Middle East in less than 25 years' time (a blink of an eye in ancient times before mass media) and that the myth could be perpetuated while eyewitnesses were still alive, seems a stretch. And this is one of many examples of writings in the Bible that scholars now believe are extremely early—writings claiming Jesus was not only real but every bit the God he claimed to be. Many scholars, both Christian and non-Christian, would date Paul's letter to a congregation in Galatia (in what is now present-day Turkey) to A.D. 48, possibly less than 15 years after Jesus' crucifixion and resurrection.

Third, the fact of the matter is that Jerry Coyne and whatever others believe the historical Jesus did not even exist are a minority among scholars and an even more extreme minority among professional historians specializing in first-century Palestine (which Coyne and Hitchens are not). Any first-century historian mentioned above (such as Richard Carrier and Robert Price) would fall within this exceptionally small minority. The vast majority of historians today have a very different view on the historical Jesus. Gary Habermas, after conducting a study of over 2,200 professional sources in the last 25 years, compiled a list of what he labeled "minimal facts"—claims that well over 95 percent of all scholars granted as fact because, when they use principles for establishing how historical certain claims might be, these facts pass with flying colors. Some of these facts include: a man named Jesus of Nazareth died by crucifixion in Palestine under Pontius Pilate; the disciples believed that Jesus rose and appeared to them in a group setting; the persecutor of the church, Paul, had experiences in which he believed he saw the risen Jesus and subsequently changed into a believer; and the skeptic (unbelieving) brother of Jesus, James, was suddenly changed into a believer after experiences in which he believed he saw the risen Jesus. Note the study does not state that all scholars believe the disciples did, in fact, see Jesus, but that the disciples believed they did.[36] Historians may then leave it to you to do what you will with those facts.

Many of the traditional explanations skeptics provide to explain belief in the resurrection can't account for all of the minimal facts. For example, a person might say, "The disciples were experiencing hallucinations brought on by guilt, a response psychologists have substantiated can happen when dealing with loss." This might be able to explain why individual disciples may have claimed Jesus was risen, each having experienced his own private hallucination. But this doesn't explain all the disciples experiencing the risen Jesus in groups or why someone like Paul, who was not a follower of Jesus and had no grief at his death, would have experiences of the risen Jesus. Another might claim, "Jesus didn't actually die on the cross," which explains how he could appear to the disciples afterward. But that would contradict the widely accepted fact that Jesus did, in fact, die on the cross. Habermas' study demonstrates that 95 percent of scholars agree that all the historical pieces are in place for a Christian to say Jesus did, in fact, rise from the dead. History does not contradict but rather reinforces our belief in Jesus as the risen Son of God.

"I can't believe in a book with such a violent God."

[36] To dig into this further, I would recommend pp. 81-120 of *The Case for the Resurrection*, by Gary R. Habermas and Michael R. Licona (Grand Rapids, MI: Kregel Publications, 2004).

There are matters in the Bible, said to be done by the express commandment of God, that are shocking to humanity and to every idea we have of moral justice.

—Thomas Paine,
US founding father

No actual tyrant known to history has ever been guilty of one-hundredth of the crimes, massacres, and other atrocities attributed to the Deity in the Bible.

—Steve Allen,
talk show host and composer

My position today is that the Bible is a diverse collection of books written by diverse and anonymous authors across several centuries. Some of it is historical, some is not; some of it is wise and timeless, some of it is cruel and barbaric. Some of it can be inspiring, but some of it is embarrassing to all but the most faith-imbued mind.

—Richard,
see above, "Listening to Richard"

There comes a point when a pastor is teaching his membership classes that part of him (the sinful part that still doesn't trust God, that we drown daily in repentance) doesn't want to turn the page. I've just taught a new Christian how God is holy and how people (obviously) are not, how this alienates people from God, and then how God fixed this divide through the substitutionary life of Jesus. I've laid the basics, maybe even tackled Genesis and evolution, and now it's time to turn to the more complete story of the Bible. Which means beginning in the Old Testament. Which means the flood and God drowning all but eight people. Which means the God of Abraham, who promised to curse those who cursed Abraham. Which means the exodus of Israel from Egypt and God's deadly plague after plague against the Egyptian men, women, and children. And that's just the first 2 out of 39 books. It's hard for my unholy, imperfect, 21st-century brain to wrap itself around how the God that is love could do these things. They do resemble barbarism. The Holy Spirit has had decades to work on my spirit and strengthen my faith, yet it still remains hard to hear.

*And so when our friends make comments like Thomas Paine, Steve Allen, and Richard above, we need to be honest about what at least **some** of their criticism is based on: God's Word. There most certainly is a tremendous amount of violence in the Bible, and a good deal of this violence is commanded by God himself and is, as Paine states, shocking. But maybe the skeptics are simply bringing to the surface an aspect of our God we'd rather leave buried deep in the Bible. Do we ever find ourselves skirting around the violence of our God, hoping no one notices, hoping no one is shocked? When we find ourselves doing this, it might be worth thinking that maybe God wants us to be shocked. The important question, then, becomes, "Why does he want to shock us?" As one case out of many, consider God's command to the Israelites as they entered the Promised Land:*

> *In the cities of the nations the LORD your God is giving you as an inheritance, do not leave alive anything that breathes. Completely destroy them—the Hittites, Amorites, Canaanites, Perizzites, Hivites and Jebusites—as the LORD your God has commanded you. (Deuteronomy 20:16,17)*

Joshua, Israel's commander-in-chief, appointed by God himself, carried out God's directives as best he could. The famous conquest of Jericho, one of the cities in Canaan, ends this way:

> *When the trumpets sounded, the army shouted, and at the sound of the trumpet, when the man gave a loud shout, the wall collapsed; so everyone charged straight in, and they took the city. They devoted the city to the LORD and destroyed with the sword every living thing in it—men and women, young and old, cattle, sheep and donkeys. (Joshua 6:20,21)*

God's desire for the Canaanites to be annihilated did not end after Joshua conquered the Promised Land. Canaanite survivors remained, and God continued to call out for their deaths. Four hundred years after Israel entered Canaan, God was still commanding the destruction of non-Israelite tribes, in this case the partly Semitic tribe of the Amalekites:

> *"This is what the LORD Almighty says: 'I will punish the Amalekites for what they did to Israel when they waylaid them as they came up from Egypt. Now go, attack the Amalekites and totally destroy everything that belongs to them. Do not spare them; put to death men and women, children and infants, cattle and sheep, camels and donkeys.'" (1 Samuel 15:2,3)*

*And even if hypothetically God did not expressly command any acts of violence in the Bible (which isn't the case, as the passages above clearly demonstrate), there's still the matter of God's providence (the belief that God guides all human history according to his will and to his own chosen end), that God in his infinite wisdom carries out his plans for history through violence. In other words, instead of **stopping** the violence, God **allows** the violence and weaves it into his master plan. Which, upon slow, sober reflection, creates a problem: If God **could** stop violence, why wouldn't he? Why would a perfect, good, and loving God not stop suffering from happening at the scale it does but instead decide to work through it? (See the previous chapter for a fuller account of the problem of evil.)*

Add to all this the tremendously hurtful things Christians say at times:

[Pat Roberston] said that the earthquake was because of a pact with the devil that the Haitians made a long time ago to get the French out of their country. A deal that has led to all the recent disasters Haiti is cursed with. Pat, you're wrong. This was mother nature, man. This was not the devil, this was mother nature doing what she does. And you need to stop doing this the day stuff happens.

—Whoopi Goldberg,
TV host, *The View*

*Yes, God reveals in Scripture accounts in which he orders people to carry out judgment against another group of people for specific sins. (Consider Jude 7.) But this does not lead to the conclusion that **all** suffering a person experiences is because of a specific sin (John 9:2,3) or that when disaster strikes one place and not another it's because that one place deserved it more than another. Few things are more incompatible with a Christian heart than saying to someone about a specific hardship they're going through, "God is punishing you because you . . ." This is not only playing God (as if you have the omniscience to make such a binding statement), but it is speaking for God, claiming you can add to his revelation, which God doesn't take too lightly. (See Revelation 22:18.)*

This can be a hard topic to discuss with our friends. And the starting point has to be honesty and sympathy:

"I've struggled with those parts of the Bible too."

"There are parts of the Bible that part of me wishes weren't there too."

"I know how terrible that sounds. But together let's see how a God who calls himself love can do things like this."

At the heart of the discussion is understanding God's relationship to justice compared to our own understanding of it. C. S. Lewis, when he was struggling to communicate ideas on this subject, once wrote, "[If] God is wiser than we His judgment must differ from ours on many things, and not least on good and evil. What seems to us good may therefore not be good in His eyes, and what seems evil may not be evil."

In other words, God by definition is perfect, and we're usually honest enough to confess we're not. And if humans are imperfect, then it follows that our understanding of morality might be imperfect as well. Maybe we don't understand justice as well as we'd like to think we do.

We would not be here if humanity were inherently evil. We'd have eaten ourselves alive long ago. So when you spot violence or bigotry or intolerance or fear or just garden-variety misogyny, hatred, or ignorance, just look it in the eye and think, "The good outnumber you, and we always will."

—Patton Oswalt,
comedian

Another important part of the discussion might be the relevant context for the accounts we read in the Bible of God's use of violence. Along with Patton Oswalt, our culture embraces the notion that humans are inherently good and so violence is never the solution. If this is the case, God's violence is always inexcusable. Yet the Bible operates within a different anthropology. Humans aren't inherently good, and a just God will certainly do something about it. Going back to the Israelites destroying the Canaanites, God gives specific reasons why he's telling the Israelites to destroy them completely. The Canaanite community had been allowing and encouraging extremely wicked and corrupting activities like child sacrifice, incest, occult practices, idolatry, and bestiality (Deuteronomy 18:9-13; Leviticus 18:24-28,20:22-23). By the time of Moses and Joshua, God had patiently given the Canaanites four hundred years to change (Genesis 15:16), but now that the Israelites, the nation God had chosen to protect God's message to the world of a Savior, were moving in, God wanted the Israelites to do everything in their power to guarantee a culture that could protect that promise. So God had given the Canaanites a generous opportunity to change and end the violence on their own, but now that opportunity had to come to an end so that God could bring about a greater good, the preservation of his rescue plan through a Savior. Is this a compelling reason for the things God ordered done to the Canaanites? Maybe not immediately compelling to our nonbelieving friends, but these are the considerations that help us better understand God's nature and what he values more than anything else: protecting the promise of a Savior.

It's almost as if the bible was written by racist, sexist, homophobic, violent, sexually frustrated men, instead of a loving God. Weird.

—Ricky Gervais,
comedian, actor

And there's considerably more to talk about as well. We could talk about how God is not interested in the killing of specific nations for racial reasons, but that he's always addressing moral and spiritual problems. We could talk about how God doesn't play favorites in regards to judgment but is as impartial a judge as they come, eventually using other nations against Israel as well. We could talk about what follows from God being the author of all life and therefore not having any obligation regarding life to anyone but himself (Deuteronomy 32:39). We could ask our skeptical friend, "Do you think acts of war or violence are ever justified?" And if the answer is yes, then a conversation can begin where you explore with your friend if God's acts fit within those conditions.[37]

But what so many have problems with, as Ricky Gervais makes clear, is the perceived incompatibility between what God does and his claim that he's the embodiment of love. What do you think will happen, though, when we begin to share not only aspects of God the judge but the heart of God the Savior? Consider talking not only about God's perfect justice over all humanity but also God's unending love for all humanity. In other words, consider exploring not only the violence commanded by God but the violence suffered by God for the eternal salvation of many. Remember, what sets our God apart from all others is not only his embodiment of perfect justice, so perfect it sometimes

---

[37] For more thorough answers to attacks on the Old Testament, see pp. 662-667 of Douglas Groothuis' *Christian Apologetics: A Comprehensive Case for Biblical Faith* (Downer's Grove, IL: InterVarsity Press, 2011).

hurts for us to talk about it, but also his embodiment of perfect love and mercy, so perfect it killed him on the cross.

"I can't believe in a book that teaches that God would send people to hell."

There is one very serious defect to my mind in Christ's moral character, and that is that He believed in hell. I do not myself feel that any person who is really profoundly humane can believe in everlasting punishment. . . . I must say that I think all this doctrine, that hell-fire is a punishment for sin, is a doctrine of cruelty. It is a doctrine that put cruelty into the world and gave the world generations of cruel torture; and the Christ of the Gospels, if you could take Him as His chroniclers represent Him, would certainly have to be considered partly responsible for that.

—Bertrand Russell,
Why I Am Not a Christian

The famous mathematician and philosopher Bertrand Russell points out two problems. The first is that the teaching of hell seems to be an extremely cruel idea, one that doesn't jive with the existence of an all-loving God. We might call this the "logical" problem of hell (because it's claiming there's an inconsistency with the teaching of hell and the Bible's notion of God). The second is the practical impact that the teaching of hell has had on humans throughout history. Russell references Matthew 5:30, where Christ says one ought to cut off the hand or gouge out the eye that causes one to sin. What seems to be boiling in the background are the centuries of Catholic men and women scourging themselves and cowering in the darkness, terrified of the flames of hell and purgatory and knowing of no way around them. We might call this second criticism the "existential" struggle with hell (because it deals with one's experience of living with the teaching of hell). Each of Russell's criticisms requires reflection.

Regarding the first, the "logical" problem of hell, consider the talk between Ivan and Alyosha in Dostoevsky's Brothers Karamozov. *Ivan, an atheist struggling with the implications of atheism, lays out before* his brother Alyosha, a novice in a Russian Orthodox monastery, one of the most compelling arguments against the Christian faith:

"Tell me yourself, I challenge you—answer. Imagine that you are creating a fabric of human destiny with the object of making men happy in the end, giving them peace and rest at last, but that it was essential and inevitable to torture to death only one tiny creature— that baby beating its breast with its fist, for instance—and to found that edifice on its unavenged tears, would you consent to be the architect on those conditions? Tell me, and tell the truth."

"No, I wouldn't consent," said Alyosha softly.

"And can you admit the idea that men for whom you are building it would agree to accept their happiness on the foundation of the unexpiated blood of a little victim? And accepting it would remain happy for ever?"

"No, I can't admit it." (The Gospel in Dostoevsky, pages 29,30)

This is another formulation of what's called the Problem of Evil (explored at length elsewhere in this book), and Ivan's formulation might be put like this: If you were God and you could not make this universe with all these people within it unless you also had to create the circumstances for one single child to suffer immense torture, would you still make this universe? And Alyosha's answer, along with most people today, would be this: no amount of good can justify the perpetuating of evil. The Christian Alyosha, along with many of Dostoevsky's Christian readers, is at a loss with how a Christian ought to respond. (The rest of Dostoevsky's novel is his attempt at responding to this problem.)

I just want to be free of the fears and anxieties and the superstitions of religion. An avenging God? One who created hell for those who don't believe? . . . I'm sorry, but no. Wrong. You're wrong. That's an insane God and therefore not mine.

—Bill Hicks,
comedian

Ivan's argument carries over even more powerfully into discussions of hell, and might be put this way: If you were God, would you create a universe in which even one baby went to hell? Could any amount of good that creating this universe might produce make up for one child suffering eternally? This is one reason why Bertrand Russell is not a Christian. This is also why so many people, like Bill Hicks, react so *emotionally to the Christian faith. How could Christ be considered a loving person if part of the way he runs the universe includes people suffering in hell? What morality would justify **eternal** suffering?*

When dealing with the Problem of Evil, sometimes Christian philosophers will try to argue that eternal life far outweighs the temporal sufferings of this world. But the Christian teaching of hell throws a wrench into that logic because suffering isn't a temporal, this-world-only thing. Instead, there are millions, if not billions, who will suffer into eternity. With hell considered, we can't argue anymore that the good outweighs the evil. Or can we?

Whatever comfort I received from believing that God loved the whole world was morally challenged by the question, if he loves them, why doesn't he save them? And for that matter, why allow them to be "lost" in the first place? During one of my more insecure childhood experiences, I was overcome with jealousy when my dog answered my friend's beckoning and not mine. Could the creator of the universe be as needy as an eight-year-old boy?

—Jerry DeWitt,
atheist and ex-pastor

And so it's only a matter of time before the character of God gets called into question. Like Jerry DeWitt, to many God seems almost petty in his jealousy when he sends people to hell for not believing in him. But how can he possibly justify these feelings and send people to hell, especially if they've been brought into this world already "lost" (not knowing who God is), maybe even without ever getting an opportunity in their lives to learn about him? As comedian Bill Burr says to God in one of his routines, "You set me up to fail!"

Heaven and hell seem out of proportion to me: the actions of men do not deserve so much.

—Jorge Luis Borges,
one of the greatest Argentine writers

We can also narrow the scope from looking at the universe throughout all of time to looking at just one life. With the Bible's teaching of hell, a person seems to be receiving from God an infinite punishment (infinite in hell) for a finite number of crimes committed within his life-time. This annihilates any idea of restitution (that is, the idea that the punishment must fit the crime) or similar judicial ideas, let alone ideas of punitive systems needing to be, at least in some respect, rehabili-tative. And so our sinful nature within us screams, "How can this even be called justice?" As Jorge Luis Borges comments, something seems out of proportion.

Then comes the "existential" struggle with hell. When hell comes up in discussions with our friends, especially non-Christian friends, there's a good chance that many of their friends and family are also not Christians. This means we're trying to get our friends on board with a teaching that includes many of their friends and family spending eter-nity in hell. Consider the following from a Yahoo answers post:

She's a very religious Catholic girl and I'm pretty much agnostic. I love learning about different religions but I don't claim any specific one as my own. She says if I don't accept Jesus Christ as my Savior I won't go to heaven. It just amazes me how she can go on through life believing that with everyone she meets. . . . You might be wonder-ing why I even care when I don't completely believe in hell. It's just that, to her, hell is the worst place imaginable and she believes I'm going there to suffer. She doesn't want me to, of course, but she truly believes that. It's depressing.

*A biblical worldview offers more than we would think in response to criticisms of hell, except that however logical or consistent our response might be, the end result is still that many people, including our friend's nearest and dearest, will still be in hell. For instance, in response to the idea that an infinite punishment is far too much for a finite number of sins, you could say that any sin is an act of rebellion against an infinitely worthy God. You could point out that sin has caused infinite harm in this world and any individual sinful act shares in all that harm. You could remember that the issue isn't only what we do, but who we are. "Surely I was sinful from birth" is a statement about **being**, not actions, and what we **are** is sinful instead of perfect. The actual sinful actions are simply what naturally flows from a sinful heart, like smoke from a fire. And one single action changes your status before a righteous judge: one murder makes you a murderer. Likewise, one murderous thought means you've got the heart and mind of a murderer. And so if God is the perfect source of goodness (which is part of the definition of who God is) and humans* have become sources of evil, then God simply can't be with humans forever. If he did, he wouldn't be perfect—unless he changes what we look like to him. And that's exactly what the Bible teaches that Jesus does for us: he clothes us in his perfect life so that when God looks at us, he sees perfection. But if you refuse those clothes, then at some point for God to remain perfect, there has to be a final "have it your way." As C. S. Lewis once wrote, "The doors of hell are locked on the inside" (Problem of Pain, page 115). So maybe hell ought to elicit at least some of the emotions it does. Maybe it ought to be depressing, especially when rightly understood.

We can add other aspects to this as well. The Christian thinker Peter Kreeft said, "If your life is Christ, then your death will be only more of Christ, forever. If your life is only Christlessness, then your death will be only more Christlessness, forever. That's not fundamentalism, that's the law of non-contradiction."

So we can talk about that. We can also talk about the dire need to share the gospel. We can talk about a lot of things. But despite how much we wrap our heads around it and despite how much we can say about it, we hate the whole idea of hell! The reality remains, people are going to hell, including some of our nearest and dearest friends. Despite how much sense we make of it, the heart wants nothing more than for it not to be true. The heart wants nothing more than to label Christianity as simply too cruel to even entertain, and then move on. Are we beginning to get the sense of the challenge of sharing this biblical truth and the reason we need to pray for patience? Are we beginning to get the sense that maybe the best approach isn't to try to argue for the reasonable existence of hell? Are we beginning to get the sense that maybe, just maybe, we need to get help from somewhere or someone else?

If we really understood the holiness of God and the wickedness of humans, as we said, hell would really not seem all that weird or unexpected. Instead, it turns out that the gospel is weird. The gospel is unexpected. We might hate the idea of hell, but God hates it even more. Despite God's perfect justice, his abhorrence of sin, and his every right to be separated forever from the people who despise him, the point of the Bible is to tell the story of a God that does everything to stop people from going to hell short of forcing them to be like him. Mark Paustian writes in More Prepared to Answer, "Deny hell and you can never see very far into the heart of Christ. . . . Deny hell and nothing Jesus did will make any sense. . . . Just what do you think his crucifixion was for?" If from the inside the doors of hell are locked, from the inside the doors to heaven were opened. *This same God who in his impenetrable wisdom allows people to live with their choice of rejecting his Son, took his wrath against imperfection upon himself when he gave the gift of his own Son. In this way, our friends' discussions of God's unpalatable justice can become discussions of God's unbelievable love.*

"I can't believe in a book that teaches so much inequality."

As long as woman regards the Bible as the charter of her rights, she will be the slave of man. . . . Within its lids there is nothing but humiliation and shame.

—Robert Green Ingersoll,
lawyer, orator, "The Great Agnostic"

Several of us finish up our Bible study together. We've just gone over the basics: we're all imperfect, God's not, that's a problem, and so God has fixed that problem through Jesus. One of the people in our group, Tiffany, joined us a few weeks ago with absolutely no background at all in the Bible. The only thing she was vaguely familiar with was the word Bible. *Tiffany is an undergraduate student at the largest university in Canada's capital city. She's studying for a degree from the university's Institute of Feminist and Gender Studies, and she's minoring in aboriginal studies (Canada's version of Native American studies). In other words, she's getting a degree in the subject of inequality. After talking law and gospel (that is, the basic biblical teachings that no one has the ability to perfectly keep God's law, but that God fixes this by sending Jesus to keep the law perfectly for us), she says, "Okay. I'm in. Tell me more." And my heart does a somersault. But my brain is already thinking ahead and tells me, "That's the easy part. Now for the hard stuff." And what my brain means is this:*

I frequently have conversations with other pastors who serve outside of the Bible Belt that go something like this: Sharing the basics of your faith isn't particularly hard. You share the law, and most people will agree that they're not perfect. Then you share the gospel, and it's fun and awesome to share, because it is, in fact, good news. Certainly not everyone you share law and gospel with becomes a Christian immediately, but you'd be surprised how many people, after building friendships with them and then patiently working through law and gospel, say, like Tiffany, "Okay. I'm in. Tell me more." Almost everything after the fundamentals of faith, though, is extremely difficult to share in a post-Christian country or a culture that has had no exposure whatsoever to Christianity and Christian thinking, except the caricatures. It's one thing to agree that you're imperfect and therefore alienated from a perfect God, but that God has fixed the problem. It's another thing to then let that gospel message permeate, change, and flip upside down all your values and truths as you begin to take in everything else in the Bible. Evolution, beliefs regarding homosexuality, the violence in the Bible (as we've just discussed), and much more are enormous cultural hurdles to get over. And in my experience, no hurdle is higher than the perceived inequality taught in the Bible, especially regarding the roles of men and women. And Tiffany and I have now arrived at this hurdle.

Just consider for a moment the cultural context of many of our friends (and most likely Tiffany): They've been taught since birth that men and women are absolutely equal in every way possible, as one of the founders of modern feminism states:

We hold these truths to be self-evident: that all men and women are created equal.

—Elizabeth Cady Stanton

They've been taught that people have complete control over their lives and bodies to do whatever they want. They've been taught that gender is a societal construct and not even really real. They've been taught that almost every culture up until this point has subjugated women, and that includes Christian cultures. Consider Katha Pollitt and Rachel Held Evans:

Can currently existing religion be disentangled from the misogyny of its texts, its traditions, and its practices? . . . a resounding NO: Misogyny not only pervades the major faiths, it's baked in.

—Katha Pollitt,
feminist poet

I left the church because I felt like I was the only one troubled by stories of violence and misogyny and genocide found in the Bible, and I was tired of people telling me not to worry about it because "God's ways are higher than our ways."

—Rachel Held Evans,
columnist

Now consider for a moment the biblical context of the gospel you're trying to share. Your Bible is a catalogue of the worst of humankind (for the express purpose of showing the world's dire need for a Savior), which includes the terrible treatment of women. And as such, Ingersoll could be taken in the right way when he says, as we quoted earlier, "Within its lids there is nothing but humiliation and shame." The plots of many accounts in the Bible center on polygamy, rape, prostitution, human trafficking, and other abuses of women, many times by their husbands or by kings who were anointed by God's prophets! Many women like Rachel Held Evans, when struggling with these accounts, have been frustrated with how Christians have responded to their questions about these accounts.

In spite of the Bible and its far-reaching effects, and in spite of the fact that the Bible is supposed to be God's eternal Word, modern human beings have advanced well beyond the Bible's teachings. In fact, we totally reject God's sexism. . . . Why do you, as a woman, reject God's Word when it comes to sexism? I would offer this possibility: We do it because the Bible's attitude toward women is completely irrational.

—Marshall Brain,
founder of HowStuffWorks

The Bible certainly teaches that there are different roles for men and women. Marshall Brain makes the comment above after cataloguing dozens of Bible passages, arguing rather well that the Bible's view of men's and women's roles is very different than our modern sensibilities. His conclusion, though, is that we ought to leave the Bible behind. After all, these roles have been abused by men throughout all of human history, one of those abuses being that men have interpreted the roles to mean men have more value in God's eyes than women. Even today it's all too easy to hear Christians say terrible things dripping with terrible *intentions like, "Women were made to serve" (an echo of Ingersoll's point on woman "being the slave of man"). How can we begin sharing **all** of our Bible with our friends like Tiffany? We shouldn't be surprised if we encounter anger and defensive posturing. Consider this:*

When people tell me I am too aggressive in my approach to feminism, I tell them that as part of a movement, I don't have time to hold anyone's hands. Hundreds of women die a year due to gender-based violence in Argentina. Mothers in the United States don't have a legal right to time paid off from work after they give birth. Ninety-eight percent of rapists will never be held in prison, or even in jail. Of course we are angry. And yes, we will be aggressive. People's lives are at stake; urgency is the only appropriate response.

—Elizabeth King,
bustle.com, "6 Common Arguments against
Feminism & Every Way You Can Shut Them Down"

Where do we begin? We begin with listening. And this includes hearing completely everything that she says, and especially acknowledging what's true about what humans in their sinfulness have done and continue to do. This also includes clarifying where possible, such as the fact that one of the ways the Bible functions is as a history book, recording events and actions that it certainly does not condone. This active listening also includes acknowledging that the Bible's teaching on men and women takes work to understand and so can easily be abused. After all, it teaches that men and women are essentially equal in value before God, yet it also teaches that God has given them different roles. And, yup, the role assigned to woman is helper.

I regard religion with fear and suspicion. . . . I think that the Bible as a system of moral guidance in the 21st century is insufficient, to put it mildly.

—Emma Thompson,
actor

Looking at how Christians have behaved in history coupled with the Bible's accounts of violence toward women and it's perhaps hard-to-understand teaching on roles of men and women, women today find the Bible a suspect source of moral codes, as Emma Thompson responds. But she may be surprised to learn that there are ways in which the Bible advocates for many of the things women are concerned about today. The model women of the Bible often include characters of independence and education, like the wife of noble character in Proverbs chapter 31. In no uncertain terms, the Bible teaches that the sexual objectification of women is wrong and that abusive marriages should not be tolerated. And the Bible is brutally egalitarian when it comes to its theological core: both men and women are responsible for the sin and suffering in this world (in fact, Adam might get more blame! see Romans 5:12), both need a solution from outside the human race, and both are covered by Christ's blood, the solution to the sin and suffering of this world. Many people don't know about these things because usually the conversation hasn't gotten this far. If we can begin with hearts sympathetic to the pain and suffering women have endured at the hands of sinful men (including sinful Christians) and if we can begin by letting them know that our God doesn't like these things either and calls us to champion the abused, neglected, and objectified, maybe the conversation can continue.

One sister sits in her bed now, finishing her evening routine of reading her Bible before she goes to sleep. She's reading 1 Corinthians 1:23: "We preach Christ crucified: a stumbling block to Jews and foolishness to Gentiles." And she tells herself she gets it. She had broken the long silence and had asked her sister why she hates the Bible so much. And starting with how unreliable the Bible is all the way to what a source of terror it's been for women, the unbelieving sister talked for what seemed hours as the believing sister sat quietly and listened. When she was finally asked to respond, the believer said quietly, "I've struggled with those same things. But that's not all I've found in the Bible." And then she quietly shared her faith. And it felt foolish at times. Very foolish. But it also felt important. So important. No one but God knew more than her how badly her unbelieving sister needed to find the love of God in that book, the love of God demonstrated nowhere more clearly than on that cross. Her sister ended the conversation with "Thanks for listening." That was a first. And a good start.

quick to listen

FRIENDS AND MEMBERS OF THE
LGBTQ COMMUNITY
TALKING TO CHRISTIANS

by Nick Schmoller

LISTENING TO RICK

This is my story. I was born February 26, 1958, in Greenfield, Ohio, in what appeared to be simpler times. In birth order, I am the middle child, but the eldest son. I was recently reminded by my parents that I was born the pride of our family: the first male, the one to carry on the family name for posterity's sake.

When I was only a couple of months old, my mother's life was transformed by a new relationship with God. This would prove to be a significant event in my life and the life of my family as well. A couple of years later my father joined her in a relationship with God and our ultimate family lifestyle.

Trying to come to terms with being gay has been an intense journey spanning several decades. While being gay is not a mental illness, the depression that came as a result of my attempting to live a life outside of whom I was created to be definitely is.

As a child, I was keenly aware of my same-sex attractions. I can remember as an elementary student staring at older guys and thinking about how beautiful they were. When I hit puberty, I was thrown into major chaos. I had been taught by my family, society, and through my religion that "normal" for a guy was having a girlfriend, eventually marrying and raising a family. It was an abomination to have feelings for another guy, and it would eventually send me to hell. I was convinced that this was true. Yet even the fear of eternal damnation could not alter my attractions.

In my later years of high school and early years of college, I spent hours in prayer and in meditation, asking God to change my desires. It never happened. This added greatly to my depression. Those who know me know that I am an extrovert, but during those years I would find myself becoming so depressed that I would not want to leave my room. I threw myself into my studies, wanting to be perfect in everything that I attempted, to fill the places where I was falling so short in my sexuality. I graduated second in my high school class and became president of many of the college organizations. People wanted to be me because they thought that I had life by the horns. Little did they know the hell I was living in.

During my freshman year of college, I met the girl that I would eventually marry. I thought that getting married and living as husband and wife would be the answer to making me straight. I was so wrong. Two months before our nuptials I was beginning to have second thoughts about how I could live this lie, but I decided to go through with it. Now, not only did I have the conflict of being inwardly gay, but I also had the guilt of having promised a "normal" life to a woman without the capability for filling that promise to the greatest extent. To this day, I love this woman more than I can love any woman, but I am still gay.

Between the winter of 1976 and the spring of 1977, God began to deal with me concerning my life's work. My personal belief is that God has designed each of us with a purpose and a plan. All people were given to me, mine to invest in and mine to influence, to lead, to inspire, to give hope to, and to introduce to God. I was called to be a pastor, a missionary, a true follower of Christ. I was called to love God with all of my heart and to love my neighbor as myself.

During my married life, my mental health was all over the charts. I would experience times of great joy, especially when my wife would become pregnant with one of our children. It was then that I would feel like I was a "real" man. Soon, though, the yearnings, impulses, desires, and extreme attraction for other guys would engulf me. I would fall into intense, severe depression, or I would act out on my desires, after which I would become smothered in self-condemnation. This condemnation would lead to deeper depression.

My wife had known for years that I had same-sex attractions, but she described it as a sin for which I could be forgiven and delivered. At one point in our marriage I fell hopelessly in love with one young man. We connected on every level. But alas, this relationship was not to be. Years later, one thing that kept my spirits lifted while doing mission work in Japan were the letters that would come to the post office from him. I would always open them there, then tear them up and throw them away so that they would not be discovered. One day I placed one in my pocket and took it home by mistake. A couple of days later, my wife discovered the letter. I came into our bedroom to find the letter open on our bed. I once again confessed and apologized, but this time it was different. I spent the next several hours in the church, pleading with God to change me. I had a choice: expose my relationship and sexual orientation to the world or bring the relationship to an end and remain with my wife to raise our family. I chose the latter and broke off all connections with him. My wife fell into a deep depression that nearly ended her life. The depression became so great that the doctors sent us back home to America. I carried the guilt with me that I had been the cause of this life-threatening hurt to my wife. It was a guilt that I would never escape.

After my children were grown, the relationship between my wife and I had become as distant roommates. Later my escape became gay pornography. In 2013, she discovered some photographs and websites and confronted me. Her words, "Rick, you have to admit that you are gay," were some of the most cutting, yet most liberating words that I had received. I replied, "Yes!"

Separation came, and it was decided that we would dismantle our home, our possessions, and our lives. I was not ready for the incredible loss that I felt. It became overpowering. The fear of the future, the unknown, the sense of hopelessness, loneliness, darkness, and foreboding overtook me. I experienced depression as never before. In my despair, I decided that it would be better for everyone, including myself, if I no longer existed. I sent a text to my children expressing my undying love, found the bottle of Ambien, and while holding it in my hand getting up the courage to consume them, my youngest son ran through the door and said, "Dad, what are you doing?" He literally saved my life. I collapsed in his arms, and he talked me through the crisis.

I went to a new town looking for a new beginning. I found a great new home. The only problem was that I knew almost no one there. My daughter told me that there was a Pride Center somewhere downtown. I googled it, got the address, and decided to walk and see if I could find it. I will never forget how I felt the first time I walked through the doors and saw the sign-in sheet and the partition hiding me from the rest of the world. I wondered what the people sitting at the bar next door were thinking about me. How were people judging me? What kind of community would I find? When I walked through the doors, I saw a couple of men sitting at the back table and talking. I went in, introduced myself, and the conversation about where I came from and how I ended up at the center occurred.

The Pride Center became my place of refuge. With the center only being open two hours a day, I would plan my day around the visit. I met some of the most interesting people, all interested in listening to my story, all accepting of who I am. It was at the Pride Center on a Sunday evening that I met a most interesting lady. She wanted to know about me, to hear my story. As I began to share, she informed me that she was the pastor of a United Methodist Church. She listened with her full attention and then asked the most alarming question: "Have you ever thought about working for a church again?" My answer was "NO!" I can remember very clearly saying to her, "How can I ever work for a church? I am gay." Her response was, "What does that have to do with anything?" I was not ready to even entertain the thought. But she invited me to come and give it a try.

My view of "church" was that it hated me and everyone like me. In their eyes I am an abomination, condemned to hell because of my sexual orientation. Oddly enough, I had still maintained my personal relationship with God. People have told me that it is impossible to have an intimate relationship with God and remain gay. They say that my homosexuality is a choice. They say all homosexuals are an abomination and will go to hell. They even treat it like a disease that God could cure.

Instead of those attitudes, I would encourage other Christians to find some LGBTQ people of faith and get to know them. Listen to our stories. Try to see us as real people—people who eat, sleep, bleed when we are wounded, and cry when we are hurt. We are so much more than our sexual orientation. We are real followers of Christ.

Most non-affirming Christians believe that being LGBTQ is a choice—that we choose to be gay. They will not allow themselves to think that God created us just as we are. I would encourage people to keep their minds open and not assume that every LGBTQ person is promiscuous or out to recruit heterosexuals into becoming gay.

Ultimately, the one who helped me realize that my spirituality and sexuality could walk in agreement was God. I am a man of faith, but all of the radical conservative Christian teachings stated otherwise. I had to hit rock bottom in my life, ready to take my own life, just to stop the pain of living behind the mask of religion, knowing who I was inwardly yet presenting myself very differently to the world. Fear was a great motivator in my life: the fear of exposure, the fear of loss of everything that I held dear, and the fear of judgment and eternal damnation. I had to get to the point of suicide to be able to listen to the voice of God. Once I was able to listen, God put key people in my life to show me that I was still valuable to and usable by God.

Every person sins and falls short of God's perfection. When you study the Scriptures concerning LGBTQ issues, remember to read the Scripture in relation to the time period, culture, and context in which it was written.

We all have our own biases due to the information that we have received and how we have been instructed. It is vital that we educate ourselves with information that is contrary to the norm. Only then can we create an informed opinion concerning truth.

LISTENING TO EILEEN

My name is Eileen. My story is a little different as I truly did not find myself or happiness until my early thirties. I grew up in a typical middle-class home in the Midwest. Both parents worked. We ate all our meals together and went to church every Sunday. I was raised Catholic and went to Catholic school all through high school. I had a very good understanding of what was or is considered right and wrong. I had the dream of marrying the man of my dreams, having a family together, and raising them just like I was raised. I had a boyfriend all throughout college and was well on the way to having my all-American family. I married at the age of 25 and thought at the time that everything was perfect and I was on my way to happily ever after. However, I soon discovered that something just wasn't right and that I truly wasn't happy. I couldn't tell at that time or, actually, for the next five years of marriage exactly what it was, but something was missing. My husband and I worked, had the same interests, laughed a lot, and had fun times together, but I just didn't feel a connection with him that I thought I should. I had never failed at anything in my life, and failing at my marriage just wasn't an option for me. I felt if I couldn't make my marriage work that everyone from family to friends would view it as a failure. So I tried to make it work.

After five years of marriage, we finally divorced and I moved on. I felt that he just wasn't the one for me and that I would find happiness with someone else. I dated on and off for the next three years, and again, no matter who I was involved with, the result was the same. There was just something missing. Throughout the years I had several friends tell me that I was gay and that I just didn't know it yet. I always dismissed their remarks rather quickly. After not finding happiness with the men I was with, I gave their remarks a little more thought and began to think, "What if they are right?" I can't pinpoint an exact "aha" moment, but I decided to try and date a girl and see if there was a difference in what I felt. I joined a dating site and was rather apprehensive as I had never been with a female, nor I had ever given much thought to being with one. I looked through profiles and emailed a couple of people that caught my interest. Long story short, the first time I kissed a woman I knew I had found what had been missing in all of my previous relationships. There was a connection that was missing with the men I had been with. I have been asked many times what that connection is, and all I can say is that it is not a sexual thing but rather an emotional connection that is incredibly strong and one that was missing before. I have been the happiest I have ever been for the past eight years. It feels very natural to me to be with a woman, and it does not feel like I am doing something wrong or sinful. I am married now with two beautiful boys and have finally found that perfect family I had been looking for. It might be different from yours, but it is still a family filled with lots of love, laughter, and acceptance.

For me, I do not have an agenda or a cause for people to understand my orientation. I simply ask that people just treat people like they would want to be treated. Just because I am attracted to another female does not mean I am attracted to every female and does not mean I am trying to convert you to be like me. It is as simple as this: I choose to love who I do just as you choose to love who you do. I believe that what I do in my home is private, and I don't advertise my lifestyle. We are simply two productive members of society who are very successful and, I believe, good role models for others. My parents and family have accepted who I am from the beginning and all they have said, to a person, is that they want me to be happy and that they have never seen me happier. I am the same exact person I was before; I just chose to love somebody like me.

I stated earlier that I was raised Catholic, and I know the teachings and what the church states very well. I have had fellow church members tell me I am going down the wrong path and have had several give me dirty looks or gossip behind my back. My first thought is that God created all of us, and I am pretty confident that he did not create thousands of gay people for us all to go to hell. I also struggle with the belief that I am going to go to hell for loving who I do, but the church could cover up all the abuse of little boys by their priests for years and they will still go to heaven. I can say that even though I still identify as Catholic, I have chosen to attend a Unitarian Universalist Church where all are accepted and the focus is on becoming a better person.

For those who want a firsthand account of how the process of dealing with a child who tells you he or she is gay and has to handle this on a national level in the public eye, I recommend *Love Ellen* by Betty DeGeneres. She tells the story of her family's background and her own personal struggle when Ellen told her the news. From her disbelief and disappointment to her journey of acceptance, love, and, most important, the understanding that this was the same daughter she had loved the first 20 years of her life. It will make you laugh and cry, and after you are finished, you too might have a greater sense of acceptance for a group of people who ask nothing more than to just be treated with respect.

LISTENING TO MARGY

In a snapshot, I would describe myself as: white, female, straight, cradle·Catholic, friend, volunteer, advocate for many causes, loyal, creative, mother, wife, vegetarian, flexible, cancer survivor, open-minded, honest, middle-aged, middle-income, LGBT ally, recovering Catholic, Unitarian Universalist, and religious-phobic.

I was born with the first four traits. The last four represent a faith journey that began the day I got my kid back. "The day I got my kid back" is an expression I use frequently when I share the story of the first time my son told me he was gay. Those first moments are usually described with words such as *shock, confusion, disbelief, grief, denial.* I can honestly say that the first thought that crossed my mind was, "Of course, now it all makes sense!" That was the day I got my kid back, my kid who had been hiding from me for roughly 10-plus of his 19 years. What a waste!

On that day I began my own process of coming out and speaking out. On the topic of religion, I am still on my journey. And as long as people use religion selectively to discriminate against our most vulnerable, it looks to be a long one too. The church was not there for my family when we needed it to be an advocate for us. That and the way they selectively emphasize some sins over others led me to no longer have need for the church.

One way Christians have led me away from religion is the way they have influenced legislation to oppose marriage equality. They talk about the societal need for traditional Christian marriage. They say that children need to have opposite sex parents or the children would suffer developmentally. They say that LGBT people are a threat to traditional marriage. In other words, when you have traditional marriage with opposite sex, two-parent families, all should be right, perhaps blessed, with one's life.

Hearing these things makes me think of my own story. I married my high school crush. Our wedding was in the Catholic Church where I grew up. We had three healthy children who all attended Catholic school. Perfect, right? Well, no.

After 15 years of marriage to a spouse who suffered from mental illness, depression, and prescription drug addiction, we divorced and I became a single parent of a 9-, 11-, and 13-year-old. Four years later my ex-husband died of a prescription drug overdose and I became an only parent. Two years later my son told me he was gay.

Now my kids are grown. And even though they grew up in a challenging environment, all three are caring, responsible adults. One served in the military for nearly ten years, one is a nurse, and one works for the State Department. So while my "traditional marriage" was not the idyllic institution many Christians describe, my children still turned out well. And just for the record, my gay son is not a threat to traditional marriage; he is the product of traditional marriage.

So here is my takeaway. No one is perfect. People are human. And humans are gay, transgender, straight, and everything in-between. The best way to protect Americans and American families is to protect and serve all Americans and all American families. I question the opinion of some aimed at protecting an ideal when the outcome is harmful to real people and families.

There are examples in recent years of transgender children who have open and supportive parents. And it is encouraging to see nature take its course in these children as they come to discover who they are and how they are comfortable with themselves. Contrast that with the despair and depression that many children are subjected to when their parents selectively apply the Bible and try to change who they are. Look at how damaging that sort of practice can be.

Some people think that LGBT people are all criminals, pedophiles, or predatory people. They think that their sexual identity is a choice or just a lifestyle that they choose to live as or not. Those thoughts and opinions only add to the discrimination that LGBT people face each day.

When my children were young, if there was something unfair that would happen, if I could make it right I would. I would decide who needed to sit in a time-out. I redistributed french fries so that they were "even steven." I kissed the ouches to make the pain go away. And there were times when I had to help my kids learn that sometimes life isn't fair.

But that should be the exception and not the rule. Now for my grown children, one is treated as a second-class citizen, somehow inferior and denied equal rights, because some believe he loves the wrong person. This is a pain so great that no mother's kiss can make it go away!

As a parent, I am tired of hearing religious reasons touted from the Bible to explain why my son's civil rights are permanently in "time-out." I don't believe amendments that attempt to ban same-sex marriage are "even steven." I see this all coming from people who hold tight to selective religious beliefs. And for this I'm not ready to accept the explanation, "Sorry, sometimes life isn't fair."

Sometimes I fear for my son. I fear that there are people driven by hate and discrimination that would try to harm him because of who he is and whom he loves. And so as a straight ally of the LGBT community, I cannot just stand by. I feel compelled to speak out.

The first question I would ask is, "Who are you to judge?" We all have our faults and failings. We all have done things wrong in the past. But how can so many sit in judgment on those who are doing nothing wrong except loving the people that they love. Even the Bible has passages that condemn that kind of judgment.

I also would encourage people to get to know an LGBT person or several of them. Just because you aren't knowledgeable about a community is not a good reason to discriminate against them. Ignorance is not the answer. Instead, you would discover that many characterizations of the LGBT community are false. They are not criminals or predators. They are people just like you and me trying to live and love in peace.

One evening as a family sits around the dinner table, a young boy brings up something that has been weighing on his mind. "Dad, why is Tommy, my classmate, so much faster than me? And why do Susie's drawings look so much more realistic than mine? I like to draw. I love to run. Why can't I be better than they are?"

"God made us all differently," the father replies. "And in fact, that's a great thing. Wouldn't it be boring if everyone were exactly the same? And sometimes we might feel like we wish we were different or better at something else, but we should be thankful for the gifts and abilities that God has given us, we should use them to our fullest, and we should be content with how we've been made."

Years go by, and now this young boy is beginning to have feelings for other boys. At first he would pray and repent when these feelings came and hope they wouldn't return. But they did. And then he thought back to that conversation around the dinner table and began to wonder. Is this one of the differences that God has given to me? My dad said our differences were things to embrace. Does that mean I should embrace these feelings too?

Then one day he's not just asking himself these questions, he's asking them to you. What do you say? But more than that, what else should you be listening for?

"We were born this way."

It doesn't matter if you love him, or capital H-I-M
Just put your paws up 'cause you were born this way, baby

My mama told me when I was young
We are all born superstars

She rolled my hair and put my lipstick on
In the glass of her boudoir

"There's nothing wrong with loving who you are"
She said, "'Cause he made you perfect, babe"
"So hold your head up girl and you'll go far,
Listen to me when I say"

I'm beautiful in my way

'Cause God makes no mistakes
I'm on the right track, baby I was born this way.

—Lady Gaga,
singer and co-songwriter, "Born This Way"

When this song was released in 2011, it became a powerful anthem for the LGBTQ community. Lady Gaga's song lyrics point to what is often the heart of the tension. How can the desires I feel be wrong, if this is how I was born—if this is how I was made? Many feel like their sexual orientation is something in which they have no choice—that this is how they have been since birth. If our perfect God is the one who brings life into the world and if God doesn't make mistakes (which is something that we can all agree with), then the natural conclusion is that anything that is part of us from birth must be from God.

It is true that there are many differences we have, in our thoughts and feelings and our spiritual gifts, that God does want us to embrace. Scripture says several times (see Romans 12 and 1 Corinthians 12 for examples) that we Christians are meant to be different from one another, just like the parts of a human body are different from one another—this is God's loving intention and design. We are the parts of the body, all serving our head, Christ, in different ways.

Is sexual orientation just another one of those God-designed differences? This is the place where our discussions with people in this community often start. And we need to sympathize with the fact that for many it is something they have wrestled with for their whole lives.

A person's sexual orientation is not something that can be recruited. It is part of who we are created to be. I can live the life that I was created by God to live and still be called a person of faith.

—Rick,
see above, "Listening to Rick"

I have had fellow church members tell me I am going down the wrong path and have had several give me dirty looks or gossip behind my back. My first thought is that God created all of us, and I am pretty confident that he did not create thousands of gay people for us all to go to hell.

—Eileen,

see above, "Listening to Eileen"

When Moses spoke with God in the burning bush, one objection that Moses raised against God's command for him to lead the people of Israel out of slavery was that he was "slow of speech" (Exodus 4:10).

God responded, "Who gave human beings their mouths? Who makes them deaf or mute? Who gives them sight or makes them blind? Is it not I, the LORD?" (verse 11). Sin can affect our human bodies so that people might be born blind, deaf, or mute, yet God still asked, "Who does this? Is it not I, the Lord?" There is comfort in the fact that God has lovingly made each of us. It is as if he says, "Sin did not make you: I made you, so take heart. I know just the work I have in mind for you to do and your handicaps will not hinder you."

Is it possible that these other sexual orientations can be part of people from birth? Whether scientific studies prove it or not, Christians probably should admit it could be so.

If it were, what would God say to people who were "born that way"? If someone complained to him about their same-sex attraction and how they wished it would be different, I wonder if God's response to them would at all resemble what he said to Moses.

We could take a cue from the Lord here. The Creator did not argue with Moses's claim that he was slow to speech, but neither would God let Moses use that as an excuse to refuse the work that God had for him, to bring freedom to the people of Israel. Likewise, whatever other failings or frailties we have in our sinful flesh, God doesn't want us to use those as reasons to disregard God's will for our lives: the important work he wants us to do.

We are told that one "discovers" that one is transgender just like one "discovers" that one is "gay." In no way do I mean to deny that there are psychological disorders to which many so-called transgenders and homosexuals are subject through no choice of their own. The problem lies in not recognizing them as disorders, and then therefore accepting them as normative behavior that should be embraced and encouraged. Does one likewise "discover" that one is an adulterer, a thief or a drunkard?

—Robert R. Reilly,
2016 article for catholicworldreport.com,
"Pope Francis vs. Gender Ideology"

The inclination to sin resides in each person's heart from birth. This is a biblical truth. While no one is free from all temptations, observation shows that there are specific sins or temptations that attack some more strongly or seem more appealing to some than others.

If we are striving to be quick to listen, we should probably avoid labeling the LGBTQ community as subject to "psychological disorders." We will be heard as trivializing their difficult emotional struggles: "Your deep feelings are really just chemical imbalances. You just need to take the right pill. You just aren't right in the head." That is how we will come across. What about the pain and isolation these people feel? We need to let them know their pain matters to us. "Mourn with those who mourn," says Romans 12:15.

But Mr. Reilly's quote goes even further, equating same-sex attraction with other sinful urges: sexual infidelity, thievery, and drunkenness. Mr. Reilly's point is valid: God doesn't want us to embrace or encourage any sinful inclination we "discover" in ourselves. Rather, he wants us to scrub them all from our hearts. But this will not come across as persuasive logic to most people who identify as transgenders or homosexuals. You can be assured that the conversation will end before it has begun. We shouldn't begin our discussions with people in the LGBTQ community by identifying them as those who revel in embracing sin. If they express helplessness or powerlessness to make these desires go away, we can sympathize with them. We can say, "It is hard to be condemned for something you don't know how to fix, isn't it?" None of us knows how to fix our sinful hearts: we must not forget that. This is why we rejoice to know that "God is greater than our hearts" (1 John 3:20).

The belief that sexual orientation is an innate, biologically fixed human property—that people are "born that way"—is not supported by scientific evidence.

Likewise, the belief that gender identity is an innate, fixed human property independent of biological sex—so that a person might be a "man trapped in a woman's body" or "a woman trapped in a man's body"—is not supported by scientific evidence.

—Ryan T. Anderson,
dailysignal.com, "Nearly Everything the Media Tell You
About Sexual Orientation and Gender Identity Is Wrong"

So often I read quotes like these, shared and cited by Christians who look to science as an answer to the LGBTQ community. Would your view of the Bible change if "scientific evidence" supported some other belief about sexual orientation? Would your view of sin change if "scientific evidence" showed that gender identity is independent of biological sex? I pray that nothing would change your opinion of Scripture.

Many Christians seem to have an interesting relationship with scientific research. Our parents and pastors encouraged us to put our faith in God's Word and not scientific "facts," because the opinions of scientists can and will change over time. But it sure does appeal to us to be able to talk like Mr. Anderson here: "You gays and transgender people, the 'scientific evidence' is not on your side."

Not that we want to let the devil monopolize all the good science, but bringing up studies like these actually can do more harm than good in our conversations. Think what an awkward situation we put ourselves in if we are too quick to cite these kinds of studies in our discussions with people in the LGBTQ community. Think what accusations we are inviting against ourselves: the accusation that we only pay attention to research that supports one side; also the accusation that we are being hypocrites, talking like we base our opinions on science, when we really base them on our holy book.[38] It is easy to talk like our main goal is to win a scientific argument, rather than a soul. It is easy for us to see case studies, where Jesus sees harassed and helpless sheep.

There may be another reason not to get too strident pointing out the lack of scientific evidence for being "born this way"—a growing num-

---

[38] Also the accusation that the "evidence" is more nuanced than we're making it out to be: One of the more prominent psychologists studying the question would say the evidence shows that one-third of the variation in human sexual orientation is caused by genetics, with males being much more "born that way" and female sexuality being more fluid. But he would be careful to point out that the opposite of "I'm born gay" isn't "I choose to be gay." (Jesse Singal, "We're Not Quite 'Born This Way,'" discussing the research of J. Michael Bailey, Sept. 1, 2016, www.thecut.com.)

*ber of people in the LGBTQ community are distancing themselves from
the "born this way" argument:*

Getting Americans to believe that people are born gay—that it's not
something that can be chosen or changed—has been central to the
fight for gay rights. The "born this way" mantra, a ubiquitous part
of the Pride celebrations taking place this month, doesn't reflect the
feelings of all members of the LGBTQ movement. Some argue it
excludes those who feel their sexuality is fluid, while others question
why the dignity of gay people should rest on the notion that they
were gay from their very first breath. . . .

"The science of whether sexual orientation is biological is pretty
sparse and full of disparate, mixed and unreplicated findings," said
Sari van Anders, a professor of psychology at the University of Mich-
igan. "So that is one reason why there is a lot of confusion about
it. Because a study will come out that says, 'This gene!' And then
another study will say, 'Oh, we didn't find that same gene, but we
found this gene.'"

It's impossible to know if we'll ever be able to map the complexities
of human sexuality, but it's more and more clear that the bodies we're
born with don't determine everything about who we are.

—Alia E. Dastagir,
front-page story in *USA Today*, June 20, 2017

*We should not assume that every nonstraight person loves the "born
this way" logic. Some don't. They say, "Why should my dignity as a
gay person depend on whether I have to prove that I can't help being
gay? I claim ownership of my feelings, wherever they came from. I am a
human being with a heart: that should be dignity enough."*

We know of hundreds of gay people who could tell stories of struggling with their same-sex attractions while diligently serving God.
These are not idolaters, people who hated God and pursued their
own desire for new and greater sexual thrills. These are lovers of
God who, nevertheless, have been attracted to people of the same
sex from early in life. They are innate (i.e., natural) homosexuals.

—Jeff Miner and John Tyler Connoley,
The Children Are Free

Imagine the pain that so many people deal with on a daily basis. The struggle of those who love God and still are attacked by temptation and filled with attractions—their struggle is real.

Whether or not their temptations can be "excused" by scientific studies, the experiences of so many who "have been attracted to people of the same sex from early in life" are numerous. Some embrace these attractions regardless of what God's Word might say. There are many who continue to love God and who search God's Word, search themselves, and sometimes, regrettably, even search the world to make sense of their attractions.

Pray to God that you would be spared from such seemingly unbearable and relentless temptations. Pray that God would help all people in the darkness of their temptations, especially those who deal with the same temptation day after day. And be present and available to listen to anyone who is in this struggle. Encourage them to not look to the world for its wisdom but to their Savior Jesus who has already defeated sin for them and the world through his perfect life and innocent death.

For years many conservative Christians supported efforts to change gay people's sexual orientation. Some still take that approach, but in 2013, the flagship "ex-gay" organization shut down and apologized for the "false hopes," pain, and trauma it caused. . . .

That approach has been called "reparative therapy." But (one doctor) discovered after he studied the issue, sexual orientation is not a choice, and it is highly resistant to change.

—Matthew Vines,
God and the Gay Christian

Perhaps you've heard about some of the procedures and practices that have been tried in the past to change sexual orientation. I'm sure you could find some horror stories about it if you tried. Why have so many of these efforts failed? One answer might be that there is some validity to the claim that there is a fixed nature to sexual orientation and attraction, or something especially enslaving about sexual sins. Another answer is one that plagues mankind in so many realms. We look to ourselves to solve our own problems.

Are there any areas where you can find yourself looking for this same solution? I think you probably can. If the temptation is worry, we try to save money for a rainy day more often than trusting God's promises. If it is other sexual temptations, we count on our own willpower, but we forget prayer, confession to fellow Christians, and the power of our baptism. The list can go on and on.

Should it be surprising that people have tried "reparative therapy" to solve temptation? It also shouldn't be surprising that man-made solutions have failed.

In conversations with people in the LGBTQ community, we must admit that horrible things have been done in the past. And telling people that all they need is the right therapy shows that we don't understand what they are truly going through.

Can God remove temptations from someone's life? Of course he can! "With God all things are possible" (Matthew 19:26). But no perfect therapy or amount of prayer guarantees that God will cure us of this specific temptation at the moment we have decided upon. Humbly, we pray that God would give everyone the strength to endure temptation and that God's will would be done in all things.

Since Scripture tells us that we're all born in sin—that it's a condition before it is a self-chosen action—we shouldn't be surprised if the Fall has in fact affected us in exactly that way. There are genetic predispositions to any number of sins such as alcoholism or anger.

The fact that it feels natural to me is not a sign of how God has created me; it's a sign of how sin has distorted me.

—Sam Allberry,
coordinator of livingout.org, interviewed for
Modern Reformation magazine

This is a good reminder for each one of us. Let us not think there is any part of our own sinful nature or our human desires that is pure. Our human nature wants to say that if God made me one way, it cannot be wrong. But sin has distorted us all.

We should not be surprised if LGBTQ people cannot recognize their desires as distortions caused by sin. Martin Chemnitz once wrote that the sin we are born with "is far removed and hidden from the sight and knowledge of the flesh, or reason, and of the world." In all truth, each of us could say, "Yes, there are things the Bible says about how we're born with sin that I can't understand either. I don't think anyone can."

And then we could add: "It's precious the way that Jesus saves us from more sin than we ever knew we had."

"This isn't a choice; it's who I am."

In time, [Josh] found it impossible to keep believing in a loving God. As he saw it, the God of the Bible required him to hate a core part of himself.

—Matthew Vines,
God and the Gay Christian

How do you identify yourself? There probably are many answers to that question. When you read a short biography of people, it might read something like this: husband, father of three, pastor, soccer player, lover of the outdoors, or something like that. Implied in that short biography is my sexuality, isn't it? I am a father. I'm a husband to my wife. While these roles are much more than just describing my sexual orientation, that's present there too.

So when Josh said that his same-sex attraction was "a core part of himself" that God required him to hate, it shouldn't surprise us. That is how our world often talks. That is how people often think. They think their sexual attractions are their identity.

What do you think Josh understood as "self"? If we could, the best start would probably be to ask Josh himself. But if "self" is merely what comes to us by human nature, if it is our animalistic tendencies towards survival, our fight-or-flight instincts and our innate desire to reproduce/find a mate, then Josh's view of "self" is correct. But if God created us to be much more than just animals, then his view of "self" is woefully lacking.

Isn't that a shame? Sex and attraction are very good and special creations of God, but why should they define what we think about ourselves? You are much more than just your sexuality. You are first and foremost a child of God (1 John 3:1,2) and a child of the resurrection (Luke 20:34-36). That is your primary identity. The other things that we enjoy, the other physical and spiritual gifts you have been given, are all built on that identity.

I fear that it is not just people in the LGBTQ community who think of their sexuality as a core part of their identity. I pray that will not always be the case. In a world that champions the freedom of sexual expression and puts it on full display for everyone to see, it becomes harder and harder for Christians not to think of themselves as mere sexual creatures. We would do well to remember that we are much more than that in Christ. And we have the privilege of sharing this amazing truth with people of the LGBTQ community too. We can offer them and everyone in this world a much greater identity that can be found only in the Savior Jesus.

The kind of sexual attractions I experience are not fundamental to my identity. They are part of what I feel, but are not who I am in a fundamental sense. I am far more than my sexuality. . . . It's easy for us to make sexual fulfillment—through Christian marriage—the goal of our life. . . . It also appears that there is a movement afoot in the States to talk openly in churches about sexuality—almost as if to say, we're not those prudish Christians; we love sex. It's almost as if we're trying to justify ourselves to the culture by making heterosexual sex a defining part of our identity too.

—Sam Allberry,
coordinator of livingout.org, interviewed for
Modern Reformation magazine

Allberry makes a point that is so often lost on people today. Our sexuality is not a fundamental part of who we are. But in this quote he cites another way that sexuality is championed today. Heterosexual sex, even sex within a Christian marriage, is often put up on a pedestal.

While sex is a gift that God does give to a husband and wife in marriage, that is where that gift should stay. A carelessly casual discussion of even marital sex does God a disservice to what he intends this gift of sex to be—a private expression of unity and love in a marriage. We would be wise to keep the sexual joys we experience with our spouse a private matter. However, sex should not be a subject that is totally taboo. Parents need to instruct their children about sex so that they don't get their thoughts about it from the world. Pastors should talk to those who are about to be married as well. There are even sections of Scripture where God vividly describes the blessing and pleasures of sex within a marriage. Certainly, those of us who are married should love our spouses and all the gifts that God gives to us through marriage. But let's not hold this up as the highest gift that one could ever imagine, or we will be guilty of leading others to have false, sinful priorities. As Paul says, "The time is short. From now on those who have wives should live as if they do not" (1 Corinthians 7:29). Finding your earthly true love can't be the Christian's be all and end all.

If we even give the impression that people are incomplete in the eyes of God until they have entered into a godly heterosexual marriage, we run the risk of alienating those who don't have such a relationship or even the desire to have one. There is such a thing as God-pleasing celibacy. Read again 1 Corinthians chapter 7. If a person is not tempted to lust after the opposite sex, that is a gift from God, an opportunity to be even more single-heartedly devoted to the Lord:

> I would like you to be free from concern. An unmarried man is concerned about the Lord's affairs—how he can please the Lord. But a married man is concerned about the affairs of this world—how he can please his wife—and his interests are divided. An unmarried woman or virgin is concerned about the Lord's affairs: Her aim is to be devoted to the Lord in both body and spirit. But a married woman is concerned about the affairs of this world—how she can please her husband. I am saying this for your own good, not to restrict you, but that you may live in a right way in undivided devotion to the Lord. (7:32-35).

Here is my identity: not whether I belong to a spouse or significant other but that I have been bought, body and soul, by the Lord—to be his own, precious to him forever.

"Those Bible passages about homosexuality aren't as clear as you think."

When you study the Scriptures concerning LGBTQ issues, remember to read the Scripture in relation to the time period, culture, and context in which it was written.

We all have our own biases due to the information that we have received and how we have been instructed. It is vital that we educate ourselves with information that is contrary to the norm. Only then can we create an informed opinion concerning truth.

—Rick,
see above, "Listening to Rick"

In the nineteenth century, experience played a key role in compelling Christians to rethink another traditional—and supposedly biblical—belief. This time, the issue was slavery. Much as you and I might be repelled by the notion, most Christians throughout history understood passages such as Ephesians 6:5-9 and Colossians 3:22-25 to sanction at least some forms of slavery. But in the eighteenth and nineteenth centuries, Christian abolitionists persuaded believers to take another look. They appealed to conscience based on the destructive consequences of slavery.

The abolitionists in their campaign against slavery [didn't argue] that their experience should take precedence over Scripture. But they made the case that their experience should cause Christians to reconsider long-held interpretations of Scripture. Today, we are still responsible for testing our beliefs in light of their outcomes—a duty in line with Jesus's teaching.

—Matthew Vines,
God and the Gay Christian

Interpretation can be a loaded word. Is it fair to say that biblical interpretation can change? God's Word is clear; its meaning unchanging. He has made his will known through it. It is our rescuing light in every darkness and doubt.

There are portions of Scripture that God-fearing interpreters and translators can't seem to agree on. But we rejoice that the message and details of God's grace to us in Christ are stated in the clearest of words, which even toddlers find joy in. Only the stubborn debate them.

At the same time, the applications of that Word can change. Throughout the history of the Christian church, as the context of ministry and life change, so do the applications of Scripture. (For example, the New Testament's directives on hair length and modest clothing, or the eating of meat with blood in it.) Applications of God's Word can and do change.

*This is something we can agree on with Matthew Vines and Rick in their quotes. In part, they are asking that people would go back to Scripture with an open mind about the applications of God's Word. While the truths and moral principles of Scripture never change, the way we **apply** those principles—that is, the way we **live them out** in our day-to-day efforts to serve one another—that will change from time to time because life's circumstances keep changing. (And our neighbors and their temptations, spiritual blind spots, and needs keep changing.) So if we are to be quick to listen, we also need to be open to listen to what others might suggest about the application of God's Word. And more than that—let's rejoice at the times whenever people express any kind of willingness to go to God's Word for more guidance and direction. Praise God for the opportunity. Express your excitement with them for the discussion. Be loving in your words. And be quick to listen.*

There are about twenty references to the story of Sodom in the Bible, and none of them says homosexuality was the sin of Sodom. One of the most extensive references to Sodom is found in Ezekiel, which says, "This was the guilt of your sister Sodom: She and her daughters had pride, excess of food, and prosperous ease, but did not aid the poor and needy. They were haughty and did abominable things before me; therefore I removed them when I saw it" (Ezekiel 16:49-50). It is clear from this passage (and others like it[39]) that the abomination of Sodom, according to the Old Testament prophets, was that they behaved with callous indifference toward the weak and vulnerable—the poor, orphans, widows, and strangers in their midst. . . .

Why then do some Christians interpret this story as condemning all homosexual behavior? We would submit that their interpretation is driven by anti-gay prejudice. Many Christians only know the stereotypes they learned in childhood. They buy into the idea that all gay men are predators and that loving relationships between inherently homosexual people do not exist. So they read the story of Sodom and see a stereotype of what they think all gay people are like. They then assume the story must be a sweeping condemnation

---

[39] Deuteronomy 29:23; 32:32; Isaiah 1:9-17; 3:9; 13:19; Jeremiah 23:14; 49:18; 50:40; Lamentations 4:6; Ezekiel 16:46-56; Amos 4:11; and Zephaniah 2:9 are referenced.

of homosexuality, because they assume all homosexuality takes the form shown in this story. In truth, this story is at most a condemnation of homosexual rape. And, as other Scriptures affirm, it is more generally a condemnation of the mistreatment of those who are most vulnerable, including strangers. It is ironic that the story of Sodom is now used by Christians to justify hatred toward another vulnerable group—gay people.

—Jeff Miner and John Tyler Connoley

The story of Sodom and Gomorrah is probably the most commonly quoted section of Scripture when discussing the topic of homosexuality. The account of the men of the city beating on the door of Lot's house when he was trying to protect his guests (who had come from heaven) is so vivid, memorable, and disturbing that this shouldn't surprise us. However, can we really be sure for what particular sin God brought judgment on these cities? When God speaks to Abraham, he complains in general about the great wickedness of the city. Other accounts of Scripture talk in general terms about Sodom's heartless abuse of those who were guests in the city. Is the destruction of these cities really only on account of homosexual sin? Jude 7 condemned their sexual immorality, but their wickedness went far beyond that.

Perhaps we should be hesitant to say that any act of judgment is on account of one sin alone. This follows in line with Jesus' teaching (Luke 13). If it is possible that this descriptive account of Scripture is not solely God's judgment on homosexuality, then it is right that we look for more clear passages of Scripture to discuss the subject. After all, if God didn't deem it necessary to tell Abraham what specific sins of Sodom and Gomorrah grieved him so dramatically, we should be careful not to speak where God has not spoken.

Orthodox Jews who follow Mosaic Law can use Leviticus to condemn homosexuality without being hypocrites. But fundamentalist Christians must choose: They can either follow Mosaic Law by keeping kosher, being circumcised, never wearing clothes made of two types of thread and the like. Or they can accept that finding salvation in the Resurrection of Christ means that Leviticus is off the table.

Which raises one final problem for fundamentalists eager to condemn homosexuals or anyone else: If they accept the writings of Paul and believe all people are sinners, then salvation is found in belief in Christ and the Resurrection. For everyone. There are no exceptions in the Bible for sins that evangelicals really don't like.

—Kurt Eichenwald,
"The Bible: So Misunderstood It's a Sin,"
Newsweek cover story, January 2015

This is a common complaint about Christians—that they pick and choose parts of the Bible to follow, that they are all about grace until it comes to sins they don't really like, and that they'll find the most obscure Bible verses to justify their position. Don't be part of that complaint. Don't use the Levitical law to tell people how to live, unless you are more than ready to also explain the beauty of how all of the requirements of Leviticus have been fulfilled in the perfect, substitutionary life of our Savior Jesus.

The next quotes refer to the following Scripture passages:
*Do you not know that wrongdoers will not inherit the kingdom of God? Do not be deceived: Neither the sexually immoral nor idolaters nor adulterers nor men who have sex with men [Greek: **malakoi oute arsenokoitai**] nor thieves nor the greedy nor drunkards nor slanderers nor swindlers will inherit the kingdom of God. And that is what some of you were. But you were washed, you were sanctified, you were justified in the name of the Lord Jesus Christ and by the Spirit of our God. (1 Corinthians 6:9-11)*

*We also know that the law is made not for the righteous but for lawbreakers and rebels, the ungodly and sinful, the unholy and irreligious, for those who kill their fathers or mothers, for murderers, for the sexually immoral, for those practicing homosexuality [Greek: **arsenokoitais**], for slave traders and liars and perjurers— and for whatever else is contrary to the sound doctrine that conforms to the gospel concerning the glory of the blessed God, which he entrusted to me. (1 Timothy 1:9-11)*

Arsenokoites and *arsenokoitai* were never an exclusive reference to homosexuals nor were they used to refer to lesbians. In 56 usages during the six hundred years after Paul first used the word, *arseno-koites* or *arseno-koitai* never refers to men in committed faithful gay partnership. And it probably goes without saying that the word was never used to describe two women in committed faithful partnership.

—gaychristian101.com

Now to *malakoi*, which is paired in context with *arsenokoitai* in 1 Corinthians 6:9-10. *Malakoi* is easier to translate because it appears in more ancient texts than *arsenokoitai*, yet it suffers other complications when translated to modern English. Older translations for *malakoi* are:

- weaklings (1525)
- effeminate (1582, 1901)
- those who make women of themselves (1890)
- the sensual (1951)

Then, just as happened with *arsenokoitais*, there was a radical shift over just a few decades. Following cultural stereotyping of gay people, *malakoi* was translated as follows:

- those who participate in homosexuality (1958)
- sexual perverts (1972)
- male prostitute (1989)

So, how did *malakoi* shift from its association with character traits to association with specific kinds of people performing sexual acts?

The King James translation of *malakos* was a good one — within THAT culture....

Malakos is associated with the traits of women as women were seen in the ancient world: morally weak, given to unnatural vices, lazy, unchaste, lustful, whorish, impure, and taking a submissive role in sex. *Malakos* was used to characterize men who lived lives of decadence; partook in excesses of food, drink, and sex; were weak in battle; prettied themselves for sexual exploits with women; or even were simply too bookish. Additionally, men who fell deeply in love with women and lost control of their passions or neglected their business pursuits were thought to be effeminate....

The historical meaning of *malakoi* presents a modern translational problem because the most consistent and best historical translation of *malakoi* really is "effeminate"—but not our modern

231

understanding of "effeminate." So when the 1552 Douay-Rheims Bible and the 1901 American Standard Version translated *malakoi* as "effeminate," the word still included the sense of all the ugly traits thought to be associated with women; it had nothing to do with gay men. *Nothing.* Today "effeminate" means "having or showing qualities that are considered more suitable to women than to men." The modern word doesn't carry the baggage of ancient negative views of women. But Paul was not writing to a world where women were of equal status to men, a world where to be a woman, or to be like a woman, was to be honorable, or to behave honorably. In light of all this, the best modern translation of *malakoi* would include in its meaning an indulgent or excessive disposition which may at times include sexual excess.

—Kathy Baldock,
canyonwalkerconnections.com, whose mission is
"Repairing the breach between the
Church and the LGBT community"

This is just a sample of the large amount of writing focused on these rather uncommon Greek words. Some (like these quotes) deny that these words have anything to do with same-sex relations. Others make the case that Paul only uses these words to condemn homosexual acts that "dehumanized" males in that society, such as forced situations and prostitution. Others say that it's not the sexual acts that are condemned but confusion of the gender roles that society considered appropriate at that time.[40]

When we are confronted with words that are unfamiliar or passages that are unclear, it is right to look to other passages that are clearer to shed light on the subject. So in discussions with people who are struggling or confused, we should search the Scriptures and study the context just as thoroughly as possible. The first purpose is to seek

---

[40] I and many others are not convinced by this argumentation. This quote from the interview with Sam Allberry seems appropriate in response to many of these arguments: "We need to remember that the kind of people Paul describes are general people. In Romans 1, he talks about women experiencing lust for women and men experiencing lust for men; he's not just talking about older men and younger boys, which you sometimes had in the Roman world. He mentions women too. In 1 Corinthians 6 he mentions both the active and the passive partner in a gay relationship, so he's not just talking about exploitative situations of homosexual rape. He seems to be talking about consensual relationships between two men and consensual relationships between two women."

God's will and his will alone. The second is to gently and genuinely help others understand.

One important thing to realize is what's at stake. What drives people who would otherwise not care about ancient Greek to dig into such Bible passages like this? If the passages are left to stand as traditionally translated, these people or their loved ones are being labeled "unholy and irreligious," on the level of those who murder their own parents, and they "will not inherit the kingdom of God." If the passages can't be retranslated or explained away, these people's claims—"I can be a practicing homosexual and still maintain my relationship with Christ"—are clearly contradicted by Christ's apostle. It would be helpful for us to sympathize with how scary this is. It could be an opening to have our neighbors explain why maintaining a connection with Christ is so important.

Also, can you help your neighbors look at the Bible's overall position on sex? Throughout Scripture, from Genesis chapter 1 on, God teaches that sex is for one man married to one woman and anything outside of that is sexually immoral. It isn't just a question of a few rare words.

Yes, it may be intimidating when discussions turn to questions of Greek translation and definitions. However, this also can be an amazing opportunity. Express joy that someone would care so deeply about the Bible—every single word of it. You can also use this as an easy way to plan future discussions on the subject. If working with Greek is something you are uncomfortable with, say, "I'm going to do some reading about what you're saying. Then we can talk about it again." Read articles or books that they suggest. You can suggest articles that would challenge their previous ways of thinking too and point them to the many liberal Bible scholars who reluctantly admit that the Bible (and these passages) condemns all homosexual lifestyles.[41] But most importantly, think about what special verses your neighbors are trying to get you to consider. As the apostle Paul uses these rather uncommon Greek words, he also includes the beauty of the gospel. No matter what sins were part of each of us before, through Christ we have been washed, sanctified, and justified through faith in Christ's death and resurrection. "Thank you for bringing up this particular verse," we can say. "Isn't it beautiful how big it makes the grace of God in Christ?"

---

[41] See for example http://barbwire.com/la2014/04/29/liberal-scholars-homosexuality/ and http://apprising.org/2009/08/10/john-shelby-spong-admits-homosexuality-is-condemned-in-scripture/

The next quote is regarding Romans 1:26,27:
Because of this, God gave them over to shameful lusts. Even their
women exchanged natural sexual relations for unnatural ones.
In the same way the men also abandoned natural relations with
women and were inflamed with lust for one another. Men commit-
ted shameful acts with other men, and received in themselves the
due penalty for their error.

The model of homosexual behavior Paul was addressing here is explicitly associated with idol worship (probably temple prostitution), and with people who, in an unbridled search for pleasure (or because of religious rituals associated with their idolatry), broke away from their natural sexual orientation, participating in promiscuous sex with anyone available.

There are, no doubt, modern people who engage in homosexual sex for reasons similar to those identified in Romans 1. If someone began with a clear heterosexual orientation, but rejected God and began experimenting with gay sex simply as a way of experiencing a new set of pleasures, then this passage may apply to that person. But this is not the experience of the vast majority of gay, lesbian, and bisexual people.

—Jeff Miner and John Tyler Connoley

These two verses from Romans chapter 1 are among several that are
often cited when talking about the subject of homosexuality. When
researching a particular subject in Scripture, I like to ask myself the
very general question, What is God trying to tell us here? And, Am I
willing to hear what God is saying, or am I trying to find passages that
back up my preconceived ideas? In many different places where God
condemns lust and sexual sins, God does point out specific sexual sins
to individually address the weaknesses of people who are tempted sex-
ually in various ways. In these verses one of the topics that God lists as
sinful are sexual relationships between people of the same sex.

Perhaps if we read Romans 1:26,27 and ask ourselves the general
question, What is God trying to tell us here? we would say, "The answer
is clear: Men lusting after men or women lusting after women is shame-
ful, an unnatural error that God will punish."

But, how can we learn to be quick to listen when talking with people
in the LGBTQ community? The quote from Miner and Connoley shows

*us another explanation of Romans 1:26,27 that a good number of those people have embraced for **why** God would condemn these sexual lusts and practices. For many it comes down to the idea of what is natural. Did God mean that an unnatural relationship is simply any that occur between people of the same sex **or** one that goes against someone's natural sexual orientation? If it is the latter, then they would argue that people who are attracted to people of the same sex are actually going against God's will by pursuing heterosexual relationships.*

And again, it is important to realize what is at stake for the LGBTQ person in the interpretation of Romans 1:26,27. If they cannot find some way around the traditional interpretation of those verses, God is calling them "shameful." God is saying he's so tired of their sinfulness that he has "given them over" to sin and lust. The next verse, Romans 1:28, talks that same way: "Just as they did not think it worthwhile to retain the knowledge of God, so God gave them over to a depraved mind." Given over to depravity, having lost the knowledge of God—these are fearsome words. No wonder our neighbors' ears are itching for someone to explain these verses away. Instead of quickly condemning them for twisting the words of the Bible, and then walking away, leaving them in their predicament, we need to consider that these are people frightened by God's holy hatred of sin, who don't know what to do with their terror. We can help them.

It seems pretty unlikely that Paul had in mind general same-sex relations. I do not mean that he thought some same-sex relations were valid. Rather, I am saying that when he talks about the despicable, he has specific practices in mind. I am suspect of the idea that Paul thought about what we know today as committed same-sex relationships and lumped them all in together. What Paul objects to and considers despicable, we do as well. In our day such practices would be called human trafficking, child abuse, molestation, and pedophilia. We, too, will not stand for such behaviors. Our culture today would be on the side of Paul, with some modifications based upon our greater biological and psychological knowledge.

—Michael B. Regele,
Science, Scripture, and Same-Sex Love

Homosexuality was most commonly practiced in those days in forms of temple prostitution, humiliation of captured enemies after war, or just the sexual extravagance and experimentation that have been mentioned before. Some could certainly make an argument that these homosexual practices are different from those that are commonly seen today.

We should recognize that for the Bible passages we would most quickly point to as condemning same-sex lusts and perversions, people in the LGBTQ community are convinced that these passages don't condemn their specific lifestyles, their "committed relationships."

How should we respond? Should we say, "Paul certainly was aware of the concept of same-sex marriage: in Paul's day even the Emperor of Rome himself, Nero, had married a man"? It may be worth bringing something like that up to challenge preconceived ideas.

But sometimes being quick to listen means looking for other ways to communicate God's message. Jesus illustrated this tactic in his ministry. In Luke chapter 18 when the rich young ruler told Jesus that he had kept all of the commandments, instead of directly denying his false claim, Jesus indirectly (yet powerfully) pointed out the sin that still lingered in his heart by asking him to sell all of his possessions and give them to the poor. We can look to do the same. One way we can employ this tactic is by illustrating how focusing on what comes naturally even to me, what appeals to my own heart, isn't always in line with the will of God.

People in the LGBTQ community aren't the only ones who act like Scripture's clear commands might not be quite so clear. Permit me to use the temptation of materialism and greed as a parallel here, since it is one that easily tugs at my heart. Why do I focus on the passages that say I can use the material things of this world for my family and my enjoyment or focus on the godly people in Scripture who had an abundance of wealth? While it is good to hold every passage of Scripture dear, it shouldn't be at the expense of other sections of God's Word. Many passages of Scripture warn me of the dangers of wealth and of obsession with the things of this world. But because my sinful nature still resides in my heart and because it always wants to justify its own desires, my natural tendency is to focus on what I want to hear.

So let's be willing to listen to what others think particular passages and their contexts mean, but also look for openings to encourage one another to listen to Scripture and not only to what our hearts, which are still darkened by sin, want to hear.

236

MR: Once again, the point is the extent to which the relationship is not the one-man-one-woman marriage intended in the beginning.

SA: Exactly. That is the foundation for all of what the Bible says on sexual ethics. And it's why we have to look at homosexuality as an application of what the Bible says about marriage.

—Sam Allberry,
coordinator of livingout.org, interviewed for
Modern Reformation magazine

While it is not the focus of this book to give arguments against homosexual relationships, this needs to be emphasized and re-emphasized when people in the LGBTQ community want to debate the Bible: Sexual relationships that are good and God-pleasing are discussed in Scripture in only one context—heterosexual marriage (for one example, see 1 Corinthians 7:2,8,9). All sexual acts, even sexual and lustful thoughts, outside of marriage are condemned without condition by Jesus (Matthew 5:27-30). When Jesus speaks about marriage, he speaks of it in the same way that God spoke about it at the beginning of time in the Garden of Eden (Matthew 19:1-12). This is the foundation for what the Bible says on sexual ethics. And that's not just in the area of homosexuality, but for all the different sexual temptations. When faced with temptation personally, we should ask if what we're being tempted to do is in keeping with God's instruction of two becoming one flesh that would last a lifetime. When talking about same-sex relationships, we should recognize that God didn't make a mistake and was aware of how times would change when he said that marriage is a man and woman united together. And when difficulties in marriage arise, we must ignore the world that says divorce is mostly harmless. Instead, we must listen to God's instruction that the marriage relationship takes precedence over every other human relationship in this world. Base all your beliefs, convictions, and discussions about the proper use of God's gift of sex on this foundation, just as God does.

"That was then; this is now."

In a 2010 study commissioned by the Episcopal Church, even revisionists acknowledged that same-sex marriage "exceed[s] the marriage practices assumed by Scripture," justifying the new ethic because it "comports with the mission of God celebrated by the Spirit in the body of Christ." Or, as those revisionists put it elsewhere, "The Holy Spirit is doing a new thing."

—Mark Galli,
editor, *Christianity Today*

The thought that the Holy Spirit would be doing a new thing has been used in the past to justify other man-made innovations in the churches. In fact, the Holy Spirit did a new thing on the day of Pentecost, according to prophecy and Jesus' own promise. This sort of thinking leads to questions, however. If people argue that exclusive, monogamous same-sex attraction is a new creation of the Spirit, why wasn't it ever prophesied in Scripture, or even hinted at? Or does that mean that God didn't know what the future would hold? Is that the reason it wasn't mentioned? Then that would mean that either God doesn't know everything or that he doesn't know what the future would hold. God knew the Holy Spirit would do something new at Pentecost, so he told us about it. We should be careful of the kind of talk that says God is doing something new outside of what he has already told us in the Word.

Historians tell us our model of loving, long-term homosexual sexual relationships did not meaningfully exist in Canaanite culture. This was a tribal culture in which it would have been virtually impossible to form such relationships. Offspring were essential to survival in this primitive agricultural economy. Moreover, there were rigid distinctions between women's work and men's work. If two men had lived together as a couple, for example, one of them would have been placed in the position of doing women's work, and the presence of a man working among the women of the village would not have been tolerated. . . .

This means that the church's explicit requirement that gay Christians commit to lifelong celibacy is new.

—Matthew Vines,
God and the Gay Christian

Vines suggests that the type of homosexual relationships that exist today, described as "loving, long-term homosexual sexual relationships," are new to this era of history. He also sets up this choice: Accept homosexuality or embrace mandatory celibacy. Mandatory celibacy would also be a new thing that God would require. So how do you answer someone who poses that choice to you? "What am I to do? I'm only attracted to people of the same sex."

One reply would be to ask, To what extent is erotic love essential to God's plan for marriage? God created and blesses sexual intimacy in marriage. But the erotic love that our society elevates as almost the sole reason for marriage is not something that God places as much emphasis on. In other words, God does not "mandate celibacy" for those who lack heterosexual attraction: they can still get married to someone of the opposite sex and focus on that other person's happiness, as Christ focused on our happiness, not his own.

Again, we could turn to 1 Corinthians chapter 7 and talk about how celibacy (for those who do not need marriage as a safeguard against their heterosexual lusts) is a blessing, not a burden.

But perhaps the best response would be to keep the conversation going and ask, "How do we know which 'new, meaningful love arrangements' are okay with God and which are not?" Then we might get an answer like this:

"Love is the heart of marriage, whatever that marriage looks like."

Human marriage, Ephesians says, is a "profound mystery" that points to the ultimate relationship: Christ's eternal union with the church. Given that Christ's covenant with us is unbreakable, our marriage bonds should be equally enduring. So the most important aspect of marriage is the covenant the two partners make.

Perhaps the dominant message about marriage in modern society is that it's primarily about being happy, being in love, and being fulfilled? What if one partner falls out of love, or they both do?

For many in our society, the answer seems obvious: The couple should seek a divorce. Why should two people who no longer love each other stay together?

But that is not the Christian message. For Christians, marriage is not just about us. It's also about Christ. If Christ had kept open the option to leave us behind when he grew frustrated with us or felt like we were not living up to his standards, he may have abandoned us long ago. But the story of the gospel is that, although we don't deserve it, God lavishes his sacrificial love upon us anyway.

In marriage, we're called to reflect God's love for us through our self-giving love for our spouse. God's love for us isn't dependent on our day-to-day feelings toward him, on how hard we work to please him, or even on how faithful we are to him. It's grounded in his nature and his covenant. Ephesians 5:1 tells us to be "imitators of God" (NASB). Because God's love is boundless, ours should be as well. That means marriage isn't, at its deepest level, just about our happiness and fulfillment. At its core marriage is also about displaying the nature and glory of God through the covenant we make—and keep—with our spouse.

If the essence of marriage involves a covenant-keeping relationship of mutual self-giving, then two men or two women can fulfill that purpose as well as a man and a woman can.

—Matthew Vines,
God and the Gay Christian

---

*When I conduct premarriage counseling classes, one of the main points I emphasize sounds much like what Matthew Vines is talking about. The heart of Christian marriage is selfless, self-sacrificing love—**agape** love. God asks husbands and wives to reflect the same kind of love with which Christ loves the church. It is a shame that this foundation of marriage is lost on so many married couples in our society.*

*We should hold God's selfless, **agape** love up high as a guiding light and an inspiration. It is the heart of the gospel. "God so loved the world that he gave his one and only Son, that whoever believes in him shall not perish but have eternal life" (John 3:16). This love of God inspires us to love in the same way. We pray that husbands and wives would love each other in this way as a vivid illustration of God's love.*

*We also should look for every opportunity to demonstrate this kind of love in all our earthly relationships. There are examples in Scripture where people of the same sex demonstrate this **agape** love in their rela-*

tionships.[42] We personally should look to demonstrate this kind of love in response to what God has shown to the world (1 John 3:16).

*However, I'm not sure where the Bible ever says that marriage is the best forum to show that love. That seems to be the real issue here. While **agape** love is the heart of Christian marriage, we must listen to what God says about marriage while we also listen to what he says about **agape** love.*

The same Hebrew word that is used in Genesis 2:24 to describe how Adam felt about Eve (and how spouses are supposed to feel toward each other) is used in Ruth 1:14 to describe how Ruth felt about Naomi. Her feelings are celebrated, not condemned.

And throughout Christian history, Ruth's vow to Naomi has been used to illustrate the nature of the marriage covenant. These words are often read at Christian wedding ceremonies and used in sermons to illustrate the ideal love that spouses should have for one another. The fact that these words were originally spoken by one woman to another tells us a lot about how God feels about same-gender relationships.

—wouldjesusdiscriminate.org

*What is their definition of **love** here? I would agree that the story of Naomi and Ruth is a story of two women in love. However, sexual love between Ruth and Naomi is never mentioned, in fact, quite the opposite. The way that they met was through the kind of marriage that God instituted—the marriage of Ruth to Naomi's son. So if this example is brought up in conversation, don't shy away from the story of Ruth. Her words to Naomi are a beautiful example of love that started when Ruth promised to leave her father and mother and be united with Naomi's son.*

The question this leads me to ask myself is, When am I tempted to do the same with stories of Scripture? This makes me think of Jacob, who knew that the promise of the Savior was his and not Esau's but then perhaps used this knowledge to justify his deception and lies. It reminds me of Moses, who heard God's command to give water to the Israelites but then abused the power that was given him to show off his own power and authority. The temptation to use God's Word out of

---

[42] For examples, see John 13:23; 21:16; and 3 John 1:1.

context to substantiate some sort of preconceived idea that I already have in my mind is always present. We should be on guard for this temptation and dishonest use of God's Word, also in our own hearts.

Marianne Duddy-Burke, the executive director of DignityUSA, an inaptly named organization of LGBT "Catholics," said, " . . . the pope doesn't understand the danger that his words can mean for 'gender-nonconforming people.'" But the Pope has shown that he profoundly understands exactly what nonconformance means and the danger it represents. In "Amoris Laetitia," he warned of "an ideology of gender" as a threat to the family.

—Robert R. Reilly,
2016 article for catholicworldreport.com,
"Pope Francis vs. Gender Ideology"

In the original creation story, procreation is not presented as the primary purpose of marriage. While Genesis 1:28 does say to "be fruitful and increase in number," Genesis 2 never mentions procreation when describing the first marriage. And despite the significance of procreation in the Old Testament, infertile marriages were not considered illegitimate. The marriages of Abraham and Sarah (see Genesis 18) as well as Elkanah and Hannah (see 1 Samuel 1) were valid even in the long years before they had a child. In the New Testament, too, Jesus may have made an exception to his prohibition of divorce, saying a couple could divorce in the case of infidelity (see Matthew 19:9). But he made no exception for couples who are unable to bear children. In Jesus's understanding of marriage, covenantal commitment is foundational. The ability to bear children is not.

Additional teachings in Scripture support the understanding that procreation is not essential to marriage. The Song of Songs is an ode to the joys of erotic love and intimacy, wholly separate from a concern for procreation. The Song centers on the delights of bodily pleasure, uplifting sexual arousal and satisfaction as good parts of God's creation. Recall, too, that in 1 Corinthians 7, Paul encouraged married couples to have sex "so that Satan will not tempt you because of your lack of self-control" (verse 5). Paul never suggested that sex was only or even primarily for the purpose of procreation.

—Matthew Vines

Arguments against same-sex marriages have been made on the basis of things like them being a threat to the family, their inability to procreate, or the lack of anatomical complementarianism. However, all of these miss the biggest point. God is in charge of how marriage is defined. Changes in legislation don't change what God has declared. Arguments based on logic and human reason don't change what God has declared about marriage. Do we do more harm than good by using these kinds of arguments in our conversations? If holes can be poked in these lines of thinking by citing examples of valid marriages without procreation or other passages cited above, that undermines the message that God has given in his Word.

MR: How do you answer someone who says, "My best friend is not the kind of person Paul's talking about in these passages, much less the kind of person who was living in Sodom and Gomorrah. My brother and his boyfriend are chaste. They are in a committed same-sex relationship, devoted to each other for the rest of their lives." How is that any different from a heterosexual couple?

SA: I want to respond in a couple of ways. The first thing to say is that it is always possible to demonstrate some kind of virtue while we sin. A daft example would be a gang of bank robbers. You might have a gang member who is a loyal gang member. He treats his gang members fairly, he looks out for them, he protects them, keeps them safe, and makes sure they all get a fair share of the earnings. But this doesn't mean that what he is doing is less sinful. It is always possible to demonstrate some kind of virtue while you sin. The presence of faithfulness and commitment in a same-sex partnership doesn't mean the partnership is good.

—Sam Allberry,
coordinator of livingout.org, interviewed for
Modern Reformation magazine

When having discussions with people in the LGBTQ community, comparing them to gang members might not be the best way to begin. However, I still think this response is very tactful and insightful. His response did not attack any person directly. **Ad hominem** attacks often lead to defensiveness. But there is value if you can demonstrate a simple flaw in someone's logic—like showing that even when you can find virtue and positive traits in something or someone, their actions can still be wrong.

Yet this truth remains: Virtue does not cover over sin. We should also ask ourselves when we might be tempted to do the same. Our sinful nature is always looking for excuses to satisfy its desires. So if we can convince ourselves that the end ever justifies the means, how is this any different than the question or scenario that the interviewer asked Pastor Allberry about? Be on your guard that you too do not fall into this temptation.

Perhaps the best way, in a conversation, to show how virtue does not equate with total righteousness, is to use examples from your own life. My desire to care for my family—while virtuous—can tempt me to neglect my neighbor or the needy. Can my faithfulness to my friends lead me to overlook my duty to warn them about the dangers of sin or even lead me to participate in them? This is the kind of self-examination we Christians should always strive to do and help others to do.

Be open to listening. Do not assume that there are no positive traits in LGBTQ relationships. Talk to others respectfully and humbly about what sin really is or how we know what it is. Challenge their thinking without being condescending.

"God doesn't want people to suffer, does he?"

While Scripture tells us not to rely solely on our experience, it also cautions us not to ignore our experience altogether. In the Sermon on the Mount, Jesus warned against false prophets, using a term that has long been understood to refer to teachers of false doctrines as well. Jesus explained how his followers could determine true prophets from false prophets. In Matthew 7:15-20, he said:

> Watch out for false prophets. They come to you in sheep's clothing but inwardly they are ferocious wolves. By their fruit you

will recognize them. Do people pick grapes from thornbushes, or figs from thistles? Likewise, every good tree bears good fruit, but a bad tree bears bad fruit. A good tree cannot bear bad fruit, and a bad tree cannot bear good fruit. Every tree that does not bear good fruit is cut down and thrown into the fire. Thus, by their fruit you will recognize them.

Jesus's test is simple: If something bears bad fruit, it cannot be a good tree. And if something bears good fruit, it cannot be a bad tree.

—Matthew Vines,
God and the Gay Christian

Jesus' instruction does seem clear here. He wants his people to look at the fruit that teachers of God's Word produce with their teaching. The point that Vines makes is that the pain and depression that so many people with same-sex attraction report can only be characterized as "bad fruit." The teaching to repress these feelings, he would say, would have to be a "bad tree" because of what it produces.

The question we should ask in this case is, Who makes the decision of what is good fruit and what is bad fruit? The only measure that is reliable for testing "fruit" is God and his Word. There are many very sad things that have happened to people with same-sex attraction due to their own actions or the actions of others. We should strive to bear good fruit ourselves and encourage the same in others. But we shouldn't let our own experiences be the judge of this fruit over the Word of God.

We also should recognize that the pain and depression of many in the LGBTQ community are real. Sympathize with that pain. And acting in love would also include bringing good fruit into their lives. Share with them the love of family and friends. Lead them to embrace the spiritual and physical gifts they have been given and to find joy and fulfillment in using them. And most importantly, vividly share with them Jesus' eternal love that will never disappear or fade.

Imagine growing up hearing from those you love and trust that certain groups of people are evil. In fact, these people are so bad, so wrong, that God himself will punish them. Imagine absorbing this hatred deep into your bones. Imagine that you then discover, at some point in your adolescence, that you are one of these people. They are the hated. You are the hated. . . .

There is abundant evidence that the prejudice we face is toxic. And when anti-gay prejudice comes from parents or religion, the effect is profound. According to University of Tennessee Knoxville psychology professor Dawn Szymanski, research shows that experiencing rejection from parents of your sexual identity is linked to traumatic internalized negativity—what psychologists call "internalized homonegativity" or "internalized stigma". The same is true when a person belongs to a religion that rejects homosexuality.

One consequence of this internalized stigma is violence: Studies of same-sex couples show that internalized homophobia is a significant predictor of violence within a relationship. Self-hatred also creates profound psychological distress: One meta-analysis found that higher levels of internalized anti-gay stigma were correlated with worse mental health. The psychological distress can include anxiety, depression, poor self-esteem and hyperarousal—a state of increased tension that includes irritability, anger and aggression.

The stress caused by internal stigma can evoke a biological response. According to Stephanie Budge, a psychology professor at the University of Wisconsin at Madison, there is broad consensus in the research community that "minority stress"—including internalized self-hatred—creates massive physical health problems. According to the Mayo Clinic, this kind of cumulative stress disrupts almost all the body's processes. Indeed, gay people who live in communities with high levels of anti-gay prejudice have a life expectancy that is shorter by 12 years.

—Jessica Nordell,
washingtonpost.com, "What happens when a
gay person grows up in an anti-gay home"

There are examples in recent years of transgender children who have open and supportive parents. And it is encouraging to see nature take its course in these children as they come to discover who they are and how they are comfortable with themselves. Contrast that with the despair and depression that many children are subjected to, when their parents selectively apply the Bible and try to change who they are. Look at how damaging that sort of practice can be.

—Margy,
see above, "Listening to Margy"

Depression, anxiety, and poor self-esteem are just a few examples of the "bad fruit" that were talked about above (in the first quote in this section) for those who try to suppress their same-sex attractions. However, there is faulty logic in the thinking that bad fruit can only come from bad teachings. Bad fruit also comes from sinful thoughts (James 1:15[43]; Matthew 15:18-20[44]).

But instead of focusing on this and meeting those who are hurting with more accusations, doesn't your heart go out to those in such pain and turmoil? So the question we must ask ourselves is how we can help. The solution that the world comes up with is to darken and harden the conscience until it can accept what the sinful heart desires. But that acceptance is not helpful. Only God can help. So our goal must be to lead people to God's solutions. That begins with repentance worked by God through his condemning law. He opens our eyes to recognize and name the sins that still lurk in our hearts and turn our backs on them. We pray for guidance and strength from the Savior who has defeated sin already. There may be times when our sinful nature still gets the best of our good intentions. But the good that our Savior has achieved and clothed God's children with in Baptism is a reminder to drown our sinful nature when it arises.

C. S. Lewis wrote, "I believe that the most lawless and inordinate loves are less contrary to God's will than a self-invited and self-protective lovelessness." Lewis's insight resonated with me even before I embarked on my study of Scripture and same-sex relationships. Lewis, of course, wasn't making a case for lawless loves. He was emphasizing the destructiveness of living in fear of love.

---

[43] "Then, after desire has conceived, it gives birth to sin; and sin, when it is full-grown, gives birth to death."

[44] "The things that come out of a person's mouth come from the heart, and these defile them. For out of the heart come evil thoughts—murder, adultery, sexual immorality, theft, false testimony, slander. These are what defile a person; but eating with unwashed hands does not defile them."

Given that we are created by a God who is Father, Son, and Holy Spirit—relational to the core—such a consequence seems at odds with God's nature. . . . It's safe to say that true Christian sacrifice, no matter how costly, should make us more like God, not less.

—Matthew Vines

Relationships are important to mankind. This was part of God's intention even from the time of creation. When he created Adam, God said, "It is not good for the man to be alone" (Genesis 2:18). Living without love from other people or fearing love is not part of God's plan for mankind. But we should work to define more accurately what kind of relationships and love God wants for us. Sexual love is not the pinnacle of love. Genuine and caring relationships are exactly what we all need. We should strive to form these kinds of relationships with all people, but especially those who are feeling the pain of living without the loving relationships that we all desire.

Paul wrote in 1 Corinthians 10:13, "[God] will not let you be tempted beyond what you can bear." But mandatory celibacy for gay Christians is more than many of them can bear.

—Matthew Vines

For many LGBTQ people it boils down to this choice: Either embrace the same-sex attractions they feel or live a life of celibacy. As said a couple times already, in that same letter of 1 Corinthians, Paul talks about celibacy as a spiritual gift that not everyone possesses. It is a gift, a blessing, an opportunity, but not for all. Can you sympathize with the LGBTQ person who says, "I am wracked with same-sex lusts day in and day out; obviously God hasn't give me the gift of celibacy"? It does **seem** *like a strong temptation with no good solutions. I'm sure there is much more that could be said about this decision that many people face. However, now let's just consider how torturous this choice could be for some. Let's empathize with the hardship that this can cause. Let's consider those temptations that continue to tug at* **our** *hearts and pray that God would show us the way to endure in the midst of suffering. But let's not only pray about our own personal temptations. Continue to pray for all who are faced with this personal struggle with temptation, that God would help them also to endure.*

Some elders and family friends I met with acknowledged that their position asks gay Christians to sacrifice something very significant: the possibility of romantic love and fulfillment. But, they stressed, that doesn't mean their position is wrong. Sacrifice is an integral part of what it means to follow Christ, and Jesus and Paul both embraced celibacy as part of their callings. All Christians who do not marry are expected to be celibate—even straight Christians who would like to marry but can't find a spouse.

As one elder said, "It depends on how you look at your situation, Matthew. I know several women in our church who held on to their hopes for a husband for years—maybe still do. But while marriage is a gift that God blesses, it isn't a right for any of us."

—Matthew Vines

This quote was a very easy one for me to read, but harder to take to heart. I have had the same thought in regard to people with same-sex attraction. Although resisting temptation may be difficult and may require sacrifice, if that is what God requires, we should willingly set it aside.

But how easy is it for you to accept sacrifice? We all understand Jesus' words and warning when he tells us that as his disciples we must take up our crosses and follow him. We know that sacrifice is part of the lives of Christians. But do we embrace it? Do we willingly accept it? I'm not saying that we should go searching out ways to sacrifice. That's not what God is asking us to do. But he does want us to have the attitude of willingly accepting sacrifice that comes into our lives. I personally, and probably all of us, could do better in modeling this attitude of willful acceptance to encourage others to do the same when sacrifice is asked of them.

We can applaud those who have sacrificed as they live for their God. We need to support those who have been asked to sacrifice for their Savior. Don't isolate them or make them feel like they are living on their own. Be there to hold them accountable, and encourage them when they are down. And share God's Word with them because, through the power of the Holy Spirit, that is where God gives us strength.

"Doesn't the Bible say, 'Judge not'?"

Do we have to worry about who's gay and who's straight? Can't we just love everybody and judge them by the car they drive?

—Ellen DeGeneres,
TV host, *The Ellen DeGeneres Show*

While this quote was obviously made in jest, I think there is a lot of thought that was put into it. Think about the amount of attention that is dedicated to celebrity relationships, whether in marriage or outside of those vows. What causes this fascination? Why do people place such an emphasis on knowing about others' sexuality and relationships? Again, I think this is the glamorization and elevation of the sexual experience above everything else. It shouldn't be our concern to investigate these sorts of matters. Does this mean that we shouldn't have any concern about the temptations that tug at people's hearts or that we should refrain from proclaiming the full counsel of God? Of course not. But we shouldn't make it seem like people owe us a confession about the afflictions of their heart instead of owing it to God.

*Ellen's comment on judging people by their cars also shows the way that this word **judging** is used in our society. The judgment that she is describing is that of people who look at other people's cars in a condescending manner, thinking how much better (or cleaner or less rusty) our car is than theirs, or how jealous we are about what someone else might drive. This kind of petty judgment—evaluating people the way we evaluate cars or other objects—this kind of pharisaical judgment that thinks more highly of ourselves than others should have no place in a Christian's heart, words, or actions. Jesus said this very thing: "You hypocrite, first take the plank out of your own eye, and then you will see clearly to remove the speck from your brother's eye" (Matthew 7:5).*

The first question I would ask is, "Who are you to judge?" We all have our faults and failings. We all have done things wrong in the past. But how can so many sit in judgment on those who are doing nothing wrong except loving the people that they love. Even the Bible has passages that condemn that kind of judgment.

—Margy,
see above, "Listening to Margy"

The Bible says, above all else, don't judge one another, love one another, don't act as a moral authority, don't speak on behalf of God, you're not better than anyone else, and the way to combat wickedness is through love and acceptance.

Yet people calling themselves Christians feel empowered to tell gay people they are sinners, that they deserve to die, and they are going to hell, because of who they love.

—14TEAMMOCKER,
brojackson.com, "Feel Our Pulse:
We Don't Expect You to Understand"

These are the impressions that so many have of Christians who speak too negatively toward people in the LGBTQ community. Some of it is off base. To say that the Bible's message "above all else" is that Christians shouldn't judge one another misses the central message of the Bible— the salvation of souls through the blood of Christ.

Too often when we talk about how homosexuality is sinful, it sounds like we too are missing what the central point of the Bible is. When we look to defend God's Word or stand up for the truth, does the main point of the Bible come through in our speech? Or does it instead sound like accusations with no possible grace? Is our main message as Christians to tell gay people "that they deserve to die, and they are going to hell, because of who they love"? Sometimes it is easy to get confused about what condemns a person before God. It is not one specific sin, or any sin, that actually condemns, since Jesus has satisfied the payment for sin on the cross. It is only unbelief that condemns. Jesus said, "Whoever believes in him is not condemned, but whoever does not believe stands condemned already because they have not believed in the name of God's one and only Son" (John 3:18). As you proclaim God's Word, keep this in mind.

There is also the warning here that we shouldn't act as a "moral authority" or "speak on behalf of God." This certainly doesn't mean that we shouldn't share God's Word. God has entrusted us as ambassadors to take his message of reconciliation to the world. We should never speak outside of God's Word as if we have God's authority. But we should be sure to speak as God does. Jesus reached out to the lost. He welcomed "sinners" and ate with them (Luke 15:2). We should do the same. Proclaim that "God demonstrates his own love for us in this: While we were still sinners, Christ died for us" (Romans 5:8). What if we were more eager to tell people about our own sins than about theirs? Would we seem more welcoming, especially since we could then tell them of the joy of forgiveness and renewal too?

It is not sinful judging to let God speak his judgments. But our great desire must be to speak also of how we are saved from his judgments through the cross of Christ. And what sense will that make if our listeners don't know what judgments they need saving from?

When we read this verse (Jude 7) in modern America, having been raised in a culture that despises gays and refers to them as "queer," it is easy to assume Jude's reference to "going after strange flesh" must mean homosexuality. For many heterosexual people, it seems unnatural or strange for a person to desire intimacy with someone of the same sex.

—Jeff Miner and John Tyler Connoley,
The Children Are Free

As students of God's Word, we would agree that in the eyes of the Lord all sins are equally deserving of hell. Although there are great differences among sins in terms of their damage to others and to ourselves, what they reveal about the condition of our hearts, and so on, every sin is an insult to his holiness and a spiteful defiance of his fatherhood over us. Yet that is not the way that homosexuality is often treated, as a sin equal to others. This quote seems to pose one suggestion as to why that might be. Is the reason that homosexuality is sometimes condemned more by Christians because this is a temptation that many people don't struggle with? I would much rather talk about a sin that doesn't tug at my heart than address something that afflicts me too. And since this is one sin that I and many other Christians don't have to struggle with, my self-righteous heart loves to judge anyone else who falls into this temptation.

For example, it is easy to condemn addiction until you struggle with dependence on something yourself. We readily condemn materialism until we have the opportunity to store earthly treasures of our own. Be aware of and resist that temptation of self-righteous judgment that seems to reside in everyone's heart, or it will derail any efforts we make to help those who are attacked in this way.

"Why don't you just show love to us?"

Research done by San Francisco State University's Family Acceptance Project, which studies and works to prevent health and mental health risks facing LGBT youth, empirically confirms what common sense would imply to be true: Highly religious parents are significantly more likely than their less-religious counterparts to reject their children for being gay—a finding that social-service workers believe goes a long way toward explaining why LGBT people make up roughly five percent of the youth population overall, but an estimated 40 percent of the homeless-youth population. . . . The resulting flood of kids who end up on the street, kicked out by parents whose religious beliefs often make them feel compelled to cast out their own offspring (one study estimates that up to 40 percent of LGBT homeless youth leave home due to family rejection), has been called a "hidden epidemic." Tragically, every step forward for the gay-rights movement creates a false hope of acceptance for certain youth, and therefore a swelling of the homeless-youth population.

—Alex Morris,
rollingstone.com, "The Forsaken"

There are plenty of individual stories of people who have been rejected by their family and their loved ones after they revealed their struggles with same-sex attraction. Our response to those who turn their backs on those who need help must be one of disapproval. In times of struggle, we must meet people in love. When there no longer seems to be a struggle but an embracing of sin, patient instruction seems to be in order. While I am not in a position to speak about individual situations, these kinds of statistics do bring questions to mind. Why are such a large percentage of young people who are estranged by their families those who struggle with same-sex attraction? And why do the majority come from Christian homes? Do Christian parents have the same reac-

tions with premarital sex, the abuse of alcohol, or any other number of sins that are common to man? Why does it seem that this particular struggle of same-sex attraction brings the strongest reaction among Christians? There may not be a single answer, but it is something that we should keep in mind.

I don't want to flatly condemn everyone who has treated family members with same-sex attraction this way. In fact, in some cases this may actually follow God's instruction to "not even eat" with people who reject God's Word and are blasphemous in their treatment of it (1 Corinthians 5:11). But that is not always the case. Many are zealous for God and just misguided in how they should act when confronted with this particular situation: they act rashly without patience, instruction, and help. I would just encourage everyone to be guided by God and his Word and not how others have responded to the same situation in the past. Casting people out of their homes in their time of temptation and need does not seem to be the best way to help people in the midst of struggle.

SA: If homosexuality is always spoken of as an "out there" issue, it will make the Christian in the pew think, "I'm not supposed to be here. I'm obviously not a Christian if I'm dealing with this." Even if it might be a struggle for the pastor to say it, the pastor has to say it—to acknowledge that this may well be an issue for some and to make that something that's okay, in a sense. We're allowed as Christians to battle with this kind of temptation, and we need to see homosexual temptation as one type of all the kinds of sexual temptation we experience as different men and women.

MR: What should we say if a same-sex couple shows up at church?

SA: Again I think people are confused on this point because we're thinking of homosexuality as a unique category. We should be asking ourselves how we respond if a sinner turns up at church. Generally, we would say, "How do you do? Welcome. Lovely to have you here. Come on in, here's the bulletin, here's the seat. I'd love to introduce you to people." That is exactly what we'd do if a gay couple turns up. It should be a word of welcome. We want people to come in; we want people to experience something of the life of the church and the core of what we believe. Therefore, it would be odd to stop them on the doorstep of the church and say, "Now, you seem to be a same-sex couple; let me quickly run through some passage on homosexuality." Doing that would imply that we want you to be sanctified before you can be justified. If any kind of sinner turns up to church, our response is, "Welcome. We would love for you to become part of our community. We would love for you to enjoy the life that goes on here, and we would love you to come to know the Lord who has met with all of us."

—Sam Allberry,
coordinator of livingout.org,
interviewed for *Modern Reformation* magazine

Allberry's comment of requiring sanctification before justification seems to get to the heart of the discussion between many in the LGBTQ community and many in the Christian church. Asking someone to live their life according to God's will before they know and appreciate what God has done for them through Christ isn't the correct order. One side talks about God's Word, and the other side often rejects what God's Word says. So there is the impasse. The love of God's Word only comes from the love of God.

I think that people who go all-out trying to convince those in the LGBTQ community that homosexuality is sinful are focusing on the wrong thing. Should we call sin "sin"? Of course. But our primary goal must not be to convince people that their sexual orientation is sinful. It should and must be an all-out effort to help them see that they need a Savior. And that Savior is Jesus. The Bible says all of our hearts are compromised and corrupted by sin. And only then, through seeing the solution in Jesus, are people able to acknowledge that maybe every desire of our hearts or rationale of our brain is not godly.

Instead of talking about one specific sin as going against God's will, we should talk about everyone's desperate need for a Savior. It's only when someone recognizes their imperfection, God's demands for righteousness, and God's solution in Christ that their hearts are receptive to what God says. Proclaim Christ crucified for the sins of all. Only then can God work sanctification and fruits of faith.

Martin Luther had a fitting quote on the same subject:
The doing away with offense [trying to remove anything that might stand in the way of the gospel] must take place through the Word of God. For even if all outward offense were destroyed and done away with, it would be to no avail as long as hearts are not brought

from unbelief to the right faith. For an unbelieving heart always finds cause for new offense. When the Jews destroyed one idol they set up ten others instead. Therefore in the New Testament we must adopt the right way to drive out the devil and all offense, namely, by the Word of God. When we redeem the heart, the devil and all his pomp and power will assuredly fall of themselves.[45]

A year and a half ago, Wheaton (College) made national headlines when a student threw an apple core at another student who, in an all-campus forum, questioned the college's traditional teachings on sexuality. . . .

After my second piece ran in the Record (concerning my sexual orientation), I received an email from the provost Stanton Jones, the former chair of Wheaton's psychology department, who has written extensively on sexual orientation and psychology. He said he was intrigued by my essays and applauded my courage and my evident commitment to Christ. Then he asked if I would be available to chat.

We met later that week. Upon entering the suite of administrative offices, his assistant told me to have a seat in the waiting area. Within a few minutes, Jones graciously shook my hand before we walked into his office and sat down to chat. To my surprise, we hit it off right away.

Jones's amiability and openness quickly put me at ease. He established his respect for me by saying that he had reread my articles. "This is exactly how I would hope students at Wheaton College would respond," he said. This, before he knew my views on whether or not I should be allowed to have a relationship with a man. Near the end of our conversation, we did discuss the ethics of same-sex relationships, since he has studied the psychology and ethics of homosexuality for much of his career, and only then did I articulate my celibate place. But Jones's primary aim was to get to know me. . . .

Jones's witness attests to Jesus' love and mercy. His desire to hear my story made a far greater impression than his scholarship would have. At the end of our hour, as we again shook hands, he asked if

---

[45] *Luther's Works*, Vol. 40, p. 59.

he and I could have a follow-up lunch. I accepted. We have shared meals together regularly ever since.

—Tyler Streckert,
Christianity Today, "What It's Like to
Be Gay at Wheaton College"

The people who shared their first-person perspectives on how we can be quick to listen to the LGBTQ community have all suggested that one of the best things we can do is to get to know people individually who are part of the community. Show your genuine love and care for them. Reflect the love that Jesus has for them too. Support them in their struggle.

Some have started message boards and networks so that people who have same-sex attraction can talk to one another and share their struggles. Some people might have the attitude of saying something like, "Don't let them talk to each other. They will just encourage that sinful behavior!" But what do we do in church each week? Don't we talk about the temptations that we struggle with individually and that are common to us all? Don't we share the joy of free and full forgiveness in the blood of Christ and share that assurance with one another in the absolution? Let's not think so little of the Holy Spirit or children of faith to think that letting people talk about their struggles will only lead them to embrace those temptations. Be the avenue that others can use to grow in their faith and relationship with God. As Proverbs says, "As iron sharpens iron, so one person sharpens another" (Proverbs 27:17).

Now the father and son are talking like they did so many years ago at the dinner table. What the father said at the dinner table wasn't wrong. But now his son needs to hear more.

It is right that we are all different. Each one of us is unique. We should acknowledge and address what we know is different about one another. The way that we can all help one another grow in our relationship with God is not to just blindly accept our differences as right and godly, but seek God's will for our lives no matter how difficult it may be.

If I don't personally struggle with LGBTQ temptations, should I be quick to look down on those who do? Should I be eager to hammer them with God's condemning laws? Or should my fondest desire and prayer be for them to trust me with their pains and give me a chance to say to them, "I know how God's words about sin can hurt—they have hurt me too—but I have also found out where to be healed from those pains and hammer blows!"

I have sins. I might get angry easily. I may have an addictive personality. I may have a tendency to stretch the truth. I might be tethered to this world more than I should.

The way that we can help one another with all these struggles is to listen to what we all struggle with. Encourage one another to turn to the all-powerful God who can accomplish anything. Say, "I'm a sinner too—and why don't we take our sins to Jesus together right now?" In this way we lead one another to our loving Savior who died to save us all. For these are God's own words and his attitude—his warning and his longing invitation towards us all:

Or do you not know that wrongdoers will not inherit the kingdom of God? Do not be deceived: Neither the sexually immoral nor idolaters nor adulterers nor men who have sex with men nor thieves nor the greedy nor drunkards nor slanderers nor swindlers will inherit the kingdom of God. **And that is what some of you were. But you were washed, you were sanctified, you were justified in the name of the Lord Jesus Christ and by the Spirit of our God.** (1 Corinthians 6:9-11, emphasis added)

AFTERWORD

Months after he submitted his story to me for this book, I asked Rob (from "Listening to Rob" in the atheists section) what the experience meant to him—the experience of contributing to this book. Here was his entire reply:

It meant there's at least one Christian out there more interested in understanding me than lecturing me.

That's what this book has been about. That's why we haven't focused on having an answer to every point and argument and accusation. There has been, throughout, an especially timely accusation we are trying to rebut: the false idea that our traditional biblical views must be uncaring, un-listening, judgmental, hypercritical, and prejudiced. We have tried to disprove that idea by modeling courtesy, by modeling an approach that says, "Let's get a realistic sense of other people's reasons for their wrong beliefs." (As one pastor has said, one big way to embrace people is to embrace their questions.) We are convinced that many Christian readers will be deeply strengthened by this demonstration of how we can follow the Bible and still be understanding, still care how other people actually think. (And strengthened a good deal more than they might have been by more exhaustive answers.)

But I don't want you to think that I personally claim to be an exemplar of caring. Maybe Rob was being more charitable to me than I deserve. He makes it sound like I was interested in him as a person—not just as an atheist "specimen" to be studied—like I really care about him and his heart. Do I?

A couple times most every week I have been praying for God to bless this project. But I don't actually remember praying for Rob or Ezra or Rebecca or any of the other people whose stories and quotes are in this book. I think I probably did, like once, back when I first got their stories. I think that shows a lack of caring.

(Yes, I did pray for them a few times as I wrote this afterword, a long time coming.)

I know that the time I have spent on this book has had a big impact on my preaching. I very regularly consider how the Bible passage I'm preaching on or the claims that it makes would come across to the kinds of people you have met here. I am convinced that this line of thought helps my messages to be more timely and address the challenges that churchgoers are facing in regard to their faith. Working on this book has also impacted my parenting and the kinds of conversations I intentionally have with my children to prepare them for the world. And those are no small things. I am thankful for those impacts.

But what about an impact on my personal witnessing or evangelism? Two of the people in this book I have known for more than half my life, but I didn't care enough to find out their stories until I (or one of the other authors) needed them for this book. Please pray for me to stop making excuses and do some personal evangelism and have the conversations that this book has been urging you to have.

*(Jesus is so patient with me. It is amazing how much he cares about **my** heart and my story.)*

*Would you give me this consolation? That at least I cared enough to help **you** care about Rob and my two decade-long friends and all these other real-live souls. That God has used me (and the authors he helped me gather here) to equip you, not just to keep hold of your own faith as challenging viewpoints confront you, not just to prepare your loved ones to run into those same viewpoints, but also to get your own patient conversations started—to care about these other souls and get to know them, to pray fervently for them and to speak thoughtfully, gently, and respectfully with them about your most thought-worthy and glory-worthy Savior.*

Thank you.

—Christopher S. "Topher" Doerr,
Broader Reach Editor,
Northwestern Publishing House

WHAT ABOUT**?**
JESUS**?**
whataboutjesus.com

We all have questions about life.
We all want _answers_ we can count on!

**Devotions, articles, and more at
whataboutjesus.com**